DECADE OF
DYSFUNCTION

THE ROAD TO TENNESSEE'S CRAZY COACHING SEARCH

MARK NAGI

DECADE OF DYSFUNCTION Copyright © 2018 by Mark Nagi.

Photographs courtesy of the author unless otherwise indicated

For information write to MeanStreets Living 12420 Fort West Drive Knoxville, TN 37934 - Attention Mark Nagi

Social Media @MarkNagi

_____

Book and Cover design by Jennifer Nagi.

First Edition Published June 2018
Printed in the U.S.A.

ISBN-13: 978-1720438274
ISBN-10: 1720438277

Library of Congress Cataloging-in-Publication Data is available upon request.

For Jennifer,
You are my sunshine...

CONTENTS

PROLOGUE

DECADE–noun: a period of ten years *(Merriam-Webster)*

DYSFUNCTION–noun: abnormal or unhealthy interpersonal behavior or interaction within a group *(Merriam-Webster)*

I'VE BEEN ASKED IF THIS BOOK IS A HATCHET JOB. It's not. I believe that this book is an accurate representation of the past ten years at the University of Tennessee, a historical account of this tumultuous period of Volunteers football, as told by the players, coaches, administrators, fans and media who lived it.

Many of you have a Tennessee story. Here is mine. I grew up a Tennessee fan, even if I didn't know what that really entailed. That's what happens when you are from Colonie, a suburb of Albany in upstate New York, and you see the Vols on TV once a year, maybe twice.

My Dad served our country during the Korean War but rarely talked about his time in the Navy. After being spending five years in the service, he came back to America and took full advantage of the G.I. Bill. John Nagi got two Master's Degrees and a Doctorate and told me frequently that he would have been a "professional student" if possible. One of his degrees came in 1968 from the University of Tennessee at Oak Ridge. The city, of course, is best known for its role in the development of the atomic bomb that ended World War II, and is a thirty-five minute drive from the UT campus.

He'd tell me stories about Tennessee, and on December 13, 1981, we packed up the family truckster, drove to East Rutherford (NJ), and watched the Vols beat Wisconsin in the soon-to-be-defunct Garden State Bowl. This was just a few days short of my ninth birthday.

Years later, I applied to colleges, and that list included Syracuse and Tennessee. I had wanted to be a sportscaster since I was seven years old, and I felt that Syracuse was the best place to go to achieve that goal. Bob Costas, Sean McDonough, Dick Stockton, Mike Tirico... the list of Newhouse School grads that have "made it" is quite lengthy.

Of course, this reminds me of a joke. How do you know that someone you just met graduated from the Newhouse School at Syracuse University?

They tell you.

Syracuse was too costly for my middle-class family. Tennessee was intriguing, but they had no campus television station. Plus, I was 17 and scared to death to go to school 850 miles from home. I chose SUNY Geneseo, a small state school south of Rochester. This was a manageable 240 miles away. For four years I got tons of experience in TV and radio. I thought that I had gained the experience that would make the transition to becoming a sportscaster in the real world an easy one. Resume tapes were sent to small towns you've probably never heard of and the responses I was getting were either non-existent or not positive. So, I had a choice to make: move back home and work the counter at Bob & Ron's Fish Fry, or go to grad school. This wasn't much of a decision.

In August of 1994, I threw some stuff in my 1990 Plymouth Horizon and headed south after choosing to attend the University of Tennessee. Football practice was beginning, and I had been hired to be one of the film guys at practice. Each day I'd hit the practice field with tripod and camera in tow and learned more and more about the Vols. On September 17, 1994, I finally had the chance to see my first game at Neyland Stadium when fifteenth-ranked Tennessee hosted top-ranked Florida. The atmosphere was incredible. I had never heard a stadium that loud. Of course, the Vols got smoked by Florida 31-0, a recurring theme for many matchups in seasons to come.

I worked for the football program throughout my first year at Tennessee. The following year I was lucky enough to earn a graduate assistantship running WUTK-FM, the campus radio station. I'd watch the 1995 season in the stands, which was a great experience in itself. Tennessee started a four-year run in which they compiled a 45-5 record, with two SEC titles and one national championship. These were the good times.

I completed my Master's Degree in 1996, and was finally decent enough to get a job in television. Granted, being the Sports Director of the ABC station in Watertown (NY) isn't the big time, but it was a start. I got to cover Syracuse football during the Donovan McNabb era, and from the minute I got to Watertown, I was already looking forward to Syracuse's 1998 season opener when the Vols traveled to the Carrier Dome. Jeff Hall's game-winning kick started Tennessee on the road to a national title.

That same season I covered Syracuse at the Orange Bowl. Two days later, I boarded an early morning flight from Miami and headed to Phoenix. I took a cab to Tempe, met my friends at some bar, and then walked to the football stadium. Tennessee would beat Florida State to win the BCS title. That night I crashed in a room with about eight other Vols fans, slept for about three hours on the top of an air conditioning unit, and then flew home. I used all my frequent flyer miles and spent money that my $24,000 salary certainly couldn't justify. My car was under two feet of snow when I got back to New York. But it was all worth it.

I worked in Watertown for three years, then Myrtle Beach for a year. I was always trying to get to a place where the big team to cover was right there in town. A place where the city lives and breathes sports... a place like Knoxville. In February of 2001, I started working as a sports reporter/photographer at WATE-TV, Knoxville's ABC affiliate. I expected to be back for a couple of years, and then move on to Kansas City, or Portland, or Milwaukee or some larger market. Because that's what you do when working in TV. You rent, you don't buy.

A month later I went out with some friends, saw a gorgeous blonde, and got her number. Next thing I knew, I was married to that Tennessee girl and we had two Tennessee daughters and I've been here ever since. Life happens that fast. So, that's my Tennessee story, and it's not a traditional one. I've lived in Knoxville longer than I've lived anywhere else, and don't expect to be going anyplace anytime soon.

My Dad and I talked about the Vols quite often. He passed away in 2003 and to this day, I think about him most every time I walk into Neyland Stadium.

It hasn't been much fun watching Tennessee football in recent years. Knoxville is a blast when the Vols are winning. In the chapters that follow we will take a closer look at Tennessee's decade-long downturn, and how those ten years led to a fan revolt that sparked a national outrage.

I really appreciate your purchase, and hope you enjoy the book.

Yours in sports,
Mark

P.S. You'll see some quotes in the book that came directly from emails or text messages in which words are misspelled or the sentence structure is improper. It is intentional that corrections were not made... You paid for this book (I hope!) and I want to make sure you are reading as accurate an account of this story as possible...

1
THE LAST GOOD SEASON

THERE WAS A TIME when trips to the SEC championship game were fairly regular events for Tennessee's football team. On December 1, 2007, Tennessee played LSU for the conference title. It was the Vols' third trip to Atlanta in seven years, and their fifth since 1997. It was an improbable, yet successful run. Not to say this wasn't a talented Tennessee roster. With a senior quarterback (Erik Ainge), a running back who gained nearly 1,200 yards on the ground (Arian Foster), a 1,000-yard receiver (Lucas Taylor) and a future NFL star starting at safety as a true freshman (Eric Berry), the Vols put together a 9-3 campaign.

"We had good players," says former Tennessee assistant coach Trooper Taylor. He coached running backs at UT and in 2007 oversaw the wide receivers. "We knew it would be a special year and it always starts with players. Those are the things you look at. Anytime you go into a season, you build on the guys that are coming back... I was thinking that we could do some special things."

But early results didn't give fans much reason for optimism. The season began on September 1 with a 45-31 loss at twelfth-ranked California. On September 15, third-ranked Florida ran it up in a 59-20 victory. That game is perhaps best remembered for when a Gators backup quarterback named Cam Newton barreled over Tennessee defensive back Dennis Rogan during garbage time. The Vols seemed to right the ship with a convincing 35-14 win over twelfth-ranked Georgia, but the good vibes were short lived.

On October 20, the Tennessee/Alabama game got the dreaded 12:30pm ET kickoff and Lincoln Financial Sports treatment. You remember Lincoln Financial Sports, don't you? The artist formerly known as Jefferson Pilot Sports? With the limited camera angles and three announcers named Dave? Yes, it was a golden era in sports broadcasting. Alabama's new coach, Nick Saban, started the game with a successful surprise onside kick, and the Crimson Tide destroyed the Vols 41-17 in Tuscaloosa. The Vols were just past the mid-point of their 2007 schedule, standing at 4-3, and only 2-2 in the SEC. Tennessee was not playing their best football, and there were even grumblings about the future of Phillip Fulmer as their head coach.

Fulmer was as Tennessee as Davy Crockett. Born in Winchester, he was an all-SEC offensive guard for the Vols. He became a Tennessee assistant coach, and eventually won what was considered by some to be a power struggle with Vols legend Johnny Majors. Fulmer joined Majors's staff in 1980, working his way up to offensive coordinator in 1989.

The Vols were one of the best teams in the nation from 1989-1991, with a 29-6-2 record and two conference titles. But heading into the 1992 season, Big Orange Country had to worry about something other than whether Heath Shuler would be an adequate replacement for Andy Kelly at quarterback. On August 25, Vols fans across the globe prayed for Johnny Majors as he underwent quintuple bypass heart surgery. The good news was that the surgery was a success and that Majors would recover. The bad news was the timing. This happened only two weeks before the season began.

Fulmer was tabbed as Tennessee's interim head coach. It was the first time Fulmer had served as a head coach at any level, but he looked like a seasoned veteran on the sidelines. The Vols went 4-0 with Fulmer in charge, including a 34-31 win at fourteenth-ranked Georgia and a 31-14 bludgeoning of fourth-ranked Florida at Neyland Stadium. Majors returned a month after his surgery for an October 3 win at LSU. The Vols had risen from twenty-second to fourth in the country and were in complete control of the SEC East.

The Southeastern Conference had expanded from 10 to 12 teams that season with the additions of Southwest Conference refugee Arkansas and independent South Carolina. They split into two divisions and would decide a conference winner in the inaugural "SEC Championship Game." The Vols were 3-0 in the conference and owned the tiebreaker against their two biggest threats in the division. They were in great position to be the first representative from the SEC East.

What followed was a three-game span that forever changed the direction of Tennessee's football program. The Vols were upset by Arkansas 25-24 on October 10. The Razorbacks recovered an onside kick in the final minutes and kicked a game winning field goal as time expired. Then Tennessee lost to fourth-ranked Alabama 17-10 on the "Third Saturday in October." It was their seventh straight defeat at the hands of the Crimson Tide.

Heading into the 1992 season, Majors had wanted a contract extension. Now, fans began to question whether Majors, Tennessee's head coach since 1977, should be on the sidelines in 1993. Since the 1960s, there has been a large rock set in the middle of the UT campus that is painted consistently by students with different messages, be they political, social, trivial, etc. After the Alabama loss, someone painted *Johnny is Back, We Want Phil* on The Rock.

"It doesn't take a lot of guts to go out and do something in the darkness and paint a rock," said Majors. "It doesn't take much ingenuity. There is the 'Legions of the Miserable' sometimes that are always going to be miserable. You don't let those affect how you approach your team."

Following a bye week, the Vols were embarrassed on Halloween in Columbia. A freshman quarterback named Steve Tanneyhill led South Carolina to a 24-23 victory. A late Heath Shuler to Mose Phillips touchdown brought the Vols within a point. But overtime was still a few years away in college football. And a tie would be tantamount to a loss for Tennessee in the race for Birmingham (site of the first SEC title game). Majors went for two points and the win, but the conversion attempt was no good. Tennessee no longer controlled their own destiny in the SEC East. In fact, the Vols would finish in third place behind Florida and Georgia.

The Vols would play at Memphis State on November 14. But the day before that game, the fifty-seven-year-old Majors announced that he was done. "Since I have not been given the opportunity by the UT administration to remain as head football coach past this current season, I am, effective Dec. 31st, 1992, relinquishing all my duties connected with the University of Tennessee." Majors would have the last two years of his contract bought out. He'd coach Tennessee's final three regular season games (all wins), and the following season would return to coach at Pittsburgh, where he had won a national championship in 1976. After the season ending victory over Vanderbilt on November 28, Majors had a parting shot for those he considered to be Judas. "I want to thank the athletic department staff, the UT faculty and school officials who've been so helpful," he said. "And, of course, I want to thank all my assistants... *the loyal ones.*"

The next day, the forty-two-year-old Fulmer was officially named as the new Tennessee head coach. "Obviously this is an exciting time in my life," Fulmer said. "It's something I've always dreamed of doing..." Fulmer had to address reports in the *Knoxville News-Sentinel* that this whole thing was basically a coup d'etat. Some believed Fulmer, Tennessee athletics director Doug Dickey and UT president Joe Johnson joined forces to push Majors out. Fulmer was rumored to be up for other head coaching jobs, and if Tennessee didn't promote him, he'd leave for another opportunity.

Fulmer denied playing any role in this transition. "I want to make it known to all concerned that at no time have I ever demeaned or conspired against John Majors, or given anyone any sort of ultimatum," Fulmer said. "I was put in the middle of a situation not of my making. I have put my love, my heart and soul into this program, and that is the reason I'm standing here today. I appreciate all that Coach Majors has done for me and I always will wish him well."

To this day, there are grudges that remain in Vol Nation over the Majors/Fulmer saga. But whether you are a Majors supporter or a Fulmer backer, everyone can agree Tennessee was able to take a final step under Fulmer that they hadn't been able to under Majors. Fulmer won SEC titles in 1997 and 1998, and on January 4, 1999, the Vols upset Florida State 23-16 to win the first BCS National Championship. It was Tennessee's first consensus national title since 1951.

Majors lasted nearly sixteen seasons as Tennessee's head coach. 2007 was Fulmer's fifteenth season in control and gearing up to be his toughest to date. They already had been outscored 100-34 by their two biggest rivals. But there was still hope for the Vols, because 2007 was perhaps the strangest season in college football history. The eventual national champion, LSU, would finish the year with two losses. FCS (formerly Division I-AA) powerhouse Appalachian State upset fifth-ranked Michigan in Ann Arbor. Stanford was a 39-point underdog when they beat second-ranked Southern Cal. At one point or another, South Florida, Boston College and Kansas were each ranked second in the nation. *Kansas!*

On October 27, the Vols were preparing for Steve Spurrier and fifteenth-ranked South Carolina. Thanks to events taking place at the World Largest Outdoor Cocktail Party in Jacksonville, UT suddenly was the leader in the race for the SEC East. "Earlier in the day, Georgia beat Florida," remembers Garrett Gooch, who was working as the sports photographer at WATE-TV, Knoxville's ABC affiliate. "After the Vol Walk I was in the media interview room before the game watching Georgia/Florida; and you could hear very loud cheering coming from the Vols locker room as Georgia was dominating Florida. Then, on the field during warmups, [Public Address Announcer] Bobby Denton announced the score and it got loud... really loud."

105,962 filled Neyland Stadium on that cool fall evening in Knoxville. They saw the Gamecocks outgain the Vols in yardage 501-317. South Carolina had 31 first downs to Tennessee's 16 and dominated in time of possession. This was a game the Gamecocks should have won going away. But with nine seconds left, the Vols had a chance to force overtime. Freshman Daniel Lincoln lined up for a 43-yard field goal. Right before he kicked the ball, there was a flinch on the left side of the Vols offensive line. Lincoln's boot was well wide to the left, but it didn't matter. The play never happened. Lincoln got another chance, now five yards further back. But this time Lincoln snuck the football inside the left upright, and the game went to overtime. In the extra session, Lincoln kicked a 27-yarder, South Carolina's Ryan Succop badly missed a 41-yarder, and the Vols had an unlikely 27-24 victory.

"I think somebody said on television the next thing we had to look forward to was signing day and the draft," a fired up Fulmer said to the media after the game. "That's stupid. That's someone who doesn't have any idea what Tennessee football is about."

"Fulmer didn't coach any different or any harder after losses," says Taylor. "He was such a rock and so consistent. That's the one thing I remember. He was so locked in and focused right then and there on the moment... Obviously we had goals, but he was so focused on the next game. He didn't venture off that."

Next week the Vols blew out Louisiana-Lafayette 59-7, but that game meant nothing. If Tennessee could beat Arkansas, Vanderbilt and Kentucky, they'd win the Eastern Division. The following Friday, nearly 200 former Vols took out an ad in the *Knoxville News-Sentinel*, pledging their support for the embattled Fulmer. Tennessee football was family, and you didn't mess with Dad. On November 10, Tennessee played one of their best games of the entire season with a 34-13 win over a sneaky competitive Arkansas team. Foster and Montario Hardesty combined for 158 rushing yards, future New England Patriot standout Jerod Mayo had a pick-six, and Berry had two interceptions as well.

"Nobody thought we could win this game," said Mayo. "We weren't surprised because we played well on defense at home all year. Our pride has been bruised all year."

The two weeks that followed saw Tennessee win games in dramatic fashion, against opponents they had beat up for decades. On November 17, Tennessee hosted Vanderbilt. Things did not look promising entering the fourth quarter with the Vols trailing 24-9. Then Erik Ainge threw touchdown passes to Josh Briscoe and

Austin Rogers to bring them within two. The game tying two-point conversion failed, but Tennessee's defense forced a three and out. A huge punt return from Dennis Rogan set up the Vols in Vandy territory, and a 33-yard field goal from Lincoln gave the Vols a 25-24 lead with less than three minutes remaining.

The Commodores got a big kick runback of their own and were ready to end Tennessee's dream of a conference title. Bryant Hahnfeldt had a 49-yard field goal attempt with 38 seconds left. That kick had the distance, but it did not have the direction. The football kept drifting... drifting.... drifting... and eventually grazed the outside of the left upright.

Tennessee had survived. Again. "I never felt like we were in a pressure situation," Taylor recalls. "We lived there all the time. I always felt the power of that 'T' and the standard with that 'T'. It was different. You put that 'T' on and it's heavy. It's not for everyone."

Tennessee didn't exactly look like the top team in the league at this point in the season, but they were still finding ways to win and if they could beat Kentucky, they would be Atlanta bound. To say that the Vols had a little momentum in their rivalry with the Wildcats is to say that Frank Sinatra had decent pipes. Tennessee had won twenty-two straight football games against Kentucky. But in 2007 the Wildcats were no patsy. They were 7-4, with victories over ninth-ranked Louisville and top-ranked LSU. They were even favored to win the Tennessee game by the Vegas sportsbooks.

It was a bitterly cold afternoon in Lexington, but the action on the Commonwealth Stadium field was red-hot. The teams combined for 1,084 yards of offense. Ainge threw for 397 yards, and a single-game Tennessee record seven touchdown passes, a record that still stands today. Kentucky's Andre Woodson wasn't too shabby either, with six touchdown passes and 430 yards. The Vols had a 17-point lead late in the third quarter, but were it not for a goal-line stand by the Tennessee defense in the final minute that forced a tying field goal instead of a game winning touchdown, this game would have been over in regulation.

These teams battled through (LeBron James/Miami Heat voice) not one, not two, not three... but four overtimes. In the second OT, Kentucky's Lones Seiber (ironically enough hailing from Knoxville Central High School) lined up for a 35-yard field goal attempt for the win.

"Their fans jumped over the wall and were ready to storm the field," recalls Tennessee fan Craig Newman, who made the trip to Lexington with his wife and friends to cheer on the Vols. But Tennessee defensive lineman Dan Williams got a great push into the Kentucky line. He elevated just enough to block the kick with his left hand and the game continued. In the fourth overtime the two teams, by now physically spent and calling on a second or third wind, swapped touchdowns. Tennessee made their two-point conversion. Kentucky needed to convert as well to tie the game and force a fifth extra session.

Tennessee rushed four linemen. Woodson took the snap and stepped up to the right to avoid the pressure. For a moment, it looked like he was going to take off for the end zone. Woodson was listed at 6'5" and 225 pounds. He was able to run over defenders much easier than your average quarterback and seemed poised to do it again. But Tennessee defensive lineman Antonio Reynolds never gave up on the play. He chased down Woodson and forced him to the turf inside the five-yard line. The ball popped out, Tennessee recovered, and that was it. Vols players jumped into the crowd to celebrate with UT fans after the game ended.

Tennessee 52, Kentucky 50. The Vols were going to the ATL. "We were the last to leave the interview room and I remember Fulmer about to do his radio hit with [Voice of the Vols] Bob Kesling," says Gooch. "Fulmer looked so happy and a great deal exhausted."

"Just consider these crazy stats. It took three missed field goals - South Carolina in overtime, Vanderbilt at the end of regulation, and Kentucky in the second overtime - to get us to Atlanta," observed Tennessee fan Justin Wear, a 2004 graduate who named his son Peyton. "We went to Atlanta having been outscored in the aggregate in SEC play."

Tennessee fans had a love/hate relationship with the Georgia Dome, with an emphasis on hate. Yes, the Vols football team won two SEC titles there, but they had lost two others in that barn as well, plus two Chick-fil-A Bowls. Tennessee men's basketball team played in eleven SEC tournaments at the Georgia Dome, and never got to the championship game. Even the Lady Vols basketball team lost the 2003 national championship to despised UConn there.

But that didn't stop Tennessee fans from showing up in droves. The Georgia Dome turned into Neyland Stadium – Atlanta style. "It was so exciting! Tennessee fans were so pumped up," said Nickie Rhoads, a Vols fan who went to the game with her Mom. "I definitely felt like it was a Tennessee crowd."

"It was the same as it always is when the Vols play in Atlanta. A big orange party," remembers Chuck Morris, a 2002 Tennessee grad. "The bars and restaurants were full of UT fans. I remember that there were daiquiri stations set up in the Georgia World Congress Center and it seemed like it was all LSU fans in line. There seemed to be a cautious optimism with the fan base. I personally was a little worried given the Vols history in the Dome over the previous years."

"I'll never forget riding the MARTA to the arena," said Kevin Hughes, a 2011 Tennessee grad who would later work in the Knoxville sports media. "Thousands of Tennessee fans screaming 'Rocky Top' at the top of their lungs. The looks on the faces of the Atlanta locals riding the train that day as drunk Vol fans screamed at 9am was amazing. My friends and I were nervous and drinking way too much, but we couldn't stop talking about how excited we were about being SEC champs in just a few short hours. I screamed the entire way into the game and definitely exchanged some words with LSU fans. I paid $12 for a 32-ounce beer with my fake ID."

The big story before the game had nothing to do with LSU's quarterback situation (Ryan Perrilloux was subbing for the injured Matt Flynn). Instead, it surrounded the future of their head coach, Les Miles. That morning, ESPN's Kirk Herbstreit, an analyst not known for having breaking news chops, reported that Miles was heading to Michigan after the season to take over for the retiring Lloyd Carr.

"I saw a chalk message written on the rear window of a Tennessee fan's car parked outside the Georgia Dome," Vols fan

Philip Kirkham told me. *"200 miles to Knoxville. 500 miles to Baton Rouge. Les Miles to Ann Arbor."*

Miles wouldn't let the rumors swell. He showed up at the podium of the Georgia Dome media room for a hastily called press conference with kickoff only a few hours away. "I'm the head coach at LSU," said an animated Miles. "I will be the head coach at LSU. I have no interest in talking to anybody else. I got a championship game to play, and I'm excited for the opportunity of my damn strong football team to play in it. Please ask me after. I'm busy. Thank you very much. Have a great day!" With that, Miles left the room.

The Vols surprised the 73,832 in attendance by pulling off a uniform switch that brought forth varied reactions among Big Orange Country. "I remember going out for pregame and the Vols were wearing orange pants with orange jerseys. Big, big mistake," says Gooch. "That uniform choice, combined with LSU predominantly yellow and white, made for one ugly looking game. Daniel Moye was an Adidas representative for Tennessee. We had a friendly relationship. He hooked me up with some gear and we chatted before pretty much every game. Anyway, I remember asking him about the pants and he said it was a struggle to get them. They were 'hiding' in some warehouse or something and barely made it to the game."

"The older fans around us didn't seem to like it because of the non-traditional look," says Morris. "Overall though it did seem to pump up the fan base."

"I noticed the orange pants as we were walking up the ramp as they were warming up in pregame and texted a buddy immediately," says Newman. "I was pumped when I first saw them and thought it would give us a little bit of a boost. Then I remembered how crappy we always played in those orange pants, thinking back to the Memphis game in 1999 when we won late in the fourth quarter."

The underdog Vols (and their orange pants) shocked the Tigers by taking the opening kickoff and marching right down the field. Ainge hit tight end Chris Brown for an 11-yard touchdown pass just three minutes into the game. As was the case quite often during the second half of the season, the Vols would be behind on the stat sheet, but within reach on the scoreboard. With 3:09 to go in the third quarter, Ainge threw another 11-yard touchdown pass, this time to Briscoe. The Vols were up 14-13, and their first conference championship in nine years was tantalizingly close.

This would be revenge, a dish served six years cold. LSU upset Tennessee in this very game back in 2001, costing the Vols a shot at the national championship. Had the Vols won, they would have played in the Rose Bowl against that memorable 2001 Miami team. Tennessee had the firepower to give that Hurricanes group a battle, at least more than the woefully overrated Nebraska squad did, but the Tigers took that opportunity away.

If the Vols could hang on, they'd keep LSU from playing for the national championship. Later that night, Pittsburgh upset second-ranked West Virginia, opening the door for the Tigers. Tennessee faced third down deep in their own end of the field, and Ainge made a throw he wished he could have had back. The pass went right to LSU defensive back Jonathan Zenon, who returned it 18 yards for a go-ahead score.

Vol Nation was devastated. "From our seats, you could see it unfolding as soon as the ball left his hand," says Wear. "It was like watching a car crash in slow motion. The Tennessee people in our area let out an audible gasp as you saw where Zenon was playing and his anticipated break. It was a movie scene where someone yelled out "NOOOOOOOOO" as the priceless antique crashes to the floor."

"In a way, that interception was the symbol of the Tennessee fan base over the past ten years," says Morris. "How many times, year in and year out, has the season started with optimism and then something falls apart."

After the successful two-point conversion, there was 9:54 remaining, and LSU led 21-14. The Vols drove inside the LSU 25 on two separate occasions in the minutes that followed. But the tying score was not to be. There was a turnover on downs, and another Ainge INT. Les Miles and the LSU Tigers would win the SEC championship 21-14. After the game, Ainge sat tall at the podium, taking the blame for LSU's winning score. "He [Zenon] made a good play. I shouldn't have thrown the ball out there," said Ainge. "I mean, just as much as he made a good play, I made a bad decision. We protected all night. The guys played hard... It's on me."

"Erik Ainge is the reason we're here, one of the reasons that we're here," said Fulmer. "We win as a team, we lose as a football team, not any one of us." Brian Rice made the trip from Knoxville to the game. "As I left the stadium, I turned to [Lady Vols Sports Information Department employees] Brian Davis and Cameron Harris and said, 'Thank God I never have to see Erik Ainge play quarterback again.'" In 2017, Brian Rice started co-hosting a sports talk radio show on WNML, The Sports Animal. Which show, you ask? "The Erik Ainge Show."

Despite the loss, Fulmer was thinking about Tennessee's seasons to come. "We're playing a lot of young people right now, which is exciting for the future, and it's exciting to watch them grow up here. It also makes you have some gray hair sometimes."

For the second straight year, Tennessee accepted a bid to the Outback Bowl. On New Year's morning 2008, they'd face Wisconsin in the Tampa sunshine, a proper reward for a team that battled game after game and nearly won the conference championship. The Vols would beat Bret Bielema's Badgers 21-17. Ainge threw for 365 yards and two touchdowns in his last game as a Volunteer.

Fulmer was beaming when he spoke with ESPN's Rob Stone. "I am so proud for these kids. They have fought and had great energy throughout the year to fight through the adversities and fight through the negativity."

It was another ten-win season for the Vols, the ninth time in Fulmer's fifteen years at the helm that Tennessee won at least that many games. This mark is even more impressive when you remember that a twelve-game regular season didn't come into existence until 2002.

Fulmer received a $350,000 raise, bumping him up to $2.4 million per year. A contract extension inked him through the year 2014. "I know he's adamant about trying to move up the ranks in SEC wins and Tennessee wins," said Tennessee athletics director

Mike Hamilton. "His plans are to coach a while, and I'm going to support him in doing that in the hopes that we'll also see some rings and trophies along the way."

Sometimes, the best laid plans never get the chance to come to fruition.

I wish I had more pictures from my sportscasting days. After some searching I was able to dig up this dandy snapshot from the 2008 Outback Bowl in Tampa.

2

A HOUSE DIVIDED

HEADING INTO THE 2008 SEASON, there was reason for optimism at Tennessee, with highly regarded quarterback Jonathan Crompton taking over for Erik Ainge. Vols fans saw positive signs from Crompton when he subbed for an injured Ainge during the 2006 season and expected big things from the Waynesville (NC) native. With his strong arm and ability to run, Crompton reminded fans of another quarterback from North Carolina that was successful on Rocky Top, 1993 Heisman Trophy runner-up Heath Shuler.

The Vols entered the season ranked eighteenth in the country. "We were preparing for an exciting year of coverage," says Wes Boling, at the time a sports reporter at Knoxville's CBS affiliate, WVLT-TV. "Both sides of the ball featured NFL prospects and numerous returning starters. The Vols may not have been in the national title conversation, but they expected to contend for an SEC crown."

Phillip Fulmer's coaching staff was one of consistency throughout most of his tenure, but he needed to replace four assistants heading into the 2008 season. That was a tremendous amount of turnover in the Fulmer era during one off-season, and the biggest change was on offense. Coordinator David Cutcliffe had resigned to become the head coach at Duke. Fulmer picked Richmond head coach Dave Clawson to replace Cutcliffe. "I am very excited about naming Dave Clawson as our new offensive coordinator," Fulmer said. "I took the attitude that this was a great opportunity for me to evaluate the coaching talent out there and find the perfect fit for a new era of Tennessee offensive football."

Clawson was only forty years old and considered to be one of college football's up and coming coaches. The commonly held belief around the UT football complex was that if Clawson did well, he could one day replace Fulmer as the Vols' head coach. "I had been a head coach at the FCS level for nine years," Clawson told me. "It was an opportunity to work in the SEC and learn from Coach Fulmer. It was a professional challenge that I was really excited about."

"Clawson was known as a master tactician who brought a lot of creativity to the table," says Boling. "The Vols had some toys to work with... Arian Foster had enjoyed a breakout 2007 campaign. There was a deep stable of running backs, and the team's top six receivers were all back from the previous season. I think Vols fans were counting on success."

Tennessee was originally scheduled to open the season on September 6, at home against UAB. But in order to accommodate ESPN, the Vols and UCLA agreed to move their game to September 1, Labor Day evening at the Rose Bowl. This was a chance for Tennessee to separate from a packed opening weekend and have a national television audience all to themselves. Tennessee did something similar four years earlier for their season opener on a Sunday night against UNLV. But that was at home, and only involved moving the game to one night later.

This time, instead of what would have basically been a tune up contest to start the schedule against the Blazers with the UCLA game the following week, the Vols had a tricky beginning to the 2017 season some 2,200 miles from home. The UAB game would be pushed to Saturday, September 13. That was supposed to be a bye week for Tennessee. Hundreds of brides and grooms across the state shed tears as their guest lists began to shrink. They knew many Vols fans would pick a trip to Neyland Stadium over a visit to First Baptist Church. Schedule significant events in the South on football Saturdays at your own peril...

Coaches and players are creatures of habit. They are all about schedules, and something as extreme as changing the football docket, even months in advance, messes with the mojo. Something felt off all night for the Vols. They picked off UCLA's Kevin Craft four times in the first half but couldn't take advantage. Crompton was shaky in his first start in nearly two years, completing less than 50% of his passes. The game went to overtime. The Bruins kicked a field goal and the moment Daniel Lincoln's 34-yard game tying attempt stayed wide of the left upright, the hot seat Fulmer had fought so hard to get away from in 2007 was hotter than ever.

"We made enough mistakes tonight to lose three, four or five football games," said Fulmer. "Whether it was offensively, defensively or in the kicking game... you can choose any one of them. These are things that are fixable."

That game in Pasadena was an early sign about just how rough 2008 would be for Tennessee. "It was a scary time after that UCLA loss in the opener," says Charles West, a 1996 Tennessee grad. "At the time we went on to say, 'Maybe UCLA will be special this season?' Then they got drilled by BYU the next week 59-0, en route to a four-win Bruins season. It was scary to think, 'What if we can't score all year?'"

The timing for a down season was not good for Fulmer, as the SEC was at the height of its powers. The national champion came from the Southeastern Conference each year from 2006-2012. In the Eastern Division alone, Urban Meyer and Tim Tebow were dominating in Gainesville. Mark Richt was still winning in Athens and Steve Spurrier was turning things around in Columbia.

To make matters worse, throughout the year there were signs that some Tennessee players weren't totally invested. "I remember that we were punished for losing to someone and we were called in really early to run that morning," says Cody Pope, who played offensive line at Tennessee from 2007-2010. "Most players were already checked out mentally and were quite intoxicated, and all the coaches showed up to watch us run. Most people who were drunk actually ran well. This gave way to an idea against Mississippi State, when one player asked me to carry a Gatorade bottle of Crown & Coke in my helmet during the game. I wasn't playing, so anything for the team. I just remember him playing really well. He graded out well too. I know it sounds wild."

Focus was an issue for Tennessee's most talented offensive player. "Arian Foster was a smart, articulate guy, and the Vols needed his leadership when the team's prospects went south," says Boling. "Instead, he said he would only conduct interviews with reporters who 'spoke pterodactyl.' When the Tennessee Sports Information Department would try to wrangle him for post-practice interviews, he'd squawk at us and keep walking. I'm sure he was as frustrated as anybody – heck he scored only one touchdown all year – but that was no way for a senior to lead a team."

On September 27, the Vols traveled to fifteenth-ranked Auburn. That game was the perfect representation of the 2008 season for both teams. "It was a great day for football," says Auburn grad Justin Cazana. "We had brought a bus down from Knoxville and hosted dozens of Auburn and UT fans at a tailgate next to the stadium. Everything about the day was great... except for the quality of football."

"The stadium was full and when the eagle was circling from the top deck, it felt like the earth was moving." recalls Prentice Elliott, who was working as a sports photographer at WATE-TV. "That Auburn experience was fantastic... right up to kickoff."

Unfortunately, the in-game action couldn't come close to matching the pre-game festivities. UT student Nathan Nease watched the game from the upper deck at Jordan-Hare Stadium. "I remember me and my friends saying, 'This is the worst football we have ever watched,'" says Nease. "It felt like we were watching a youth football game. Neither team could move the ball or get out of their own way."

Crompton completed only eight passes, and they went to eight different Vols for a total of 67 yards. Gerald Jones had the best day among Tennessee pass catchers with one reception for 14 yards.

Auburn wasn't much better. The Tigers lone touchdown came when Crompton and Foster botched a handoff and Jake Ricks fell on the football in the end zone. Both teams combined for only 417 yards of offense and 24 first downs. In the fourth quarter, the Vols and Tigers combined for eight punts and seven straight three and outs.

They should burn the fourth quarter tape, bury the ashes with a shovel, and then bury the shovel.

"I was on the sideline shooting the game with the rest of the photogs and it was standard practice to switch ends of the field to make sure you were in position for the best plays," says Elliott. "After a while, everyone with a camera gave up. We all stopped moving because of the sheer amount of punts."

All Tennessee needed to do was make one first down and they'd be in Daniel Lincoln's range for what was potentially a game winning field goal. It never happened. Auburn finally got a first down when Kodi Burns completed a pass to Montez Billings on a play in which Burns was nearly tackled for a safety (naturally). That allowed Auburn to run out the clock.

Auburn 12, Tennessee 10. "Adversity will challenge us, and we will see where we really stand," Fulmer said.

"It was bewildering," says two-time Auburn grad Brian Stultz, who watched the game with other AU alums at Bar 515 in New York City. "To be honest, I never thought for a second that Auburn was going to lose the game, and I think a lot of that had to do with how bad Tennessee was. The bar, usually loud and full of atmosphere, was completely dead. It was almost like everyone was thinking, 'OK, just let this game end.'"

"As we exited the field, it was the first time I'd ever heard such vitriol aimed at the coaching staff," Boling remembers. "Tennessee fans were leaning over the railing hurling criticism at Fulmer, and I think it was the first moment I thought his job might be in jeopardy. I overheard a couple of defensive linemen cursing Crompton on their way to the locker room."

As the season went on, the chatter about Fulmer's future at Tennessee continued. The players were not overly concerned because of what they were being told by their coach. "We were hearing about Fulmer being on the hot seat," says former Tennessee defensive back Derrick Furlow Jr., who today is an entrepreneur, speaker and author of *"What's Next: How to Transition Like a Champion."*

"Coach Fulmer talked to the team and said that [the administration] promised that he wasn't going to be fired," says Furlow. "He said he was going to be here and that he wasn't going anywhere. That was comforting."

But Fulmer's job was never in as much peril as it was on October 25, when the 3-4 Vols hosted second-ranked Alabama. Nick Saban was building a bulldozer in Tuscaloosa. It wasn't just that Tennessee lost that night 29-9. It was that approximately 15,000 Alabama fans had found their way into Neyland Stadium and took over the building. A week later, Tennessee dropped to 3-6 after a loss at South Carolina. Nick Stephens, now installed as Tennessee's starting quarterback for Crompton, threw for only 134 yards. He also gave up a pick-six. Overall, the Vols gained a paltry 207 yards. "The frustration of the offensive team right now, on a scale of 1 to 10, is probably a 10," admitted Fulmer after the game. "I appreciate the players getting back out there and working so hard. There were a lot of hurt feelings in the locker room because that is not the way Tennessee is supposed to be. It's not what they came here for."

Tennessee fans were split. On one hand, this had the potential to be a second losing season in four years, something that hadn't happened since 1980. On the other hand, the Vols were one interception away from winning the SEC only a year before, and Fulmer was a beloved, future hall of fame coach. On a personal note, I was working as a Sports Anchor/Reporter at WATE-TV that season and was tasked with editing a Phillip Fulmer retrospective package that would be ready to go in case Fulmer was fired. It's the type of thing that you have prepared in advance if a notable figure is gravely ill. It felt nearly as morbid putting that piece together. We were all waiting for an announcement.

The pressure was on Tennessee athletics director Mike Hamilton. But he had the backing of key power players, both on and off campus, to make a move if necessary. He had caught lightning in a bottle with the hiring of Bruce Pearl to coach the men's basketball team in 2005. Pearl turned the Vols into an SEC powerhouse, with a regular season title and three NCAA tournament appearances to that point. More recently, in 2007, Hamilton showed fans that he was willing to make a move when he fired baseball coach Rod Delmonico after eighteen seasons and 699 wins, including three trips to the College World Series. Hamilton was about to make the most important decision of his tenure. It would have a massive effect on Tennessee football for the next decade.

On Monday, November 3, 2008, the most gut-wrenching press conference in the history of the University of Tennessee occurred, as Phillip Fulmer announced that he would be stepping down at the end of the season. Fulmer was being forced out. It's difficult to overstate just how big a deal this was in Knoxville and across the state.

That press conference aired live at 5pm ET on television stations in the Tri-Cities, Knoxville, Chattanooga, Nashville and Memphis. Satellite trucks surrounded Neyland Stadium. ESPN broke into their regular programming for the press conference as well. I was in the room that day, and the tension in the air was thick. Many in the athletics department were not happy with Hamilton's decision. Emotions were high for everyone involved, fans and boosters, players and alums, students and secretaries, reporters and ushers.

When a teary-eyed Fulmer said, "I love Tennessee too much to let her stay divided," a significant segment of the fan base felt it. Even if they wanted Fulmer gone, they didn't want it to be this way. This was a man who led Tennessee to two SEC titles and a national championship. This was a man who had given 34 of the past 40 years of his life to the University as a player, an assistant coach or a head coach.

This... was a *Tennessean*.

In Clay Travis's terrific book, *On Rocky Top*, which chronicled Tennessee's 2008 season, he wrote, "Watching Coach Fulmer deliver his speech is like watching your Dad cry. It's agonizing and uncomfortable as Fulmer chokes on several words."

Sometimes, when a coaching change happens, players are relieved. But in this case, there was almost unanimous anger on the part of the Volunteers. "About forty-five minutes or so before the press conference began, I sat down on the front row of the seating area to speak to a friend who was working for the student radio station," says Roger Hoover, a student writer at UTSports.com that season. "While we talked, the room became flooded with nearly the entire football team cramming into that tiny spot. It became hard for some reporters to get in their normal spots for press conferences, but this was anything but normal. [Offensive lineman] Anthony Parker sat next to me, and right across from me half-seated on the stage was [defensive end] Wes Brown, who cried throughout the press conference. We had never seen Coach Fulmer or the players so emotional."

"We walked as a team from the meeting at the complex to the stadium to show unity and respect for him," remembers Pope. "A lot of us felt useless. We couldn't do anything to make the university take him back and the damage was already done. A lot of people were lost as Coach Fulmer was a more than a coach to them. He supplied stability for a lot of guys that never had it."

"How do you do this to our guy, our leader? He helped us grow as men," Furlow said. "You gave him your word and then it changed. We were mad. You don't lie to him and you especially don't do this in the middle of the season, after all he gave for UT."

"Fulmer was a father figure to a lot of us and we felt like the boosters and the AD were making a huge mistake," says Daryl Vereen, a Tennessee linebacker from 2007-2011. "We just made it to the SEC championship game the year before and continued to have good recruiting classes year after year. We knew by doing that, Tennessee wouldn't be the same for a while, if it was ever going to be the same again."

Fulmer was visibly moved by the support he received from his players. "That's what we're about," he said. "Some people may not understand that as well as others. When you're in the homes of these young men and you work eighteen hours a day with the coaches, you sacrifice a lot. It's in the name of Saturday afternoon, but it's not really about Saturday afternoon at all. The reason we all got into coaching was to have that relationship we have. A lot of people don't ever get to experience it and I've had it for a long time."

Fulmer has a son and three daughters. The hundreds of players he coached were also family. One of his former players is now his son-in-law. Fulmer's daughter Courtney married Robert Peace, a Tennessee linebacker from 2000-2003. When Fulmer was done speaking and left the room, Hamilton stayed at the podium to answer questions from reporters. Tennessee's players then stood up and walked out on Hamilton, some yelling at him as they departed.

"Emotions were high," remembers Furlow. "We had Fulmer's back and family sticks together. No one was happy with the decision. It was terrible how they went about it and we didn't like it. We wanted to make the administration know that we'd ride with him."

"I think change is never easy in life, in high school, college or beyond, and we will get through this process," Hamilton said from the podium. "It will be a painful process... but in the end the University of Tennessee will move on and Phillip [Fulmer] will be a part of this process in the end... we want him to be a part of the University of Tennessee."

I've been told that the initial plan was for UT President John Petersen to be sitting with Fulmer and Hamilton from the start of the press conference. Instead, the media-averse Petersen chose to stand in the back of the room, and then bolted midway through the event, leaving Hamilton to take the blows alone. "It seemed at certain points that Hamilton might not make it out of that presser," says Elliott. "From fans to players to coaches, they all expected so much more, and then to have the season devolve into a literal worst-case scenario was too much."

Tennessee lost the following week at home against lowly Wyoming. The Vols had no desire to be on the field that day, and their play proved it. But Tennessee didn't lay down. First, there was a 20-10 win at Vanderbilt, giving Fulmer a 15-1 record all-time against the Commodores.

The final week meant the Kentucky game. On Thanksgiving, Tennessee continued its "Last Tackle" tradition. This happened at the end of the last practice of the regular season. Fulmer would say some words about each of the seniors, who then would jog down the line and take out a tackling dummy dressed in the jersey of that week's opponent. Some seniors would go at the dummy with a WWE style "Stone Cold Stunner" or a "People's Elbow." Others would simply tip the dummy over with a slight touch, to the disappointment of their teammates. On this occasion, Fulmer obliged his players and took a turn himself. "I kind of got in on a cleanup block," Fulmer told reporters on Haslam Field. "I didn't have to hit it. It was already on the ground, so I just cleaned it up a little bit."

November 29, 2008 was "Phillip Fulmer Day" at Neyland Stadium. Fulmer would "Run Through the T" for the final time, this time with his family. Video tributes played on the Jumbotron. The nation's longest active win streak by one team over another would continue, as Tennessee beat Kentucky 28-10, leaving Fulmer a perfect 16-0 against UK. It was the Vols' twenty-fourth straight win over the Wildcats. The Vols also avoided the eight-loss nadir, something Tennessee had never reached in a single season.

Phillip Fulmer's record as Tennessee's head coach finished at 152-52. "It was a tough transition and November felt like a month-long funeral," says Hoover. "Coach Fulmer had put so much into building the program his way for sixteen seasons and it always felt like he'd coach there forever."

After the game, Fulmer was be carried off the field by offensive linemen Anthony Parker and Ramon Foster. This was a fitting end for a man who, even with his coordinator and head coaching success, was always an offensive lineman at heart. Fulmer held the game ball up high in his right hand, as the fans that stuck it out through the raindrops chanted his name. "I feel like that's the way a legend should go out, on top," said Tennessee defensive end Robert Ayers. "Coach Fulmer is a legend of college football and he is always going to be remembered at the University of Tennessee for being a great guy and a great coach."

The coaching community is a tight-nit group. Many of Fulmer's counterparts stood up for him in those final weeks, including the coach he just defeated. "I think it's a tragedy," said Kentucky head coach Rich Brooks. "I think it's a sad commentary on the coaching profession. Phillip Fulmer is a quality act, an outstanding coach... It's a crime to see people like that forced out of the profession."

"I've been so blessed," said Fulmer. "I'm sure it's going to take a few days [to sink in]. I guess my wife will kick me out of the house because I don't have anything to do now."

Tennessee could never get the "Clawfense" to work the way they wanted. "There were a lot of things I learned the hard way that I think I benefitted from," says Clawson. "I would have loved to take that learning curve and have that help Tennessee the following year, but it was not meant to be." In his previous stops at Fordham and Richmond, there was a gradual improvement on offense from season to season. At Tennessee, they didn't have that kind of time.

Crompton and Stephens alternated as the starting quarterback and in this case the old adage was correct. If you have two quarterbacks, you really have none. "Crompton was a kid we really wanted to get on the edge," remembers Clawson. "So much in what we designed was to get him on the edge and have run/pass options. Before the UCLA game he got a high ankle sprain, and that limited him the whole year. We weren't able to get him on the edge and put him in those situations because of the ankle. We tried to make him a pocket passer and I don't think he was comfortable doing that. I don't know if we maximized his skill set. That's the responsibility of the coordinator and I didn't do that."

"Dave Clawson was one of the nicest coaches that you will find in the NCAA," says Pope. "Unfortunately, I think he felt as if he had to recreate the wheel. He had guards and tackles flipping sides, one side quick and the other side strong. This confused even the smartest group of guys on the team, a group that let up only five sacks the year before."

"I think Clawson didn't have the right players to fit his system," says Tennessee grad Chris Newman, a student at UT during that fateful 2008 season. "I don't think I would have given him another year, but with players that fit his system, they could have thrived. I believe he has done well for himself since his short tenure with the Vols."

Clawson would become the head coach at Bowling Green in 2009. Five years later, he was named head coach at Wake Forest, and has led the Demon Deacons to two straight bowl game victories heading into the 2018 season. "I think I am a better coach because of that year, but I certainly didn't like the way it ended," says Clawson. "I loved working with Coach Fulmer. He was a great leader of that program and the type of coach you'd want your son to play for."

"What I'll remember about that season is how quickly it went downhill," says Elliott. "It was the start of a very strange time for Tennessee football." The firing of Phillip Fulmer was also the first big hit to the status quo at Tennessee. Brian Davis grew up a Tennessee fan in Jackson, and worked in women's athletics at Tennessee for thirteen years.

"It felt like a family. Phil's daughter Allison played on the softball team, so he was always around," Davis says. "Everybody seemed to be on same page in athletics with everyone pulling in the same direction. I'd look over and see Fulmer and Pat Summitt sitting together watching the game. I knew everyone in athletics had my back. It felt like a big family. Once Fulmer was fired and Mike Hamilton got his group in there, that's when it changed. When the outsiders came in... they didn't know what it was like before at UT. When they came in it started to change things. You didn't feel you could trust everyone anymore. There wasn't the same level of support."

Two days after Fulmer's last game, the Vols officially welcomed their new head coach, someone who was a 180 degree turn from "The Battle Captain" in every respect.

A new era of Tennessee football was about to begin. But no one could have known just how brief an era it would be.

In the Fall of 2008, I brought my daughter Lillian (2 1/2 years old at the time) to the UT football complex. She loved running around on the indoor field and pretending to score a touchdown. But soon thereafter things began to change within the Tennessee athletics department. Thanks in large part to the firings and resignations of many long-time employees, much of the family feel that was a hallmark of the program was lost.

3

THE LANE TRAIN

LANE KIFFIN WAS BORN INTO A FOOTBALL FAMILY. Son of legendary college and pro football defensive coordinator Monte Kiffin, Lane's childhood was spent on the football fields of Fayetteville, Raleigh, Green Bay, Buffalo, and Minnesota. After three seasons as a backup quarterback at Fresno State, he passed up his final season to become a student assistant coach for the Bulldogs. With that, a career was born.

Things really took off for Lane in 2001, when he was hired to coach tight ends at Southern Cal. He would serve under Pete Carroll in a variety of positions for the Trojans, including co-offensive coordinator. Those were the Matt Leinart, Reggie Bush, LenDale White championship teams that lit up the scoreboard. Those were the squads that came to your town, stole your girl and drank your booze.

Early in his tenure in Los Angeles, Lane got a glimpse of his future while working on recruiting. "When we were at USC as young assistants, me and Steve Sarkisian… we'd watch all the anonymous questionnaires come in," Lane told me in a February 2018 interview. "Who are your top five schools… Florida State was on all of those lists. Maybe a surprise was that Tennessee was on a ton of them. And these were kids from all across the country, five-star players. I remember seeing video of a Vol Walk. I saw a recruiting video where they had that online... L.A. doesn't have that type of atmosphere two hours before a game. We had nothing like the Vol Walk. Seeing that, I always had a picture of the passion there and that it was a top ten to fifteen job in the country."

Seven years later, Kiffin was paying attention to the events in Knoxville. "I researched it when it came open at the time and it was a premier job," Kiffin says. "It was one that we could go and really win at. It was more of a football town. Jimmy Sexton is my agent and we started the interview process there with Mike Hamilton and the committee, and I just kept getting excited about it."

Word started to leak about Phillip Fulmer's replacement in the days leading up to the Kentucky finale on November 29, but Tennessee wouldn't make anything official until that game was complete. On Sunday, November 30, Lane Kiffin was named as the twenty-first head coach of the Tennessee Volunteers, and was formally introduced the next day. Kiffin was only thirty-three years old, but had already built an impressive resume. He relished the challenge that lay ahead. "The SEC at that point was maybe the strongest it ever been or will be when you look at that next year with Alabama and Florida being the number one and number two teams in the country," Kiffin says. "That's not even talking about Mark Richt, Steve Spurrier, Les Miles... and it was great players everywhere. Why not go and try to beat the best?"

Part of the appeal to Tennessee athletics director Mike Hamilton was that this wasn't just the hiring of Lane Kiffin, but the hiring of a team of coaches that would get the Vols back where they belonged. Lane's father Monte would be the Vols defensive coordinator. Monte was the well-respected sixty-eight-year-old defensive coordinator of the Tampa Bay Buccaneers, and he was willing to take a pay cut to coach with his son. Ed Orgeron, the energetic former Ole Miss coach, would be the Vols assistant head coach, recruiting coordinator and defensive line coach. Jim Chaney would be the offensive coordinator, coming to Knoxville from the St. Louis Rams, although Lane Kiffin would be the one calling the plays. Throw in guys like Lance Thompson, Willie Mack Garza and

David Reaves (Lane's brother-in-law at the time), and you had a coaching staff that was all about crootin'.

"By finding these coaches as SEC schools, that's addition by subtraction," Lane told *Sports Illustrated* in February 2009. "I have to play Alabama every year, and I basically stole their best guy [Thompson]," I have to play South Carolina. I took their best guy [Reaves]… Ed Orgeron was going to be LSU's recruiting coordinator. I went and got him… I like to joke that we'd have the best recruiting class in the country right now if I'd spent as much time recruiting players as I've spent recruiting coaches."

Hamilton wasn't always sold on Kiffin. He kicked the tires on a few different coaches, including Air Force's Troy Calhoun and Cincinnati's Brian Kelly, who would eventually take the Notre Dame job. There was another coach considered that make Tennessee fans wonder what might have been. Today, TCU's Gary Patterson is considered to be one of college football's best coaches. The folks at TCU have built a statue of him in front of their football stadium, thanks to a 159-57 record in 17 seasons running the Horned Frogs program (very similar to Fulmer's 152-52 mark in over 16 seasons at Tennessee). In November 2008, Patterson was up for the Vols job, but Hamilton decided to go in a different direction.

In 2017, Patterson told ESPN's Chris Low, "Tennessee didn't think I could handle the big stage. My wife and I went to dinner with them, and I could tell they had already decided on Kiffin… I think a lot of these AD's now are more interested in hiring guys who're going to win the podium than they are in hiring football coaches, and there's a lot more to it than if you're going to win championships."

Winning the podium? Kiffin did just that on day one. A packed house filled Neyland Stadium's Wolf-Kaplan Center to welcome Kiffin that Monday. "When you actually spend time with Lane, you see his unbelievable energy, and his incredible focus on the competitive nature on the recruiting process," said Hamilton. "He's charismatic, he has a plan for everything he is doing, and he is a tireless worker. He will assemble a great staff, and we will support his efforts in doing that."

When it was Kiffin's turn to speak, he immediately sent a shot across the bow of the SEC's biggest battleship. "I'm really looking forward to embracing some of the great traditions at the University of Tennessee, for instance the Vol Walk, Running Through the T, singing 'Rocky Top' all night long after we beat Florida next year. It's gonna be a blast, ok? So, get ready." Fans and boosters applauded in the room, and across the state.

"It probably wasn't as premeditated as people think," Kiffin recalls. "It was literally sitting there, jotting down some notes. Mike Hamilton was there. [Agent] Jimmy [Sexton] mentioned, 'Hey, you can get them really excited by saying something about winning in The Swamp.' That's really where that came from. In general, there was a plan that we need to install confidence in players and the fanbase because they had been beaten up the last few years. There were some lopsided losses, and Florida and Alabama were rolling and Florida was really rolling, so part of that was by design."

While some Tennessee fans didn't like the bravado, many ate it up. For years Fulmer stayed mostly silent while Florida coach Steve Spurrier took jabs at the Vols. "You can't spell Citrus without U-T" was the most well-known Spurrier blast. The Vols played the Citrus Bowl in 1995 and 1996, the same years Florida was playing for national championships. While Tennessee had turned the tide in their rivalry with Florida at the end of the Spurrier era and during the Ron Zook years (the Vols won four of their seven meetings from 1998-2004), that changed when Urban Meyer showed up in Gainesville. UT had lost four in a row to Florida. The idea that Lane wanted to poke the big bear was a delicious prospect.

"For friends my age, all of us juniors in college, that's the type of attitude that not only resonated with us, but that we craved," says Tony Geist, a student when Kiffin was hired and now a two-time graduate of the University. "The dude oozed swagger and it was exactly what college kids wanted to see."

The first time Lane Kiffin ever set foot in Knoxville was the night before that press conference. There was no way for him to know just how big a deal the Vols were in that town. In Los

Angeles, SoCal football was a newsmaker, especially back when L.A. had no professional football team. In L.A. there are approximately 700,000 other things that a person can to do there on any given day. It's a city of four million people, most of whom cared more about Brad and Angelina than who won the Heisman.

In Knoxville, it's Tennessee football that runs the show. When the Vols are good, the local economy is better. The hotels and restaurants are packed, and the souvenirs fly off the shelves. If the Vols are winning ten games and competing for SEC titles, it's like printing money here. But Kiffin needed to put together a roster that was going to win football games. The Vols had gone 5-7 in 2008, but would lose only one player (Robert Ayers) to the 2009 NFL Draft. Disgruntled yet talented running back Arian Foster was graduating. He went undrafted, but would go on to rush for 6,527 yards in the NFL.

The Vols learned quickly that the past meant nothing. "Lane didn't care if you were an All-American or if you were a walk-on, his message was very clear. If you want to play you will need to earn it day one," says former Tennessee offensive lineman Cody Pope. "It's hard not to want to play for that. It hurt some player's egos a little bit... guys that had played or started before, they suddenly had to earn their spot."

The roster Fulmer left Kiffin was not lacking in talent. Safety Eric Berry was hitting his stride entering his junior season. Foster's backup, Montario Hardesty, was ready to pick up the slack on the ground. In all, six players from Kiffin's 2009 team would be taken in the 2010 NFL Draft. Kiffin also had what was potentially a top-ten recruiting class to work with that Fulmer had been securing. Kiffin had to decide which of those players he wanted, and who he was going to nudge away from Knoxville.

Fulmer had verbal commitments from two quarterbacks for the Class of 2009, Phoebus (Hampton, VA) High School's Tajh Boyd and Midlothian (TX) High School's Bryce Petty. According to a June 2015 article by Nathanael Rutherford that was posted to the Rocky Top Talk website, Kiffin told Boyd's father that he would honor his scholarship, but that Boyd didn't fit his system. Boyd would decommit. As for Petty, ten days had gone by after Kiffin's hiring and he and his family still hadn't heard from him. Petty got the hint and decommitted as well. Boyd became a standout at Clemson, with Petty also having a great deal of success at Baylor.

Kiffin spent the first two months after he was hired crisscrossing the country, eventually landing what would be ranked by 247Sports as the eighth-best recruiting class in 2009. Lane Kiffin spoke about his class on National Signing Day and... Story time? Story time! *(Ok, I'm taking liberties with the topic but heck, I'm the one writing this book and I think it's a fun story. I hope you do as well.)* A couple of days before National Signing Day (Wednesday, February 4) I had the day off work. Our daughter Lillian was two years old, and we recently had found out that my wife Jennifer was pregnant with our second child. Emily was born on September 17.

Sportscaster hours are awful, especially during football and basketball seasons. I tried to make the most of my time with Lillian. On Monday, February 2, I took Lillian to one of those open gym type places in town. You know, the kind of place where the kids get to run and jump and have a ball and hopefully be tuckered and sleep through the night when they get home. The bad part of those places is that they are basically big petri dishes. So many germs...

The next day, Lillian was sick. She caught whatever bug they had festering around that place. That was a long day and night, but she was bouncing back by the time I left for work on National Signing Day. Tennessee was holding a press conference later that afternoon to talk about the Class of 2009, so I was on my way to the football complex. Back then, Tennessee held its press conferences in their old Football Hall of Fame. They set the podium up in the front of the room with trophy cases to each side and a few rows of chairs in the middle. Cameras had their own podium in the back of the room. I took a seat in the front row.

About a minute before Lane was going to start speaking, I started to feel warm. Really warm. Like, too warm. Oh no. Not now. Yeah, the 24-hour bug that Lillian caught had made its way to me. Lane started talking about the recruits, and I was going to get sick.

The winter coat I was still wearing made it feel like your Grandma's house in December, ninety degrees and rising. The problem I ran into was the real estate. The tiny room at the Hall of Fame was packed. I couldn't go backwards and the sides were blocked by trophy cases. I had a choice. Either make a scene and run out in front of Lane Kiffin during the press conference, or try to outlast the queasy feeling, and risk throwing up on the new Tennessee football coach in front of a live television audience.

I chose Option B. Lane probably talked for about thirty minutes, and during that time I was sweating like Nixon. Finally, Lane was finishing up (thank you baby Jesus) and then immediately introduced his recruiting coordinator Ed Orgeron and asked him to step to the podium. My reaction? $%#! I had missed my opening, and now I was afraid of throwing up on a wild man hopped up on Red Bull. So Orgeron spoke for probably fifteen minutes, and I'm sweating like an extra in *Cool Hand Luke.* Things could get bad at any second. I can't remember if things really went "viral" back in 2009, but if they did, I bet this would have. By the grace of God, the Vols' assistant coach finished his talk. I calmly walked out of the football complex and felt the sweet cool Knoxville air on my face. I was gonna be ok.

I got home, immediately went into the bathroom, and proceeded to make a nest by the commode for the next eighteen hours. I told my wife to take Lillian to her mother's house in Kingston. Remember, Jennifer was pregnant so the last thing I wanted was for her to be around me in this state. Jen ended up getting the bug anyway, as did Jen's Mom. That darn gym... And that's the tale of how I almost threw up on Lane Kiffin.

Now back to the crootin' talk. The Class of 2009 was a group big on flash. Five players from Rivals.com's top-100 made the list, safety Janzen Jackson, tailbacks Bryce Brown and David Oku, linebacker Jerod Askew and wide receiver Nu'Keese Richardson. Lane Kiffin was so proud of the Richardson pull that he decided to take a swing at Urban Meyer during a celebration breakfast event. Kiffin had the mic, and let it fly.

"I'm gonna turn Florida in right here in front of you. While Nu'Keese was on campus, his phone keeps ringing. One of the coaches said, 'Who's that?' And he said, 'Urban Meyer.' Just so you know, you can't call a recruit on another campus. I love the fact that Urban had to cheat and still didn't get him."

Of course, Urban Meyer hadn't broken any SEC or NCAA rules by calling Richardson while he was on a UT visit. Florida demanded an apology, and the SEC publicly reprimanded the Vols' first-year coach. In a statement released by the University of Tennessee's Sports Information Department, Kiffin said: "I apologize to Commissioner Mike Slive and the SEC, including Florida AD Jeremy Foley and coach Urban Meyer. My comments were not intended to offend anyone at the University of Florida."

During that same recruiting cycle, Kiffin allegedly told Alshon Jeffery, one of the top high school players in South Carolina that he'd end up pumping gas for the rest of his life if he stayed in-state and played for the Gamecocks. Jeffery said that others heard the conversation with Kiffin on speaker phone. Kiffin has denied saying this to him. Jeffery did end up signing with South Carolina and has become a Pro Bowl wide receiver in the NFL. He caught a touchdown pass in Philadelphia's win over New England in Super Bowl LII.

The Bryce Brown recruitment in particular was met with skepticism around college football. That whole thing was, well, shady. A man named Brian Butler identified himself as Brown's "trainer and handler," and recruiting updates about Brown were sold for $9.99 a month or $59 a year. It was like VolQuest, but all the news was only about one dude. Brown had been committed to Miami for a year. His brother Arthur was playing for the Canes. But Bryce didn't sign on National Signing Day. A month later, he announced that he was heading to Knoxville.

"I remember seeing that Tennessee signed Bryce Brown - then the number one running back in the country, I believe – and I was stunned," said Jesse Smithey, who was the high school sports editor at the *Knoxville News-Sentinel*. "I didn't even want to know what really went on behind the scenes to get Brown to commit and sign with the Vols. I'd bet good money it wasn't Tennessee's rich tradition or that the campus 'felt like home.'"

The NCAA looked into Brian Butler's relationship with Bryce Brown, and whether Brown's amateur status was in jeopardy. Eventually, Bryce Brown was given the ok to play for the Vols. A couple of weeks after National Signing Day, long-time Tennessee athletics department employee David Blackburn was promoted to Senior Associate AD for Administration and Football Operations. Blackburn was well respected on campus, a Tennessee grad that worked for both Johnny Majors and Phillip Fulmer. "David has served as football operations director in the past and has worked closely with Coach Kiffin and his staff since their hiring," said Hamilton in a statement. "He has been a tremendous asset for me on the administration side and will become an even greater asset to UT Athletics in this increased role."

This move was significant... not that Blackburn was initially on board. "Mike asked me to go, and I said I didn't want to," Blackburn told me in 2018. "I felt that would put a nail in my coffin. I never thought I'd get back to being a deputy AD." Three weeks after he was originally approached, Hamilton and UT Interim President Jan Simek didn't ask Blackburn again. This time, they *told* Blackburn that he was taking the job.

"I got it," Blackburn says. "I took it as a badge of honor to do what I could for the school. It was not something I wanted to do at the time, but after four to five months I was glad I did it because I was now a watchdog for UT and the coaches, and it helped me grow as an administrator." Blackburn would set up an office inside the football complex and be able to keep a closer eye on Lane Kiffin and his staff, while working with them directly in the months that followed.

"That was Mike's plan," Kiffin says. "I thought it was a great plan, not knowing ton about UT history and connections to the people. David had been there for years, knew the ins and outs of the university and all the people around there. He was working with Mike to come over to football operations to help us and that was really good."

"I give credit to Mike and Dr. Simek," says Blackburn. "They saw it could get out of control. They needed someone in that role to guide that staff because they could see problems coming. I think it would have spiraled." That coaching staff lived on the edges, some more daring than others. Shifting Blackburn's priorities might have been one of the most important decisions ever made in that department.

Despite the coaching staff screw-ups, none of which were program shaking by themselves at this point, Vols fans were ready to roll, buying their official "It's Time" t-shirts and thinking more and more about the upcoming season. Over 51,000 fans attended the Orange & White spring game on April 18, the most fans to show up at Neyland Stadium for that contest in thirty-three years. When the season began on September 5, an announced home crowd of 98,761 watched the Vols handle Western Kentucky 63-7. The following week, Jonathan Crompton threw four interceptions as the Vols lost 19-15 to a mediocre UCLA team.

The most highly anticipated game of the college football season happened on September 19, when Tennessee traveled to Gainesville to play top-ranked Florida. The Gators certainly remembered Kiffin's prediction from that introductory press conference, and not only didn't want Tennessee to sing "Rocky Top" all night long, but they wanted to embarrass the Vols. Urban Meyer was known for holding grudges, and would run up the score if the opportunity presented itself.

Most experts predicted a blowout. The Vols played conservatively. Crompton threw two more interceptions and had only 93 yards passing. Kiffin wasn't going to force things, even playing with a deliberate pace while only down two scores in the fourth. Florida won 23-13, but rarely has a ten-point loss felt more like a victory. For many Vols fans, simply not being run out of Ben Hill Griffin Stadium was enough. In their previous visit to Gainesville, the Vols lost by 39. After the game, Kiffin told reporters that all the trash talk was by design. "I think it worked perfectly," he said in the cramped visitor's media room. "It took all the pressure off our players."

Crompton continued to struggle, but a switch was flipped on October 10, when the Vols surprised Georgia 45-19. He passed for 310 yards and four touchdowns. Lane Kiffin has received a great deal of credit for getting the most out of his fifth-year quarterback, and deservedly so. Crompton played well the rest of the season. "I look at guys first based off talent and just seeing his arm talent and his prospects as a pro. There was a reason he was a five-star quarterback," Kiffin says. Crompton was so impressive that he was picked in the fifth round of the 2010 NFL Draft by the San Diego Chargers.

On October 24, the Vols were 3-3 when they played at top-ranked Alabama. Tennessee was a massive underdog, but Monte Kiffin's defense was stout that afternoon, allowing only four Leigh Tiffin field goals. With three and a half minutes to go it looked like Alabama was going to survive an uncharacteristically sluggish game. They led 12-3 when Eric Berry recovered a Mark Ingram fumble. From there it was a short Crompton touchdown pass to Gerald Jones, followed by an onside kick recovery. Suddenly, the gritty Vols had a real chance to pull a gargantuan upset.

With 48 seconds left, Crompton found tight end Luke Stocker for a big gain down to the Alabama 27-yard line. The clock stopped while they moved the chains. The Vols had no timeouts. They wanted to get the ball closer for Daniel Lincoln, but Kiffin also was fearful of a mistake. Instead of spiking the ball on first down to stop the clock, they gave the football to Montario Hardesty, who was stopped by Alabama defensive back Javier Arenas for no gain. The clock kept ticking. Tennessee was going to take their chances on a 44-yard field goal attempt.

It had not been a good day for Lincoln. He was short on a 47-yard field goal and had a 43-yard field goal attempt blocked by Alabama's large lineman, Terrance Cody. Lincoln was not in tip-top condition. He was recovering from a quad injury and could not elevate the football the way he wanted. It made the earlier block by Cody an easy one. But here, with the game in the balance, the Vols prayed that he could give Tennessee its first win over a top-ranked team in twenty-four years. Instead, Cody plowed through the line, got a hand on the football, and the Lincoln kick never had a chance.

Regrets for Kiffin about the late game playing calling? He has a few. "You always look back. When you are in the heat of it, it's happening so fast," Kiffin recalls. "As things slow down, obviously we were struggling with field goal kicking that day. Playing the number one team in the country you are thinking, 'Hey we are in field goal range to win this thing.' At the time you are thinking what if you do screw it up? What if there is a sack or an interception? Then everyone is saying, 'why did you do that? Why not just take the field goal to beat the number one team in the country?' But now? They had Javier coming off the edge. I wish I woulda had the bubble screen there and thrown it." Tennessee had more first downs, more yards of offense and more minutes of possession. After the game, Kiffin shook hands with Nick Saban, telling the veteran coach that he would never lose to him again.

"I remember 2008 was the first year UT started making students pay for football tickets," said Geist. "A few games in somebody painted, 'We started paying, you start winning!' on The Rock. Kiffin may not have gone undefeated, but he made the choice to pay for tickets a really simple one. 'Will I be entertained? Is this a guy that won't take crap from Meyer or Saban? Can he restore us to glory?' We went from resigning ourselves to Florida and Alabama being blowouts to really thinking we could go toe to toe with them in year one, which was a huge switch from walking into a slaughter."

A week later, the Vols hosted twenty-first ranked South Carolina. There were rumors about Tennessee wearing black jerseys for the first time in eighty-seven years, but the Vols went through warmups in their orange tops. When they came out of the locker room before kickoff, the black jerseys were there. These things looked like they fell off the back of a truck that was headed to the discount outlet store, and some traditionalists were disgusted watching the Vols run through the T without the orange. But most of the crowd was on board, loud and proud on a rainy Halloween night as Tennessee cruised to a 31-13 win.

Lane Kiffin 1, Steve Spurrier 0.

"Sometimes I feel Tennessee tradition can hurt in recruiting because young players like to see things like that," says former Tennessee linebacker Daryl Vereen. "Never underestimate what team's attire does to a decision for a teenage kid trying to pick a school."

"Lane was fun, energetic, and challenged us every day," says Pope. "Some days were harder than others and he and his staff did a hell of a job making football fun and fresh."

Tennessee students were energized as well. The Vols were not going to win the SEC, but nobody in the league wanted to play them at that point either. "We weren't little brother anymore," said Geist. "We were the younger brother that discovered creatine and weights, hit the gym every day, and may not beat you in a fight right now. But you'd remember you were in a brawl and if it happened again next year, you may get your ass whooped." Tennessee was 5-4 and getting ready for a road game at Ole Miss on November 14. Things were going fine for Kiffin on the field. Off the field he and his coaching staff were still making secondary NCAA violations, but the pace had slowed considerably.

Early in the morning of November 12, the narrative changed. Jackson, Richardson and Mike Edwards were taken in on charges of attempted armed robbery. At least one of the players was wearing Tennessee gear as he was arrested outside a convenience store just off the UT campus. That footage aired on WVLT-TV, and soon was picked up by national media as well. Jackson and Richardson were two of Kiffin's prize gets in his first recruiting class. A few days after the arrests, Kiffin booted Richardson and Edwards off the team, while suspending Jackson for two games.

Kiffin's 2009 recruiting class will go down as one of the most underachieving in college football history. The other top-100 players would later transfer (Brown, Oku) or were kicked off the team (Askew). "The perception was that Lane recruited well, but a lot of people started to realize that this was done with smoke and mirrors," said ESPN's Chris Low. "That recruiting class was a paper tiger and that proved to be the case."

Tennessee would finish the 2009 regular season at 7-5, before getting drilled by Virginia Tech in the Chick-fil-A Bowl, yet another defeat in the Georgia Dome. However, a 7-6 record was reason for optimism.   It appeared that brighter days were ahead for Tennessee football.

Then came January 12, 2010. A date which lives in Tennessee infamy.

4
LANE'S MIDNIGHT RUN

SOUTHERN CAL HEAD COACH PETE CARROLL had rebuilt one of college football's traditional powerhouses. Under his direction, from 2000-2009, the Trojans won 97 games and lost only 19. They also won national championships in 2003 and 2004. Carroll was happy, living in the California sunshine, looking much younger than his fifty-eight years. He had turned down more than a few overtures from NFL teams to return to the pros. So, it was a bit of a surprise when on January 9, 2010, Carroll accepted the head coaching job with the Seattle Seahawks. "I do not expect to ever be able to top what we just did," said Carroll. "I think it's just been a beautiful time together. It hurts to separate right now... but it can't keep on going, because I can't pass up this opportunity."

Lane Kiffin wasn't anticipating his old boss packing up the moving truck. "I saw it on the ticker," Kiffin says. "I think I was in San Antonio at the U.S. Army All-American Bowl doing visits with kids that week. I was in the hotel and saw it on the ticker on TV so that's how much I knew."

The timing was... interesting. Was there another reason why Carroll was leaving USC? For years the NCAA had been poking around the Southern Cal athletic program. There were lots of questions surrounding Heisman Trophy winning running back Reggie Bush, and multiple reports of improper benefits that he and his family received from an agent. Southern Cal athletic director Mike Garrett needed a new football coach. National Signing Day was a little over three weeks away, and the Trojans wanted to keep the Class of 2010 together. In Carroll's last season, the Trojans went 9-4. Certainly nothing to sneeze at, but at Southern Cal, an Emerald Bowl victory over Boston College wasn't exactly a reason to hold a parade.

Carroll had no previous Southern Cal ties before he got to La La Land, but traditionally, USC likes to make important hires within the family. John Robinson had two tours of duty as the Trojans head coach. Ted Tollner was Robinson's offensive coordinator who was promoted to head coach when Robinson left for the NFL's Los Angeles Rams in 1983. Carroll's predecessor, Paul Hackett, was a former Trojans assistant coach. Garrett himself won the Heisman Trophy as a running back for the Trojans in 1965 and would be replaced as Southern Cal's AD later that same year by another former Trojan, Pat Haden. It wasn't shocking to learn that Garrett was looking at coaches with at least one Southern Cal entry on their resume to replace Carroll.

Lane Kiffin loved his time at Southern Cal. He spent six years as a Trojans assistant coach and was now paying attention to what was going on with his former boss. His current boss was aware as well. "In our conversation the previous week about Pete potentially going to Seattle, I had asked Lane about the USC job and his interest," Mike Hamilton told me in 2014. "He indicated that it would be of interest to him. As a result, we both discussed where he might be on USC's priority list of candidates and agreed there would most likely be other candidates more likely to be selected initially."

The first name to hit the rumor mill was an obvious choice. Oregon State coach Mike Riley spent four years as the Trojans offensive coordinator in the mid-90s and was in the middle of his second stint in Corvallis. The Beavers had been very competitive in the Pac-10, winning 36 games over the previous four years, including an upset of then number one Southern Cal in 2008. But

Riley wasn't excited about the prospect of replacing the ultra-successful Carroll. (Ask Ray Perkins what it was like stepping in for Bear Bryant.) Former Trojans Jeff Fisher (Tennessee Titans) and Jack Del Rio (Jacksonville Jaguars) also said no. Southern Cal was trying to replace a legend while knowing that the NCAA hammer could drop at any minute.

Even with those issues, Lane Kiffin seemed like a long shot. He and his coaching staff racked up lots of NCAA secondary violations during his first year at Tennessee. Hiring Kiffin would basically be Southern Cal's not so subtle way of telling the NCAA to "bring it on." Plus, Kiffin had only been at Tennessee for one season, and hadn't proven that he was ready for the Southern Cal job. Of course, he hadn't proven he was ready for the Vols job either, and that hadn't stopped Tennessee from hiring him.

On Tuesday, January 12, Tennessee fans were satisfied. The football team had already welcomed their early enrollees, including 4-star quarterback Tyler Bray from California, and 4-star linebacker Jacques Smith from Ooltewah, about an hour south of Knoxville. They were big parts of a recruiting class that was projected to once again be in the top ten in the nation. Elsewhere on campus, the men's basketball team was only two days removed an emotional victory over top-ranked Kansas. Head coach Bruce Pearl had kicked star forward Tyler Smith off the team, and suspended three others, following early morning arrests on New Year's Day on drug and weapon charges. The undermanned Vols put the game away when Rutledge's own Skylar McBee hit a desperation three pointer in the final minute.

Life for the Tennessee sports fan was good. But that was about to change, because Lane Kiffin was negotiating to return to Southern Cal. He had been in Orlando attending the American Football Coaches Association Convention. "It wasn't just a conference," Kiffin says. "[SEC commissioner Mike Slive] had a coaches meeting there. I land at a private airport and [Southern Cal] faxed me the contract to us. I get that contract and Jimmy [Sexton] is down there as well. I don't know whether I'm going or not. I haven't even read the contract yet. So, I go into the meeting. Nick Saban is actually the chair that year. He and the

Commissioner are up front and the rest of us SEC coaches are in there going over an agenda of items. I'm half listening. I'm actually reading the contract in front of me that no one knows I'm reading."

Former Tennessee offensive lineman Cody Pope remembers the events of that night very well. "Me, Nick Reveiz, Luke Stocker, Shane Reveiz, Austin Johnson, Daniel Lincoln and Nick Stephens were just all hanging around the apartment," says Pope. "We were in the middle of dinner eating while Nick got a call from his Dad [former Vols kicker Fuad Reveiz] saying there was some noise about Lane going to USC. Once we all got a mass text simultaneously telling us we had a team meeting out of nowhere later that night, the rumbles started to become more and more relevant."

"I was at Best Buy with about five or six of the guys. We were using our gift cards that we got at the bowl game," says former Tennessee defensive back Derrick Furlow Jr. "All of our phones start buzzing. We got a mass text saying there was a 9pm meeting. A meeting that late? We knew something had happened. So, we get to the checkout. You know how Best Buy has all those TV's? The news that Kiffin took the USC job came across on the ticker. That's how we learned he was leaving."

Kiffin had wanted to tell his team in person that he was leaving for his "dream job," but couldn't get back in time. His team knew the story before Kiffin ever got to the UT football complex. Word spread quickly. On VolQuest.com, Brent Hubbs started a message board thread that was simply titled, "Guys, it's true." WVLT-TV broke into programming with the story shortly after the VolQuest posting.

Players originally skeptical of Lane after the Fulmer firing had bought into his vision completely. Now, they'd face more uncertainty with yet another coaching change. Kiffin explained to his now former players why he was leaving. It didn't go well. "It was a very tense and frustrating meeting," says former Tennessee linebacker LaMarcus Thompson. "Lots of not so happy words were exchanged."

"The meeting was complete chaos with a lot of yelling and smart comments across the room. Some of the players had been drinking," recalls former Tennessee linebacker Daryl Vereen. "The older players kind of understood the game and had just kind of gone through this with Fulmer. But the younger players couldn't believe what they were hearing. They felt betrayed and lied to. I remember the anger and confusion on the faces of players like Marlon Walls and Corey Miller who had arrived there on a Lane Kiffin recruiting lie, saying he will stay at UT."

"The players that had been brought in by Phillip Fulmer had been sold on stability and family," says Brian Rice, who was now working in UT Athletics media relations. "That's what they had come to expect from Tennessee. That's what everyone in the country expected as well. Kiffin ran things like a business." The departure of Kiffin was hardest for the early enrollees. They had only been on campus a few days. For Bray, this was even more frustrating. His immediate family had recently moved to Tennessee from California, having no inkling that the coaching staff he committed to wouldn't be there.

Then there was the Ed Orgeron factor. "The only thing that had everyone upset was that Coach O called some of the recruits and specifically told them not to go to class," said former Tennessee defensive lineman Daniel Hood. "One of them had their phone on speaker and we heard Coach O telling them not to go to class. When we confronted Kiffin about it, he said he didn't know that that was happening, and he didn't initiate it. He then said he hadn't hired anyone, so it had no merit."

Lane's comments may have technically been correct, but everyone knew the deal. Lane was going to Southern Cal and taking some of his coaching staff with him. Orgeron and Lane's Dad, Monte, were the two most valuable assistants on that coaching staff, so they'd go west too. This entire sequence still bothers many Vols fans to this day. Orgeron was telling Tennessee's most recently arrived players not to go to class, presumably so that they could transfer, perhaps even follow them to USC. Lane's departure was already going to gut the Tennessee football program and leave that 2010 recruiting class in shambles.

They were not only burning down the house. They were pissing on the ashes.

"If that was happening, that would be operating without knowledge of the rules," said Tennessee athletics director Mike Hamilton the following day. "I consider it unethical."

Orgeron told *The Los Angeles Times*, "Yes, I did call recruits to clear up any questions they had… In my knowledge, I followed the rules correctly. I make tremendously strong ties with families in recruiting."

"It was expected from that staff. They would do anything to win games and win the recruiting battle," says Vereen. "Those were two young studs [Jacques, Tyler] so it was expected that they would try to take those guys. I'm assuming they stayed because they had already been lied to before."

Lane didn't bring everyone from that coaching staff to the Southern California sunshine. According to *The State* newspaper, Kiffin hadn't told his brother in law, Tennessee quarterbacks coach David Reaves, that he was going to Southern Cal. Reaves ended up at New Mexico. Some other assistant coaches didn't know about the situation until they saw the story break on the ESPN ticker.

The reaction of Tennessee students was intense, over the top, and riveting. "I was in my apartment in Andy Holt that evening when a student started running down the halls yelling about a riot taking place near the athletic complex," reminisces Tennessee student Chris Sharpe. "We ran over to one of the entrances of Stokely and watched." Stokely Athletic Center was across the street from the Tennessee football complex. Sharpe and his friends saw hundreds of their fellow students show up, many with the intention of blocking cars from leaving the complex. Back then a one lane road led into and out of a small parking lot located directly behind the indoor field. That's where the coaches parked. If Kiffin was going to depart, there weren't many options.

"By the time we got back to campus there was a riot going on," says Furlow. "I saw police looking straight at a guy that started burning a mattress. What? Wow!"

"I was one of the first ones there, and shortly thereafter members of another fraternity rolled up in a pickup truck and had a mattress and a set of drawers in the back of it," remembers

Tennessee student Ben DeVault. "They were loading things up to take to the dump when the news broke, and like me wanted to check out the student reaction. People were screaming, yelling and cussing Kiffin in general, hoping he would come outside. At some point during the gathering, the fraternity guys I saw earlier unloaded their stuff into the street and set it on fire."

"I think the clear upward trajectory was a huge reason for the outrage," says Geist. "We saw a team that was making noise with a first-year coach, knowing next year's team was going to be better. The guy had two undersized walk-ons on his offensive line and brought them within a field goal of taking down the eventual national champions."

And while everything was crazy outside, some students had actually gotten into the football complex, where a press conference was going to take place. Lane Kiffin, of all people, was going to address the media. That press conference added to the insanity of the evening. First of all, there was no obligation on the part of the University of Tennessee to allow him to address the media while on the UT campus. He could have been escorted off campus immediately after resigning because Lane at this point was no longer a university employee. Oh, and Lane had some ground rules too. He didn't want television cameras to be rolling at the beginning of his talk to the media.

This caused a verbal brawl involving Knoxville media members and Tennessee's Sports Information Department. Most reporters agreed to those restrictions, while a few, led by WBIR-TV News Director Bill Shory, refused to go along with it. The main argument being that the television media, specifically the three local stations, were going to get less access than everyone else. The video of that skirmish is a YouTube classic.

Eventually, Kiffin tired of waiting. He abandoned his restrictions and walked into the cramped quarters of the Gordon Ball Boardroom. Wearing khakis and a plain, untucked white golf shirt fitting such a rushed moment, Kiffin gave a brief statement. "Thanks for coming, guys. This was not an easy decision. It's something that happened quick... a decision that myself and my family made. We've been here fourteen months. The support has been unbelievable here. I really believe that this is the only place I would have left here to go, to go to Southern Cal. There's so many people to thank so I'm just gonna be generic and say thanks to all the Tennessee people and the way they welcomed myself and my family. It's been an exciting time. And I know I can walk out of here and say this. We've been here fourteen months and there's not one day that I didn't give everything I had to the Tennessee program. And I know, just looking at that team room and knowing the players coming in on this roster, and what's going on in development, that we are leaving here fourteen months later a lot better team than we were fourteen months ago. So, I appreciate you guys coming and thanks again for all your support."

On Left: Tennessee Sports Information Director Bud Ford
On Right: WBIR-TV News Director Bill Shory   *(Courtesy: YouTube)*

It took exactly one minute for Kiffin to utter those words. He immediately left the room, ignoring questions shouted from the media. *"What does this mean for recruiting, Lane???"*

"That whole thing, that part of doing it that way and the whole press conference... I take a lot of heat over that," Kiffin told me. "But I was doing the abnormal thing, which I believe was the right thing to do. I was trying to get to my players first, so they don't hear it from someone else. I'm trying to sit down with the media to explain this is why I'm taking this job. My kids being born there, the memories of USC... This is why I'm doing this, and I want to thank you guys for a great year of covering us. That's what I was trying to do, and I was advised against it by everyone. They said, 'Just get on the plane and go to L.A. You don't need to go back to Knoxville. Just get to L.A. and take the next job.' I said no, that's not the right thing to do. I wanted to explain to my players and explain to the media but that all backfired."

While this was going on, the campus unrest continued. Kiffin didn't depart the football complex until approximately 4am, long after the student unrest had subsided. Monte Kiffin took no chances and slept in the football complex that night. Lane boarded a plane for Los Angeles the next morning.

"I was surprised in the backlash by the students and the burning of things. That part was surprising," Kiffin says. "But I was also surprised because people leave jobs all the time... I always said the media that blasted me for it... they go from FOX and ESPN and CBS or whatever it is all the time. But that's why you have contracts and why you have buyouts in them. You leave? You gotta pay. I was surprised because it happens all time. Did Willie Taggert get killed for going from Oregon after one year to Florida State, where he hadn't even been before if I recall, let alone a dream job? Versus a place I spent six years at? I just think it was combination of a lot of circumstances and that's why it became such a big story."

Fans were stung by this departure and found ways to express their anger. Many posted videos on social media of themselves setting the Lane Kiffin "It's Time" t-shirts on fire. A Knoxville attorney named Drew McElroy took a different path. He paid $262 to file paperwork with the Knoxville City Council's Public Properties and Facilities Naming Committee. He wanted to rename the waste water treatment plant near the UT campus the "Lane Kiffin Sewage Center." The application was denied. A year after Lane Kiffin left Knoxville, Frontier Firearms in Kingston (located about a forty-five minute drive from the UT campus) had an idea on a way to raise money for Second Harvest Food Bank.

"Shoot Coach Lane's Bobble-Head Day."

"That's what sports is about. They have teams, villains, teams they don't like, coaches they hate. I think Kiffin will go down, in

Tennessee fans book, as one of those people," Frontier Firearms owner Brant Williams told me at the time. For five bucks, you could shoot live rounds at bobbleheads of Lane or Monte Kiffin. Second Harvest would back out of the fundraiser. Frontier Firearms cancelled the event.

"It's funny, the entire state wanted to kill this guy when he left," says Pope. "I never heard any players that actually play for him say anything bad about him."

"I didn't take it personal," Furlow says. "I knew it was a business move. After Fulmer was fired, my perspective changed. A coach might want to be at a particular level or have a dream job to go home to their comfort zone. I didn't like that my teammates would have to start over and go through it again. But I still would play for him today."

Vols fans were coming to grips with having a head coach leave on his own accord, and after only one season to boot. Lane was telling Tennessee, *it's not you... it's me.* For 32 years, Tennessee football had two head coaches. Johnny Majors and Phillip Fulmer were both Tennessee legends. Knoxville is where they most wanted to be. They were invested in the program as players before they were coaches. Majors should have won the Heisman Trophy in 1956 and Fulmer was a standout at guard. Majors chose to retire in East Tennessee, and Fulmer will do the same. Lane Kiffin, on the other hand, bolted after 13½ months, leaving a burning Big Orange Country in his rearview.

Tennessee would eventually receive four years of probation due to NCAA violations that happened under Lane Kiffin's watch. There were twelve secondary violations over a ten-month span. Kiffin's assistant coach, Willie Mack Garza, paid for the travel and lodging of recruit Lache Seastrunk and his Mom in 2009 during an unofficial visit. This was considered "unethical conduct" by the NCAA since Garza was aware that he was breaking the rules when he did it.

The parting of Lane Kiffin and Tennessee, as abrupt and controversial as it was, wasn't the worst-case scenario here. In the years that followed, the role that David Blackburn played as UT's Football Operations Director was brought to light. Without

Blackburn serving as an overseer while guiding Kiffin and his staff, who knows how far things might have gone in terms of NCAA problems.

"I think they viewed Tennessee as maybe being hurt for a bit," recalls Blackburn. "We weren't doing as well as we were in the 1990s. Lane was so young then and he is so much more mature now, but he will always be a free spirit. He started at eighty miles per hour, which was too fast for everyone at that time. Lane and his staff embraced me. They knew I had a history at the school and they tightened it up. We came out with no major violations."

As it turned out, Southern Cal didn't go as planned for Lane Kiffin. The NCAA did indeed drop the hammer on the program due to the Reggie Bush scandal. USC was banned from the postseason for two years. They lost thirty scholarships in three seasons. Despite those punishments, Lane Kiffin had his team ranked number one to start the 2012 season. But they struggled and finished 7-6. The move back to California did not help Kiffin with his maturity issues either. He gave a twenty-nine second press conference. He wouldn't allow opposing teams to do walkthroughs at the L.A. Coliseum. He allegedly had players switch jersey numbers *during* a game to try to fool an opponent on a two-point try.

It was a lot of small things that added up, just like when he was in Knoxville. Five games into the 2013 season, after a humiliating 62-41 loss at Arizona State, Lane was fired by USC Athletics Director Pat Haden. The dismissal occurred at a private airport near LAX. Lane was pulled off the team bus, which then left without him. He had to find his own way home. Lane Kiffin went 28-15 as Southern Cal's head coach.

Looking back, does Lane Kiffin wonder what might have been if he had stayed at Tennessee? That NCAA situation certainly plays a part when he thinks about it. "Those were such extreme penalties," Kiffin says. "The *Los Angeles Times* the next day basically said that USC has death penalty... that you can expect a half-empty Coliseum and four to five wins a year. Even when those penalties came down I was like ok, it stinks that we won't be able to make these championship runs for a while until we get our numbers back. When you do get fired people forget that you did lose all of these scholarships, and that you aren't supposed to be winning ten games every year like we managed to do in our second year. Then you say, what would it have been like back in the SEC? Would you still be there? You'd have this rivalry every year with Saban. We were so close in that first game."

He eventually found his footing at Alabama, serving as their offensive coordinator for nearly three years, helping the Crimson Tide win a national title in 2015. His departure from Tuscaloosa was (surprise surprise) not a smooth one. Alabama head coach Nick Saban fired Kiffin a week before the 2016 national championship game. Kiffin was taking the head coaching job at Florida Atlantic, and Saban didn't believe Lane was giving enough attention to the title pursuit. With Steve Sarkisian now handling play calling duties (yes, Lane's co-offensive coordinator at USC), Alabama lost in the final seconds against Clemson. Chaos follows Kiffin wherever he goes. Love him or hate him, he's never boring. And he certainly wasn't at Tennessee.

For Vols fans, Lane's resignation was a shocking dose of reality. Tennessee is historically one of the winningest programs in college football. This is the program of Doug Atkins and Reggie White. Peyton Manning and Condredge Holloway. Heath Shuler and Hank Lauricella. Eric Berry and Al Wilson. General Robert Neyland. For the first time since Doug Dickey left for Florida in 1970, Tennessee had a coach say that they would rather be someplace else.

Kiffin's decision was felt from Mountain City to Memphis and by Vols fans no longer living in the state, but whose hearts have never left. Dickey returned to Tennessee as Athletics Director in 1985, a position he held until 2002. It's a safe bet that we won't see Lane Kiffin become Tennessee's AD in 2025.

The night Kiffin quit, Hamilton was in Colorado, meeting with DISH Network. He immediately flew back to Tennessee but didn't get into Knoxville until the early morning hours. The clock was ticking. National Signing Day was three weeks away. Hamilton had to find Kiffin's replacement.

Tennessee did not choose wisely.

5
Derek Dooley Gets His Chance

THE MORNING AFTER LANE KIFFIN'S RESIGNATION, Tennessee began to adjust to a new normal. The first step was finding out who was going to be in charge for the time being. Tennessee assistant Kippy Brown was named interim head coach the night everything went down. According to some players that were in the room when Kiffin told the Vols he was leaving, Brown was a major reason why things didn't spiral out of control. Brown was a calming influence in those charged moments and had the respect of the team.

"Last night's meeting was very positive," said Brown during a press conference the following day. "Every one of those guys came up and said 'Coach, thank you.' Because they were mad, and sometimes when you are young you look for things to be mad about. You just have to explain, 'Hey, welcome to life.' That's the way this deal is. You're gonna have bumps in the road. But how you react to those bumps is what separates you from being successful or unsuccessful."

Kippy Brown was a "Vol For Life." He's a Sweetwater native, which is located about a forty-five minute drive southwest of Knoxville. Brown was hired by Kiffin just a few weeks earlier to be the Vols' wide receivers coach and passing game coordinator. This was going to be Brown's third tour of duty as a Vols assistant. He helped Tennessee get the nickname "Wide Receiver U" due to his recruitment and coaching of pass catchers like Carl Pickens, Alvin Harper, Anthony Miller and Tim McGee.

Brown let the media know that he hoped the interim tag would be removed. He wanted to be the next head coach at Tennessee. "I was told that I am [a candidate for the job]. I think that I'm a legitimate candidate for the job, I do," said Brown. "The reason that I say that is that I'm very confident in my ability to coach, to recruit. I've proven that when I was here before. I've coached at Tennessee on SEC championship teams. I've gone into out of state areas and brought back All-American recruits. I feel that I am a legitimate candidate."

"Kippy is one of us," Hamilton said at that same press conference. "He is a fine, fine individual, considered to be one of the great coaches in America and will represent us in the right way."

Hamilton started searching for that next head coach shortly after Kiffin's resignation. "Everybody knows that we are going to be hitting a live recruiting period time again," said Hamilton. "This is an absolutely critical time for our program... so we will work very diligently towards trying to bring closure to this process as quickly as possible.

Hamilton then added what would prove to be an ominous line. "I would rather be a day late, and make sure we got the right person."

Finding the right person was not going to be easy. It wasn't going to be Phillip Fulmer. While Fulmer still had support on campus, going back to the well would reopen all those wounds from 2008. Multiple coaches would turn Hamilton down, including Texas defensive coordinator Will Muschamp. "They tried to get Muschamp and were willing to pay, but he just wasn't interested," said ESPN's Chris Low. "It was too big a rebuilding job. He felt that a bigger job was coming, and he was right." The following December, Muschamp was hired at Florida to replace Urban Meyer.

Air Force coach Troy Calhoun was a finalist when Kiffin was hired but didn't pursue the job when contacted again. Hamilton was not in a position of power, of course. National signing day was drawing ever closer, so if it was a college coach he was going after, they'd be doing to that school exactly what Kiffin did to Tennessee.

This forced Hamilton to go down a road he didn't necessarily want to when he offered the job to Duke head coach David Cutcliffe on Thursday, January 14. Truly, this would have been the best-case scenario for Tennessee. Cutcliffe had two tours with the Vols totaling nineteen seasons. His successful recruitment of Peyton Manning in 1993 and 1994 changed the Tennessee football program forever. "Coach Cut," as he is affectionately known, is one of the best coaches, developers of talent, and recruiters in college football, and he would have been a popular choice to save the day in Knoxville.

Negotiations progressed so far down the line that a North Carolina television station reported that Cutcliffe was taking the job. But things got bogged down when Cutcliffe told Hamilton he wanted to bring his coaching staff with him to Knoxville. Cutcliffe didn't want to see any of his assistants possibly be out of a job because of a decision that he made. Hamilton wasn't completely on board with that prospect. Cutcliffe told Hamilton that if he didn't hear from him that evening that he should take his name out of the running.

It was very similar to the situation Cutcliffe experienced when he was the head coach at Ole Miss. Following the 2004 season, he was told by Rebels athletics director Pete Boone that he would have to make changes to his coaching staff if he wanted to keep his job. Cutcliffe refused and was fired. In 2010, he was staying loyal once again. Cutcliffe woke up on Friday, January 15 as the head coach of the Duke Blue Devils, a position he still holds heading into the 2018 season.

While Hamilton was striking out on the coaching search, Kippy Brown was keeping things together in Knoxville. Was hiring him as the head coach in 2010 the best play? The players liked him. He was a good recruiter, and had decades of experience. And he was a Tennessee guy. Having him in charge would unite the Vols fanbase as well. But Hamilton kept looking.

Hamilton said in the past that he had a list of coaches ready, just in case something unexpected happened. Now, Hamilton had to be far down on that list. One of the more interesting possibilities was Houston head coach Kevin Sumlin. The former Oklahoma co-offensive coordinator had gone 18-9 in his two seasons running the Cougars program. However, Hamilton never got to Houston, because the job search ended in Ruston, Louisiana.

Derek Dooley had a southern football pedigree. His Dad, Vince Dooley, was the legendary Hall of Fame coach at Georgia. Derek was a walk-on receiver at Virginia, and part of the Cavaliers' ACC championship winning team in 1989. Football didn't appear to be in his future when Dooley got his law degree from Georgia in 1994. He spent two years practicing law in Atlanta. But for Dooley, football was a sickness that had no cure. He went back to Georgia as a grad assistant in 1996, and then spent three years as the wide receivers coach at SMU. Dooley's big break came when Nick Saban brought him onto his staff at LSU in 2000 to coach tight ends and to be his recruiting coordinator. He followed Saban to the NFL's Miami Dolphins as well. In all, Dooley spent seven seasons working for Saban.

Shortly before Saban left the Dolphins for Alabama, Dooley was hired as the head coach at Louisiana Tech. Later, Dooley would add the title of athletics director. You don't often see someone wear both hats these days. But Dooley, a noted control freak, loved the concentration of power. The high point of Dooley's tenure as the Bulldogs head coach came in 2008, when Louisiana Tech finished 8-5, good enough for second place in the Western Athletic Conference. They also beat Northern Illinois in the Independence Bowl, La Tech's first bowl game win in thirty-one years.

That success, however, was sandwiched around a 5-7 season in 2007 and a 4-8 mark in 2009. Dooley was 17-20 in three seasons as a head coach and not on anyone's radar. But at this point, Hamilton had to be desperate. They started with option A, were down as far as option G or H, and National Signing Day was drawing ever closer. Surely Dooley realized that if not for the extreme situation, he would never have been considered for the Tennessee job at this point in his career. It was a chance to play with the big boys. It was an opportunity to get out of his father's shadow and make a name for himself in the Southeastern Conference. It would also mean a significant raise, with resources he simply didn't have in Ruston.

Dooley wasn't going to say no. And he didn't. "We spent a lot of time during the brief search to replace Kiffin talking about Derek Dooley's resume," remembers WNML's Josh Ward. "My co-host Will West was in the middle of explaining why Tennessee could not hire Dooley when [WNML's] Jimmy Hyams came onto our show that Friday afternoon to report that Tennessee was indeed hiring Dooley. Will and I couldn't believe that's what Tennessee decided to do."

If there was a true low point during this coaching search, it came that same day, when Kippy Brown interviewed for the head coaching job at Tennessee. This interview happened *after* Tennessee had already decided to hire Dooley. It was an embarrassment, and an appalling way to treat the well-liked Brown. He would leave Knoxville once again to become the wide receivers coach of the Seattle Seahawks. Brown was on the Seahawks coaching staff when they won Super Bowl XLVIII. He retired from coaching in 2015. Had Tennessee hired Kippy Brown for the 2010 season, would they have had success? Who knows. If they did, then you could have given Brown the job on a more permanent basis. If he failed? At least you had a year to get your program back on stable ground, and you didn't make a panic hire.

Tennessee made a panic hire in Derek Dooley.

The University of Tennessee officially introduced Derek Dooley as their twenty-second head football coach on Friday, January 15. He and his family flew into Knoxville's TAC Air that night, and were whisked to the UT campus for a 9pm press conference in a fleet of black SUV's. You would have thought the President was in town. Dooley was a below .500 coach coming off a losing season. He had no Tennessee ties. He was a kid who once took a few turns around an abandoned parking lot in a Chevette and was now being given the keys to a Cadillac.

Yes, it was a Cadillac that desperately needed an oil change and some new tires, but it was still a Cadillac.

"When we hired Derek Dooley, I did the same thing that everyone did," says former Tennessee wide receiver Jayson Swain, who today hosts "The Swain Event" sports talk radio program in Knoxville. "I went on Google and found out who he was. It was a big letdown. We are Tennessee and we can't get any better than this?"

People joke about the importance of "winning the press conference." But on this day Tennessee really needed Dooley to put on a good show following what had been a brutal 72 hours. And Dooley did just that. He was self-deprecating. He had a southern accent. He had great hair. Heck, his son was named Peyton. He understood the importance of this job. Perhaps most importantly, Derek Dooley came across as the anti-Lane Kiffin. "I have a lot of respect for coaches in this league, and I'm always going to conduct myself in that manner," said Dooley.

"We are excited to welcome Derek and Allison to the University of Tennessee family," said Hamilton in a statement released by the University of Tennessee. "Derek is one of the bright young coaches in America. He understands our league and the competitive environment in which we compete."

"The night of his press conference, a few of the players showed up, including running back Bryce Brown," says Kris Budden, who was working as a sports anchor at WBIR-TV in Knoxville. "We asked him if he ever heard of Derek Dooley. His answer, 'Not until this afternoon.'"

"I had no clue who Derek Dooley was," admits former Tennessee linebacker LaMarcus Thompson. "But the team wanted to give him a chance because we wanted to win."

"My first impression of Derek Dooley was that he didn't deserve the job and got it because of his Dad," says former Tennessee linebacker Daryl Vereen, who would now be playing for a third head coach in three years.

One thing that Dooley was not was a guy who liked to promote his football program. A story I've been told comes from that first day. During negotiations, Dooley and Tennessee athletic administrators talked about how often he would speak to boosters and alumni groups, how many times he would go on the Big Orange Caravan, etc.

Folks, that opening press conference wasn't exactly White House Press Secretary Sarah Huckabee Sanders exchanging barbs with CNN and MSNBC. This was 30 minutes of "Coach, Welcome to Rocky Top" type questions. And I'm using the word "questions" quite loosely here. It was as friendly a scene as a football coach will ever have.

When the press conference ended, Dooley shook some hands and took a few pictures. He then walked past those same athletic administrators and said, "Ok. That's one," and continued out of the room. Derek Dooley was getting a six-year deal starting at $1.8 million per season, and he wanted to make sure they knew that the press conference should count towards his number of required speaking engagements.

Dooley had to go right to work to secure the Class of 2010, and he made the best of a bad hand. Dooley picked up 4-star receivers Justin Hunter from Virginia Beach and Da'Rick Rogers from Calhoun (GA). Rogers's recruitment was helped when Dooley also gave a scholarship to a 3-star quarterback he didn't necessarily need, Rogers's high school teammate Nash Nance.

A troubling sign for the future of the Vols football program came shortly before the 2010 season began. Tennessee was scheduled to play a home and home series with North Carolina in 2011 and 2012 but wanted to push the series to later in the decade. When North Carolina refused to do that, Tennessee decided to buyout the contract. Hamilton told ESPN, "We're playing this fall with 71 or 72 guys on scholarship and we want to get our program back to where we need to be. We wanted to lighten the load a bit."

In 2011, Tennessee's out-of-conference schedule became (FCS) Montana, Cincinnati, Buffalo and MTSU. In 2012, Tennessee's out of conference schedule was now N.C. State, Georgia State,

Akron and Troy. That isn't exactly a murderers' row of opponents. Canceling the North Carolina series allowed Tennessee to have an eighth home game in 2011, and that extra revenue more than made up for the cost of buying out the UNC deal. But it also cost Vols fans a rare trip to Chapel Hill to face an opponent they hadn't seen since 1961. In the recent past, Tennessee scheduled out-of-conference games against the best teams in the nation, including Notre Dame, Miami, and UCLA, amongst others. The perception that a program like Tennessee was running from North Carolina, in football of all sports, was tough to shake.

Going into the 2010 season no one was expecting Tennessee to contend for an SEC title, but the fans gave Dooley their full support. Over 99,000 showed up at Neyland Stadium for their season opener against UT-Martin. Over 102,000 were there for losses to top ten foes Oregon and Florida. When Tennessee escaped with a double overtime win over UAB on September 25, players celebrated like they just won a national championship.

Tennessee needed something to change. On October 2, the Vols played at twelfth-ranked LSU in Baton Rouge. LSU dominated on the stat sheet, outgaining the Vols in yardage 434-217. But the Tennessee defense forced four turnovers and the Vols offense played conservatively. With less than twelve minutes to go, quarterback Matt Simms scored on a three-yard touchdown run, and Tennessee had a 14-10 lead. With 1:21 remaining, LSU had a fourth and 14. Make a stop and the Vols would win. But Jarrett Lee found Terrence Tolliver for a 20-yard gain down to the Tennessee 18, and the drive continued. Eventually, LSU had second and goal from the Tennessee two-yard line. There were only 32 seconds left and the Tigers had no timeouts.

Anyone who watched LSU during this era knew two things. First, Les Miles was the luckiest coach in college football. Some of his decisions were unconventional, but they often worked. Second, Les Miles was awful at clock management. AWFUL. The sequence that followed would fit both categories. Quarterback Jordan Jefferson took the snap out of the shotgun. He ran to the right side, and was stopped at the one-yard line by Nick Reveiz and two other

Vols. And this is when the madness began. LSU alternated Jefferson and Jarrett Lee at quarterback the entire day. Jefferson had only completed three passes against the Vols while Lee had sixteen. LSU would have rather had Lee in the game at this point. It was now third down. If Lee threw an incompletion, you'd get to run at least one more play.

Instead, you had anarchy. Jefferson looked to the sideline for a play while three LSU players ran onto the field. By rule, Tennessee then would get the chance to make their own substitutions. And the clock... kept... ticking... Finally, everyone was lined up. LSU needed to spike the football or run a play. CBS play-by-play announcer Craig Bolerjack called the action: *"Down to four... down to three... Ohhhh! Jefferson wasn't ready for it! It is over! It is over in Baton Rouge!"*

LSU center T-Bob Hebert had snapped the ball quickly to try to beat the clock, and it went past Jefferson. Players fell on the football and the game was indeed over. Tennessee had won 14-10. Derek Dooley hugged defensive back Marsalis Teague. A wild celebration was on. The Pride of the Southland Marching Band was playing "Rocky Top." Chris Sharpe was on the trombone. "I can still see in my mind Matt Simms running over to celebrate with the band," said the 2012 Tennessee grad. After nearly nine months of bad vibes stemming from the Lane Train leaving the station, Tennessee fans had reason to celebrate. Dooley was waving his players off the field. Some had already run down the tunnel to the locker room. But the referees were staying on the field for some reason. Perhaps there was an unsportsmanlike penalty on LSU?

The call was made. "Illegal participation... on the defense... twelve men on the field. Half the distance to the goal. Replay third down."

Most of the 92,932 at Tiger Stadium went crazy. LSU was going to have one final chance with an untimed down. During the madness of the moment, the Vols ran four defenders on the field to match the LSU substitutions. Slight problem. Only three players ran off the field. And one of those players ran back before the snap. That's right... The Vols didn't have twelve men on the field. They had *thirteen*. "The coaches were on two separate pages," remembers former Tennessee linebacker Daryl Vereen. "They were calling two separate personnel [packages]."

So now, the Vols had to regroup for one final play. Tennessee coaches were perplexed. Dooley fumbled with his headset as he rushed to put it back on. Seconds later, Jefferson pitched the ball to Steven Ridley. Reveiz shed a blocker and got a hand on the ball carrier, but Ridley wouldn't be stopped until he carried the football a few inches over the goal line.

Despite their best efforts, LSU had won 16-14. Tennessee's players walked off the field stunned. Some were crying. Derek Dooley was angry, throwing his headset on the ground before making a beeline for the locker room. Les Miles ran him down for what was their second postgame handshake in less than five minutes. Dooley was still shaken when he addressed the media. "Sometimes things happen in life that you don't understand," Dooley said. "Sometimes things happen in life that you don't think is fair, and you have to deal with it and that's where we are."

This was the first in a series of unexplainable losses for Tennessee over the next eight seasons. It was something that Vols fans got numb to with each passing experience. The Vols did not respond well to the LSU ending. In the next three weeks they were outscored 120-48 in losses to conference rivals Georgia, Alabama and South Carolina. But the schedule got easier, and freshman Tyler Bray took the reins of the offense. The Vols won their next four games in high scoring, exciting style to finish the regular season at 6-6, and earn a spot in the Music City Bowl on December 30. Improbably, the Vols would play in the postseason.

"I think there was as much hype as realistically possible for a 6-6 team headed to a bowl like the Music City Bowl," says Daryl Hobby, who was working as a Sports Anchor/Reporter at WVLT-TV. "Vol fans love Nashville. Who doesn't like the honkytonks and Broadway. The Vols were sitting on a 2-6 record after October. Any bowl game should have been welcomed." (This also earned Dooley a cool $40,000 bonus by getting Tennessee to a bowl game.)

The Music City Bowl produced the strangest ending in Tennessee football history. Yes, even weirder than the LSU game. The Vols were basically the home team against North Carolina on a cold Nashville night at LP Field. Bray kept up his hot streak, with 312 yards passing and four touchdowns. With only 31 seconds left, Tennessee led 20-17. North Carolina had the ball on their own 20-yard line. Surely there wasn't enough time for them to get into field goal range. Well, a 27-yard completion was followed up by a launching penalty on Tennessee's Janzen Jackson. Eventually, the Tar Heels had the football on the Vols 25-yard line with 16 seconds left. They were in field goal range.

With no timeouts remaining, UNC would have to throw the football close to the end zone or near the sideline. Instead, for some reason they ran the ball up the middle, gaining only seven yards. There was mass confusion on the Tar Heels sideline. Players ran on and off the field. Were they spiking it? Were they trying to kick a field goal? There might have been sixteen UNC players on the field at one point. The clock struck zero. The Vols rushed the field with unbridled joy.

Derek Dooley shook hands with Tar Heels head coach Butch Davis. For media facing deadlines, the race was on. "The referee declares that the game is over. I need to get this video back to the station ASAP," says Hobby. "I start to high tail it out of the stadium and to the satellite truck in the parking lot. I remember nearly colliding with the big stage that was making its way onto the field for the trophy presentation."

Tennessee would finish the year at 7-6 and...

Wait a minute. Oh no. Not again. "I get to the concourse and a Vol fan who was heading back in tells me, 'The game isn't over,'" says Hobby. "He explains in a Nano-second what happened, so I high-tail it back to the field."

On review, the referees determined North Carolina had too many men on the field, but that quarterback T.J. Yates had spiked the football with one second left. So, they'd back the Tar Heels up five yards. North Carolina would have a chance to tie the game. Casey Barth drilled a 38-yard field goal under extreme pressure, and we headed to overtime.

Bray tied the game in the first extra session with a touchdown pass to Luke Stocker. He immediately turned to the North Carolina bench, and gave a double throat slashing motion. It wasn't seen by the refs, but the video clip became a Tennessee fan favorite for years to come. Those few seconds were peak Bray. He threw a perfect pass that only Stocker could catch, and followed it up with a taunting gesture. At Tennessee, Tyler Bray had a million-dollar arm and a fifty-cent head. Of course, karma came back and bit Bray in the second overtime, when Carolina's Quan Sturdivant picked him off. Barth kicked a chip shot, and the Tar Heels had a controversial 30-27 double overtime Music City Bowl win.

"I had a sick feeling when the thing hit zero because I've been there," said Dooley after the game. "I didn't celebrate this time because, I don't know, there will be a lot of things brought up for discussion in the offseason on end of game management and end of game rules. I hope there will be."

Dooley was right. In the offseason a new rule was implemented by the NCAA. In the final minute of each half, if a foul, an intentional helmet removal or an injury stops the clock, the opponent is given a ten second run off option. If the offense has a time out remaining they can use it. Otherwise, ten seconds will be taken off the clock.

This rule would have given Tennessee the win in Nashville. Obviously, it was too little too late for the Vols. Tennessee finished Derek Dooley's first season at 6-7 but easily could have been 8-5. They lost games because they had thirteen players on the field, and they lost games when their opponents had sixteen guys on the field. But with talented, young players returning at the skill positions, some Vols fans felt that brighter days were ahead.

Inside the football complex though? The head coach wasn't exactly inspiring devotion. "Dooley was very arrogant and acted like he had all the answers for everything," says Pope. "He constantly was arguing with assistant coaches and/or coordinators about silly things that typically he was totally wrong about."

The Vols would have to work through that internal strife if they were to turn things around.

6

ROMMEL'S DEMISE

TENNESSEE'S CLASS OF 2011 featured players that were expected to make an impact, with six of them ranked in the ESPN 150. That included wide receiver DeAnthony Arnett, linebacker Curt Maggitt and mammoth offensive tackle Antonio "Tiny" Richardson. The twenty-seven players Dooley signed put Tennessee in the top fifteen nationally, with a best ranking of eleventh by Scout.com. That group gave Vols fans reason for hope, but it was news off the fields and courts of play that was dominating the Knoxville sports scene. In the lead up to the 2011 season, University of Tennessee athletics would be a place of drastic, and devastating change.

First, popular men's basketball coach Bruce Pearl was fired by Tennessee athletics director Mike Hamilton. This came following months of controversy after the NCAA charged Pearl with unethical conduct. Pearl wasn't originally truthful with NCAA investigators when they asked him questions about a cookout at his home that recruits attended. More violations were discovered in the months that followed.

Pearl held a tearful press conference on September 10, 2010 when the original violations were announced. "I've made some serious mistakes, and for that I'm truly sorry," said Pearl. "I let everybody down... I love the University of Tennessee. I want to coach here the rest of my life." The presser was interrupted multiple times by a pesky fire alarm (there was no emergency). These were moments of levity that underscored the serious tone of the moment. Pearl would be suspended by the SEC for eight conference games in 2011, leading to the creation of the infamous "Bruce Pearl timeline" graphic, which listed all the key dates and recent transgressions. It would be a prominent part of ESPN's broadcasts of Tennessee basketball games that winter.

He received public support from Hamilton and UT Chancellor Jimmy Cheek throughout the season. Tennessee fans wanted to stick with Pearl, even if the NCAA brought down severe penalties. Pearl had the misfortune of breaking rules at a time when the NCAA actually seemed to care about member institutions breaking rules. North Carolina ran a fake college for decades with hardly any punishment, but Pearl was getting clipped for a BBQ.

A couple of days before the Vols were set to face Michigan in their NCAA tournament opener in Charlotte, Hamilton went on WNML radio in Knoxville. Instead of sticking to the script and saying that the NCAA investigation was ongoing, and that Pearl was his coach, Hamilton changed course. He said that the "jury was still out" as to whether Pearl would be back as the Vols' head coach next season.

Vols players were furious at Hamilton's comments. This was when he decided to speak up? The biggest game of the season only days away! A source close to the basketball program told me at the time that Hamilton apologized to Pearl, saying that his comments were misinterpreted. But the damage was done. The Vols looked lethargic from the jump against Michigan. This was a team thinking about everything but basketball. Tennessee lost by thirty points, and Pearl was dismissed three days later.

Pearl, whose contract had been terminated by Tennessee after the initial violations came to light, still received a nice parting gift. He took home $948,728 in salary and benefits from the University, even though they weren't obligated to pay him a single penny more. "If anyone ever deserved to be fired for cause, it was Bruce

Pearl," a former UT athletic department official told me. "And they paid him $1 million."

During the Bruce Pearl era (2005-2011), the Vols played a fun, up-tempo style, with likeable players to boot. They made six straight NCAA tournaments, with three Sweet Sixteen stops and one Elite Eight, the only time in program history that they have advanced that far in the NCAA tournament. They also won the 2008 SEC regular season title.

On February 23 of that same year, second-ranked Tennessee played at top-ranked Memphis. It was a star-studded affair, with Peyton Manning, Justin Timberlake and Priscilla Presley in attendance. The Vols upset the rival Tigers 66-62. The following day, Tennessee would be the top-ranked team in the nation for the first and only time in program history. From a dollars and cents standpoint, Pearl was, well, money. He made Tennessee games a happening. They sold out the gym on weeknights in January. Black curtains that covered empty seats in the second level became a symbol of the Buzz Peterson era. Under Pearl, those curtains were put into storage. Thompson-Boling Arena got a huge renovation, and Pratt Pavilion was built as a desperately needed practice facility for the Vols and Lady Vols basketball teams.

The rise of Bruce Pearl and Tennessee basketball was an unexpected one. He turned a dormant program into an SEC powerhouse and had a swagger that energized UT fans. But off the court issues would lead to Pearl's downfall.

None of this occurs without Pearl. UT students loved Pearl's bravado, cockiness, and of course, the winning. If Pearl asked the student body to invade Chattanooga, 25,000 students would have marched down I-75. In 2010, Tennessee came within a bucket of the Final Four. A year later, there was great uncertainty surrounding the future of the Vols program with Pearl's departure. He would be replaced by Missouri State coach Cuonzo Martin, someone whose character was not in question.

On May 24, Hamilton fired another coach whom he had hired, baseball's Todd Raleigh. The Vols went 108-113 during Raleigh's four years in the dugout. This was an easy decision, as Tennessee failed to advance to the SEC tournament even once, going 42-78 in league play. Raleigh would receive a buyout of $331,657.33.

Then, on June 7, Hamilton announced that after eight years as Tennessee's Athletics Director, he was resigning. "The last several years at UT have been marked by turmoil, fractures and the development of camps," said Hamilton at the same podium where Phillip Fulmer wept two and a half years earlier. "This is not healthy, nor is it productive for our university."

The football and basketball programs were both under investigation because of Lane Kiffin and Bruce Pearl's loose interpretations of the rule book. But Hamilton received a $1,335,000 buyout, while Tennessee was awaiting their turn in front of the NCAA committee on infractions.

It looked for a time that LSU athletics director Joe Alleva was going to be the choice to replace Hamilton. But at the last minute, Alleva backed away from a deal. That flirting did lead to a raise for Alleva. This wouldn't be the only time that simply speaking to UT got somebody a bonus. How would things have turned out at Tennessee if Alleva had taken the Vols' AD job? "That would have been a complete disaster," a former Tennessee athletic department official told me. Alleva has been a polarizing figure in his own right in Baton Rouge.

Eventually, Tennessee hired sixty-two-year-old Dave Hart as Hamilton's replacement. At the time, Hart was working as the

Executive Director of Athletics at Alabama. He was basically the second in command in that department.

On August 22, 2011, the worst news of all for the Tennessee family became known publicly for the first time. Lady Vols basketball coach Pat Summitt, the greatest representative the University of Tennessee has ever had, revealed that she was diagnosed with early onset dementia. She would coach one more season and then retire with 1,098 victories, the most NCAA wins all-time in women's or men's basketball history.

With this backdrop, Tennessee fans wanted so badly for the 2011 football team to have success. They needed a distraction from the squabbles and the sadness. The Vols started the season 2-0, including what was one of Dooley's best wins in his time at Tennessee, a 45-23 victory on September 10 against Cincinnati. The Bearcats were coached that day by a former Brian Kelly assistant named Butch Jones.

Dooley's talent evaluation was often spot on. One story sticks out during preparations for the 2011 game against the University of Buffalo. "He's [Dooley] in the staff room watching film," remembers Jimmy Stanton, who was working as the Associate Athletic Director for Communications at Tennessee. "He says 'Man, this kid is as good as any in the country. Best player we will play face all season.' I said that we had some pretty good teams on our schedule, but he said that this kid was gonna make ten Pro Bowls. I walk away thinking that our coach thinks a sophomore linebacker from Buffalo is gonna be the first pick in the NFL Draft." Kahlil Mack wasn't the first pick in the 2014 NFL Draft. He was the fifth. Mack has played four pro seasons and been a Pro Bowl choice three times.

Tennessee was 3-1 (the lone loss to Florida, naturally) before hitting their toughest stretch of games. In a four-week span, they fell to Georgia, top-ranked LSU, second-ranked Alabama, and ninth-ranked South Carolina. Three of those games were played at Neyland Stadium.

A big reason why the Vols took a turn for the worse was injuries. Their spectacular wide receiver, Justin Hunter, tore his ACL during the Florida loss and was done for the season. Quarterback Tyler Bray broke his thumb in the Georgia game and missed a few weeks. Bray's replacements did not fare well. Matt Simms was ineffective and true freshman Justin Worley looked like a true freshman. The Vols were a mess. And when Arkansas destroyed Tennessee 49-7 in Fayetteville, the Vols were 4-6, and still winless in SEC play. But there was good news. Bray was coming back from injury. If the Vols could continue their winning ways over Vanderbilt and then Kentucky, they'd be 6-6 and once again postseason bound.

James Franklin's Commodores were 5-5, confident, and improving during his first year in Nashville. Yes, they had only beaten Tennessee once in twenty-eight tries, but anyone that watched these teams play in 2011 realized that this would be a pick 'em type game. The Vegas sportsbooks had Vanderbilt listed as a slight road favorite. Past the midway point of the fourth quarter, the Commodores led 21-14. Tennessee had fourth and goal from the 5. Dooley elected to kick a field goal. It looked like Sean Richardson blocked the Michael Palardy kick, but officials ruled that he didn't touch the football before he ran into Palardy. This gave Tennessee another shot.

Dooley, perhaps realizing that getting this close to the end zone again with a rusty Bray at quarterback was going to be tough, changed his mind and went for it, now from the two-and-a-half-yard line. Da'Rick Rogers had one-on-one coverage and Bray went right to him. Rogers made a terrific juggling catch for the game-tying score.

Prentiss Waggner would intercept Jordan Rodgers, the future star of ABC's "The Bachelor" at the Vols 35-yard-line, and the game would go to overtime. Vanderbilt got the ball first. Rodgers fired a pass for Wesley Tate. Defensive back Eric Gordon, a Nashville native and former Mr. Football award winner in the Volunteer State, stepped up and snagged the football. On first glance, it looked like his left knee touched the ground. Whistles blew, but Gordon smartly kept on running, 90 yards to the end zone. That runback was proven to be the right decision as replay showed that his knee stayed off the turf. Tennessee had a 27-21 overtime victory against their in-state rivals. In the press box, Tennessee offensive coordinator Jim Chaney shouted, "We finally got a break!"

The locker room after the game was the site of a wild celebration. Tennessee's players put Dooley on their shoulders and threw him into the air, which led to one of Dooley's most memorable lines. *"The one thing that Tennessee does is always kick the shit out of Vandy!"*

"After the game, a Tennessee player told me he was proud the Vols had become bowl eligible," says WNML's Josh Ward. "I had to tell him that was only their fifth win."

The Vanderbilt victory meant that the Vols were back on track for the postseason. The next week they'd go to Lexington to play a Kentucky Wildcats team UT hadn't lost to since 1984, a streak of twenty-six meetings. Win that game and they'd go to a bowl, probably the Liberty Bowl on New Year's Eve. Tennessee hadn't played in that game since 1986, and the Memphis based bowl knew they wouldn't have any trouble selling tickets if the Vols were eligible.

But UT needed one more win to get there. Losing to Kentucky simply was not done at Tennessee, and certainly it wouldn't happen this year. The Vols were seemingly motivated in playing for a bowl berth. The Wildcats were 4-6, and losers of six out of their last seven games against FBS opponents. Also, Kentucky was forced to start a 6'5" senior wide receiver named Matt Roark... at quarterback. Their top two signal callers were out due to injury. Roark hadn't played quarterback since he was tearing up defenses at North Cobb High School in Acworth (GA).

Watching the Kentucky offense against the Vols was like going back in time... a time when throwing the football was still thought to be a fad. Roark tossed only six passes all afternoon, completing four of them for a whopping 15 yards. But he gained 124 yards on the ground, and led the offense with confidence. The Vols ran for a paltry 61 yards. Bray completed only 15 of 38 passes. And when Taiedo Smith intercepted Bray on fourth and 17 in the final two minutes, the unthinkable had happened.

Kentucky 10, Tennessee 7. Wildcats fans stormed the field as if UK just won the conference title. "What an amazing game," said Kentucky head coach Joker Phillips. "If we lined up the last twenty-six years, how many quarterbacks have we had, probably fifteen? Who would pick Matt Roark as the guy that broke the streak?"

Dooley did the mandatory post-game press conference in the small visitor's media room at Commonwealth Stadium. "Well, it's a real bad ending to a real bad season," said a somber Dooley. "It's hard to say much more than that. Our biggest fears were realized... give Kentucky a lot of credit. They played a lot more inspired football than we did."

In the days that followed, the motivation of players was put into question by Vols fans. Bray and Rogers in particular were criticized for a perceived lack of enthusiasm. "There was a rumor floating around that some guys didn't want to play in a bowl game, so they weren't playing as hard," said Worley. "I heard that a few times but don't think that was the case. It was just a day we couldn't get things to go right for us."

This was the time when Derek Dooley, the leader of the Tennessee football program, needed to rally the troops. That meant both his players and the fanbase. He needed to explain that this was a bump in the road, and that the team would learn from this adversity and be ready for 2012. Instead, Dooley hid in an underground bunker for thirty-eight days. Is that true? Hey, it could be! After all, Dooley spent more than five weeks with no public appearances, no press conferences, no Vol Calls segments and no social media posts. That last part wasn't a surprise as Twitter, Facebook, etc. simply weren't Dooley's cup of tea. During those thirty-eight days, Tennessee had key players in the Class of 2012 de-commit. They also saw most of the coaching staff resign. Only offensive coordinator Jim Chaney and quarterbacks coach Darrin Hinshaw stayed in Knoxville.

In addition, a media firestorm was brewing because of Dooley's tone deafness. Tennessee wide receiver DeAnthony Arnett had a very good freshman season, with twenty-four catches for 242 yards and two touchdowns. He was the Vols top recruit in the Class of 2011 and living up to his billing. But Arnett wanted to transfer to Michigan or Michigan State in order to be closer to his father, William, who had serious health issues. Dooley wouldn't allow the transfer, stating Tennessee's policy to deny transfers to schools they play and/or recruit against. Obviously, Dooley could have said that Tennessee recruits against any Division I school since they contact hundreds of prospective student-athletes.

Scout.com ran a statement from Arnett on December 29. "I need to be there for my dad and with my family while still pursuing my goal of being the best student-athlete I can be,"

Dooley came across as being heartless, and Tennessee was run through the gauntlet of public opinion. This was seen as a head coach that was making millions of dollars a year keeping a teenager from being near his ailing father. Media members had made multiple requests to speak with Dooley about this topic and others, but were denied.

The belief was growing, both locally and nationally, that Dooley was playing his fiddle while Tennessee football burned. Dooley wasn't scheduled to speak publicly until National Signing Day, February 1. But I was told by a source that new Tennessee athletics director Dave Hart ordered Dooley to end his silence. At the time, Hart was tasked with the merging of the men's and women's athletics departments at Tennessee, which would take place in 2012. This had been discussed for years, and it took someone like Hart, a Tennessee outsider, to see it through. Had he been in Knoxville for more than a few months, and not been concentrating on that major task, the Kentucky game might have been Dooley's last as the Vols' head coach.

Finally, on January 3, Dooley held a press conference and addressed the Arnett situation. "I want you guys to know that the most important concern for me is the welfare of our student-athletes. I also have a responsibility to Tennessee, and so I needed some one-on-one dialogue with DeAnthony. These are big issues. They're complex. They're emotional... I'm very comfortable carving out an exception for him when he makes his request, which is not until today because our offices have been closed... I'm really supportive of DeAnthony. He has a great future as a person and as a player..."

Arnett would transfer to Michigan State. From a strictly football perspective, it wasn't the right place for him, as he caught only twelve passes in parts of four seasons as a Spartan. But the Dooley/Arnett saga proved that Dooley simply couldn't read the tea leaves. There was no way that situation was going to end well. He tried to play it off during the press conference, saying all the negative press was really just a misunderstanding. He was blaming social media for spreading the news. But how could Dooley say he was supportive of Arnett, while at the same time making him wait weeks to secure his future?

Nothing was going right. Dooley tried to calm the nerves of Vols fans, but that was tough to accomplish. "I think it's understandable why there could be a perception that it's [Tennessee's football program] not good right now," said Dooley. "But I'm not concerned at all about what's real because what's real is this program has been put in the last twenty-two months on as good of a foundation as we could ever do... I can't control what people think and perceive. I can only control what's happening and going on inside the building."

The control that Dooley may or may not have had was up for debate. The reality was that all the uncertainty did indeed have an effect on what prospective student-athletes thought about Tennessee. The 2012 class didn't give Vols fans any reason to celebrate. The class was ranked twentieth nationally according to 247Sports. And there was a glaring absence in the group of twenty-two players. Dooley signed a class with no offensive linemen. No offensive tackles, no offensive guards, no centers... An SEC team having an entire recruiting class without a single offensive lineman was unheard of. This was immediately panned and used by a future Tennessee coach as an excuse for issues up front.

At LSU, Dooley was Nick Saban's recruiting coordinator. At Tennessee, it appeared that he enjoyed recruiting about as much as a trip to the DMV. "The majority of our area high school coaches said that they had regular contact from other SEC coaches," said

Stephen Hargis, Sports Editor at the *Chattanooga Times Free Press*. "But they didn't even know who was responsible for recruiting their school for UT because they had never heard anything from the staff... It had reached the point where many of those high school coaches were downright angry at the lack of communication from UT."

Hargis added, "They felt Dooley and his staff didn't care about their support, and when they reached out to Dooley they had either never heard back or had felt he was arrogant and condescending to them."

"Dooley's staff did a really poor job of communicating with prospects and coaches at the high school level," says Ward. "There are countless stories of them apparently forgetting to contact highly touted prospects on their board for weeks at a time."

It was clear that the roster desperately needed an upgrade. But there was excitement for the upcoming season with the return of the talented Tyler Bray, Justin Hunter and Da'Rick Rogers for their junior seasons. JUCO transfer Cordarrelle Patterson was expected to make an immediate impact at receiver and in the return game.

Dooley had to make a bunch of hires due to seven assistant coach departures, the most important of which being at defensive coordinator. Tennessee wanted Clemson DC Kevin Steele for the position. Steele previously had been on the Vols coaching staff twice under Johnny Majors in the 1980s. But his Tigers gave up 70 points to West Virginia in the Orange Bowl, making that move impossible. Another potential hire for the DC opening was Buddy Green, who had just finished his tenth season at the Naval Academy. He interviewed for the job. Green was the former head coach at UT-Chattanooga and had experience in the south as a former assistant at LSU, Auburn and N.C. State.

Instead, on January 13, Dooley and Tennessee settled on Sal Sunseri, the Alabama linebackers coach. Sunseri hadn't been a coordinator since serving in that role at Alabama A&M in 1999. "The chance to work with Derek Dooley, who has been around championships and knows what it takes to build an elite program, combined with the rich tradition of the University of Tennessee makes this opportunity so exciting to me," said Sunseri, who was bringing twenty-seven years of coaching experience to Knoxville. "I am fired up to work with all the young talent on the defensive side of the ball."

Much like Tennessee had to adjust to a new offense under Dave Clawson in 2008 (with disastrous results), the Vols were forced to move from the 4-3 to a 3-4 base alignment under Sunseri. Following the Orange & White game, which concluded spring football practice, Sunseri expressed optimism in the transition to the 3-4. "We're right on track," he said as reported by the *Chattanooga Times Free Press.* "We're doing a lot of good things. I'm extremely excited about where these kids have come with it... I'm pleased with these kids. Am I satisfied? No. Are we ever going to be satisfied? Probably not."

Overall, this was another long off season for Tennessee as the public relations hits kept coming. In July, according to a Knoxville Police Department report, Tyler Bray was accused of throwing beer bottles at a parked car from his balcony at the Landings Riverfront Apartments. Charges would not be filed. WVLT-TV reported that the victim, Bradi Hudson, said that Bray told her he would pay for the damages to her 2008 Ford. In August, Bray had to appear in court after he was charged with operating a personal watercraft without a permit and in a reckless fashion on Tellico Lake. Bray was "hotdogging" on a jet ski, about a hundred yards from a TWRA officer on July 4. Charges were later expunged from his record.

Neither incident was a huge deal. But if you are the starting quarterback of an SEC team, it's an awful look. It will dominate the news cycle, especially in the summertime when there are no games being played. Derek Dooley and Tyler Bray was a marriage of convenience. Dooley didn't recruit Bray, and Bray had no desire to play for Dooley. But if Dooley and Bray could find a way to get along, it might mean big things for both of them. However, Dooley's unwillingness to publicly discipline his star quarterback did Bray no favors.

In late August came more trouble when Da'Rick Rogers was kicked off the team for what was called at the time "a violation of team rules." Rogers immediately transferred to Tennessee Tech in nearby Cookeville. During a press conference announcing the transfer, Rogers admitted to failing multiple drug tests at Tennessee. The Vols would have to find a way to replace his SEC-leading 67 catches to go with 1,040 yards receiving from the previous season. Dismissing Rogers wasn't a rash decision. Dooley finally reached his limit with one of his most talented, yet troubled players.

"Dooley had a silver spoon background but had a soft spot for the kids who had nothing," a former UT athletic department employee told me. "Making a difference in their lives was a priority for him. Often when a kid got in trouble, even if the kid couldn't play, he'd say, 'If I run this kid, where will he go?'"

There was a perception in the locker room that everyone wasn't on the same playing field. Dooley didn't appear to have an open-door policy for all his players. "I really believe that Coach Dooley was a smart guy," says Charles Folger, who spent five years in Tennessee's football program. "He did, however, from a lowly redshirt walk-on's perspective, choose favorites and really only had relationships with a select few. There would be times that I or other players who were lower on the totem pole would say 'hi' in the hallway and the general responses were few and far between."

Even with an offseason to forget, Dooley had a spring in his step when he walked into the Wynfrey Hotel in Hoover, Alabama for the annual SEC Media Days. He had a talented group and was going to let everyone know it. "Our roster's in place," Dooley boasted. "We have a full 85 on scholarship. We have nineteen starters back... I know, of course, the SEC has enjoyed taking advantage of our tough times. But there's a nice mood on our team right now that you're not going to have Tennessee to kick around anymore."

Overall, a successful football season for Tennessee was crucial from an economic standpoint as well. A few days before the season opener, the UT athletics department announced a $3.98 million deficit for the 2011-2012 fiscal year. Their reserve fund was nearly depleted, standing at less than $2 million. "It is critical that our athletics program be financially healthy and that its budget is sustainable," said UT Chancellor Jimmy Cheek. "We are committed to having premier athletics programs at the University of Tennessee, and to do that, we must develop a financial model that pays for these programs while also building up the necessary reserve funds."

Tennessee started the season in the Chick-fil-A Kickoff Classic on August 31 in their personal house of horrors, the Georgia Dome. They'd face North Carolina State; a team with future NFL draft picks Mike Glennon at quarterback and David Amerson at cornerback. The Vols were remarkable on this night. Bray threw for 333 yards and two touchdowns. The newly arrived Cordarrelle Patterson looked like a chess master playing against a novice. Patterson had a 41-yard touchdown catch and a 67-yard touchdown run, both in the first quarter. Yet another option emerged on the Tennessee offense as Zach Rogers toasted Amerson for a 72-yard TD reception. Marlin Lane and Rajion Neal rushed for a combined 128 yards and the Tennessee offense accounted for 524 yards. Sunseri's defense recorded a safety and intercepted four passes. Tennessee pulled away in the third quarter and won 35-21. If the offense could click like this and the defense hold its own, the Vols would be a contender in the SEC East.

"It's one game. All that matters is that we are 1-0 and we have to clean up a ton of mistakes," a measured Dooley told reporters. "We're not going to pat ourselves on the back because we won one game." The victory snapped Tennessee's five-game losing streak in the Georgia Dome, dating back to the 2001 SEC title game.

"After the N.C. State win everyone on that team thought we would have an incredible season," said former Tennessee fullback Ben Bartholomew. "We had some of the best talent in all of college football."

Big Orange Country was fired up. "I expected an SEC championship appearance during the preseason, and more so after the N.C. State game," remembered Terrance Pryor, a Tennessee fan from Lafayette.

"I was sitting in the corner of the end zone where Zach Rodgers burned David Anderson, the top DB in college football at the time, supposedly," says life-long Vols fan Eli Breece. "I remember watching CP take the reverse for a touchdown and outrun everyone and score."

Michael Greene is a three-time Tennessee grad and fifteen-year Vols season ticket holder that attended the game. "Dooley broke the curse of the Georgia Dome. I remember thinking that we finally turned the corner."

The Vols won a tune up against Georgia State the following week 51-13. But everyone was getting ready for the annual grudge match against Florida on September 15. There was a serious buzz around a Tennessee football game for the first time since Lane Kiffin was barking at Urban Meyer. Both teams were ranked in the top-25 and it appeared that the Vols finally had the talent to matchup with the hated Gators.

ESPN College GameDay set up shop at UT's Circle Park. Country music star Kenny Chesney was the guest picker and it was no surprise when the 1986 graduate of nearby Gibbs High School predicted a Vols victory. Chesney gave *Smokey IX*, the Bluetick Coonhound Tennessee mascot, a smooch on the GameDay set. For the rest of the day, Vols fans were getting properly fueled on campus, with the Vol Navy, at Calhoun's on the River, and at the bars on the Cumberland Strip. Confidence was sky high in Big Orange Country. Yes, Tennessee had lost seven straight games to Florida, but they never had this kind of firepower during the streak.

The Vols led 14-10 at the break. In the 27 games Dooley had coached at Tennessee, the Vols were 13-0 when leading at halftime (and 0-14 when trailing after intermission). With just over five minutes left in the third quarter and trailing 20-13, Florida coach Will Muschamp thought his team needed a spark, and called for a fake punt on fourth and 9 from his own 42. The Vols special teams unit wasn't fooled, made the stop, and the offense had now had great field position.

Most of the sold-out crowd of 102,455 was sensing the knockout blow. Tennessee could prove right now that Dooley was correct, and that the SEC would not have Tennessee to kick around anymore. Instead, Bray was sacked for a loss of ten yards on the first play of the drive. Matt Darr would end up punting into the end zone, and Florida had new life. The next 18 ½ minutes were a nightmare for the Vols. On the first play of Florida's next drive, Trey Burton took a shotgun snap, ran to the sideline, and then outraced Marsalis Teague for a game tying 80 yard score. Burton was the Gators' fullback who took snaps out of the Wildcat formation. The odds were pretty good that he was running the entire time. Exactly what Sunseri's defense was doing on that play is anyone's guess. Then you had a Bray interception, two Jeff Driskell TD passes, and a Caleb Sturgis field goal. It was a collapse in every way possible from Tennessee.

Bray finished the game with seven straight incompletions. The only pass caught by a guy in orange went to Dooley himself on the sideline. He spiked the ball in frustration.

Florida 37, Tennessee 20. The streak was up to eight. The Tennessee offense had averaged more than 38 points a game through the first four weeks, and on September 22 they exploded at fifth-ranked Georgia for 44 points and 477 yards. Slight problem: The defense gave up 51 points and 560 yards, dropping the Vols to 0-2 in conference play.

"We are better in a lot of areas, but we have to shore up the run defense," said Dooley. He was absolutely right. Georgia's Keith Marshall and Todd Gurley combined for five rushing touchdowns and nearly 300 yards against the Vols. Tennessee had a much needed bye week to try to correct their defensive woes before facing three more nationally ranked opponents: At Mississippi State, home for Alabama and then back on the road to play South Carolina. But before the next game, something else happened at Tennessee that made national news. And it had nothing to do with football.

A Tennessee student named Alexander Broughton was allegedly hospitalized in late September after what was called a "butt-chugging incident" at his fraternity house. He denied having practiced an alcohol enema. *The Knoxville News-Sentinel* reported that Broughton's blood alcohol level was .45, five times the legal limit, according to a UT Police report. On October 2, a press conference was held in front of the Torchbearer statue at Circle Park (yes, a stone's throw from where College GameDay set up a couple of weeks before). Broughton was there, as were his Pi Kappa Alpha fraternity brothers. Broughton's lawyer, a man named Daniel McGehee, addressed a pack of local media, and somehow was able to make a bizarre situation even weirder.

"Mr. Broughton denies each and every allegation whatsoever that has been inferred that he may have been a gay man. He is a straight man. And he thinks that the idea of the concept of butt-chugging is absolutely repulsive."

When asked to explain what did in fact happen, Broughton uttered four unforgettable words.

"It's a long story."

Tennessee became a laughing stock. "Butt-chugging" entered the national lexicon. Orange t-shirts were printed with a dog that looked like Smokey and a funnel connected to his backside. Signs referencing the alleged incident could be seen weekly all season on College GameDay. That press conference actually happened. I still can't believe it happened.

For Derek Dooley there was physical pain to go with the emotional stress of sitting at 14-16 as the Vols head coach, with no wins over a ranked opponent. Dooley had surgery to repair a fractured right hip on October 9 and would coach the Vols from the press box. Doctors told him that he had to have the surgery and couldn't put it off until after the season.

Even with two weeks to prepare for the Bulldogs, the Vols defense didn't show much improvement. Patterson did have an exciting 98-yard kickoff return for a touchdown. A late Bray touchdown pass to Bartholomew pulled Tennessee within three points, but the Bulldogs won 41-31. A state trooper brought Dooley down from the press box in a wheelchair after the game.

"We are not very good right now," admitted Dooley. With each loss, the number of critics swelled. The following week,

Dooley's old boss Nick Saban brought top-ranked Alabama into Neyland Stadium. "I was on the field and saw Alabama come out and every Tennessee player stopped and stared at Saban and those red helmets," said Nashville TV sports anchor Joe Dubin. "I turned to my friend and said, 'Bama is going to kill them. Tennessee has already lost.'"

Dooley was back on the sidelines for the game, this time on crutches. He also had an orange stool that he sat on close to the field of play because, you know, having a guy that can't easily move sitting a few inches from large, fast men playing a violent, physical sport is a great idea. Much like in 2008, Crimson Tide fans took over the building. The Vols defense gave up over 539 yards of offense along with 44 points. Near the end of the first half, the Vols trailed 23-10. They had the ball on their own 22 with 1:24 left on the clock, plus two timeouts. Bama was getting the football to start the second half. There was lots of time to get into field goal range. Instead, Dooley elected to let the clock tick to zero. Boos rained down across Neyland Stadium.

You are playing the number one team in the land and you are a 20-point underdog. Why not try to get some points there? "I understand people being upset with me," Dooley said after the game. "We're down 13, which is fine. It's not the end of the world... If we were moving the ball well, I'd have been more aggressive. I wanted to get out of there without making it any worse. We were not playing well on offense."

The final tally of the game came on fourth and goal from the Alabama 3, with only 3:57 left on the clock. Dooley elected to have Michael Palardy kick a chip shot field goal. The Vols were down 34 points at the time. Alabama beat Tennessee 44-13. The Vols were now 3-4, and 0-4 in conference play. Hope was fleeting.

Had Dooley been more popular with alumni, specifically players who built the program, he might have survived this stretch. But he was very similar to Saban in one respect. Dooley wanted complete control, from the construction of the indoor facility expansion, to the placement of garbage cans in the football complex. (Yeah, I'm not kidding about the garbage cans.) That autonomy got him on the wrong side of the guys who came before him in Knoxville.

What was it like for alums at Tennessee during the Dooley years? "Terrible," said former Tennessee defensive back Derrick Furlow. "Here's my first encounter with Dooley. Me and [former Tennessee wide receiver] Quinten Hancock are in the training room after the NFL combine. The guys we just played with are out there practicing. We wave, don't say much. We go and workout. Condredge Holloway walks up to us. He says, 'I won't tell you to leave, but Dooley isn't so sure about players coming and going.'"

Holloway is a Tennessee legend. He was the first African-American quarterback in SEC history and has worked in the UT athletics department for decades. Dooley looped him and others in the department in on enforcing a policy that was not taken well by alums. He was making it difficult for them to maintain a connection with the program. "Dooley was twenty yards away. He sent someone else to do his dirty work," Furlow says. "He could have introduced himself and been respectful to the guys that helped build the program. But it went downhill from there. This made zero sense. We got to NFL Pro Day and the same thing happened. It was a really a bad beginning."

"It was weird to hear guys that just finished the year before that would be hanging out at practice being told they had to leave," said former Vols wide receiver Jayson Swain. "You have guys that love Tennessee with a passion. They met their wives here and their best friends here. Being told to leave hurt them. It ate them up."

Dooley's policy required alumni to call the football offices before they came to practice or entered the football facility. Dooley addressed a question from the *Knoxville News-Sentinel's* Dave Hooker on this topic at one of his weekly press conferences. "Why are they getting concerned about that, because of things that are getting said that did not come from me," an irritated Dooley responded to Hooker. "How confusing it this? [Dooley mimics phone call] 'I want to come to practice.' 'OK' [mimics hanging up phone]. I mean, when you go to somebody's house, you don't just walk in. What's so hard about that?"

"I got called by several players that wanted me to bring more publicity to this policy," recalls Hooker. "Many of those players still have ties to high school prospects. Some coach camps. Some had sons who would be prospects. Dooley didn't get that. He quickly turned a recruiting tool into a hindrance."

If you ask media members and fans what the best part of Dooley's tenure at Tennessee would be, they'll likely say his press conferences. They were rarely boring, and often unpredictable. In October 2010, WBIR-TV's Kris Budden asked Dooley a question about Tennessee's inexperience and the issues that caused. Dooley responded by comparing his players to the Germans on D-Day.

Wait, what?

"Right now, we're like the Germans in World War II. Here comes the boats. They're coming. You have the binoculars, and it's like, 'Oh my God, the invasion is coming.' That's what they did, they were in the bunkers. It's coming. They call [General] Rommel. They can't find Rommel. 'What do we do? I'm not doing anything until I get orders. [Dooley pretends to look into binoculars] Have you gotten Rommel yet?'"

Dooley quoted Shakespeare and Bruce Hornsby and talked about the Pythagorean Theorem. He had a graphic installed on the double doors leading onto the field in the indoor complex that is supposed to read "Opportunity is Now Here," but it also looks like *"Opportunity is Nowhere."* He stressed shower discipline to the media after some Tennessee players got staph infections. He brought an orange ceramic dog to the practice field to promote positive thinking the day after losing at Arkansas by 42 points. And Derek Dooley's Mom, Barbara, went on sports talk radio shows to rip sportswriters that criticized her son, who she lovingly referred to as "Precious."

During the Dooley era, this graphic was on the doors leading to the indoor field at the UT football complex. Dooley wanted his players to read "Opportunity is Now Here." Most everyone read "Opportunity is Nowhere," which was a fitting description of those three seasons at Tennessee. The Vols went 15-21 during Dooley's tenure, including a woeful 4-19 mark in SEC play.   (Picture courtesy 247Sports)

Entertainment was never a problem for Derek Dooley. Winning games was the issue. In October 2012, Tennessee needed a big victory, and they need it soon. South Carolina was the last ranked opponent on the Vols schedule. This game showed off the best and worst of Tennessee football. Bray threw for 368 yards and four touchdowns, but the Vols defense once again failed to stop their opponent. Star running back Marcus Lattimore was knocked out of the game with a knee injury that cost him his pro career. His teammates played on for him, racking up 510 yards of offense in a 38-35 Gamecocks victory.

Perhaps the biggest insult of the season for Tennessee happened a week later against Troy. Bray threw for 530 yards and five scores. Patterson had 219 yards receiving and a touchdown. Hunter chipped in 181 receiving yards and three tallies. If you look at those numbers, you'd think the Vols won by 40 against a Trojans team that was 4-4 out of the inferior Sun Belt Conference. Instead, Troy accounted for 721 yards of offense, the most that a Volunteers team had ever given up, and they have played football at Tennessee since the nineteenth century. The Vols actually trailed late in the fourth quarter but rallied for a 55-48 win. This happened against Troy. I feel that this should be written again. Tennessee gave up 721 yards... to TROY.

"Sal Sunseri is a fine position coach, but he was in over his head trying to run the entire defense," says Ward. "He had to get help during the season once everything started to fall apart."

If the Vols defense had played at the same level of Sunseri's practice field vulgarity, they never would have lost a game. "Sunseri's language and outbursts can't begin to be described, even in the context of a football coach," said Grant Ramey, who today is a sportswriter at GoVols247.

On November 10, 4-5 Tennessee hosted 4-5 Missouri. It was the Tigers first trip to Neyland Stadium in this, their inaugural season in the Southeastern Conference. The game got the dreaded 12:21pm SEC Network treatment, the modern-day version of the Jefferson Pilot Sports slot. Still, it was a beautiful fall afternoon and a great day to watch some football. But the Tennessee student sections were as empty as a Chick-fil-A on a Sunday.

Bray put up great numbers yet again, with over 400 yards passing and four touchdowns. Tennessee led by 14 points midway through the third quarter. The Vols played better than the Tigers on both sides of the ball. They gained more yards and had more first downs. In the final minute, the defense was trying to close the door while up seven. All they had to do was stop a fourth and 12 and they'd have their first SEC win of the season.

Sunseri had the Vols rush three men, with a spy waiting to see if quarterback James Franklin was going to run. Franklin had all day to throw and created more space by rolling to his left. Somehow, receiver Dorial Green-Beckham was alone in the end zone. Beckham tiptoed the sideline, secured the grab, and with 47 seconds left, the game was tied at 28. Still, the Vols had two timeouts. They had Bray, Patterson, Hunter, and Rogers. After a short kickoff to avoid the dangerous Patterson, Tennessee had possession at their own 39-yard line with 43 seconds remaining. If they picked up about thirty yards, they'd be in Palardy's field goal range. Bray threw an incompletion, and then a screen pass lost a yard. Still there were 30 seconds to go. They could call time out and... and... "If you were to hear how loud the boos were when Dooley didn't go for the win at the end of regulation, you would have thought a sold-out Neyland was witnessing two top teams playing," says Breece.

Dooley had a gassed defense and a record setting offense, many of whose players made NFL rosters. Yet he elected to take his chances in overtime. "I didn't want to go third and 10 and have to punt and all of the things that could happen there," Dooley told reporters. "We had the ball back on the last play in the same scenario. So, we just went in for overtime. We had the offense and I just had confidence in them. The first two plays, I was pushing it. We screwed up both of those plays - poor execution."

Bray gave Dooley a death stare as he walked to the sideline. "You had one of the best offenses in the country and a defense that was terrible," says Tennessee fan Chuck Morris. "Bray's reaction was typical of the fans that day and all season to be honest."

In the fourth overtime, Tennessee had fourth and 3 from the 17. Dooley went for it. But the Missouri defense kept a Bray to Rogers pass from being completed for a first down. On Missouri's possession, Tigers kicker Andrew Baggett drilled a 35-yard field goal, and that was it.

Missouri 51, Tennessee 48. The writing was on the wall for Derek Dooley. There was no way that he was going to survive as Tennessee coach. There would be a new man in charge in 2013. But there was still one more insult to come for "Precious." A week later, the Vols had to play at Vanderbilt. Traditionally, this was a fun trip for Tennessee and their fans. The Vols would fill Vanderbilt Stadium and leave with a victory. The Vols were the big brothers, always ready to push their little brothers into the lake from the dock. But in 2012, the Commodores were pretty good. They were 6-4 and already bowl eligible. Vanderbilt's players certainly remembered Dooley's *"Kick the shit out of Vandy!"* locker room comment after the 2011 game.

"It was disrespectful and you're damn right we thought about that all year," says Kyle Woestmann. He was a Commodores outside linebacker/defensive end from 2011-2014. "[Head coach James] Franklin played 'Rocky Flop' for like ten days straight in the locker room. That was enough to make us come out and make sure a statement was made. We wanted to punish UT. We knew they had some struggles in 2012 and that it would be a great year to dominate them."

Franklin fired up the student section during warmups. They were expecting to see the Commodores beat Tennessee for what would only be the second time in thirty-six years. "I remember [defensive coordinator Bob] Shoop sitting in the locker room telling [defensive back] Andre Hal that he would have two interceptions and he did and telling me I'd have a sack and I did," said Woestmann. "We knew the talent on our team was elite enough to be very competitive."

Tennessee was not beating Vanderbilt on this night. Following a tipped pass interception in the second quarter, Bray was benched by Dooley. Bray returned in the third quarter and finished the game with a season low 103 yards passing. The Commodores won 41-18, their first victory over the Vols in Nashville since 1982. This game was the outlier in that 2012 season. For once, the UT offense couldn't keep pace.

"If we'd had just a top-40 defense that fall, Tennessee could have won ten games," says Greene. "That offense was truly elite, probably the most explosive since 2001. Sadly, as good as it was, Sunseri's defense was apocalyptically horrid."

Just like the decision to hire Dave Clawson helped cost Phillip Fulmer his job in 2008, the choice of Sal Sunseri would basically be the end of the line for Derek Dooley in 2012. The next morning, Sunday, November 18, Dooley did his television coaches show. While it was airing on WVLT-TV in the Knoxville market, the station ran a bottom line scroll. VolQuest.com was reporting that Dooley had been fired by Hart. It was surreal. Dooley was on screen as Tennessee's head coach at the same time text was on screen detailing that he was no longer Tennessee's head coach.

"When Coach Fulmer was fired, former players and staff were very upset," said former Tennessee defensive back Fred White, a key member of the 1998 national championship team. "Players addressed their feelings to the national media about how they were not happy with the firing. When Dooley was fired? No one said a word. You do the math."

Derek Dooley will be remembered as one of the worst head coaches in SEC history. In nearly three seasons under Dooley, the Vols went 15-21. They were only 4-19 in league play, and 0-15 against nationally ranked FBS opponents. Tennessee might have avoided large NCAA sanctions under Kiffin, but the Dooley years were a de facto death penalty. "I am sorry we could not generate enough wins to create hope for a brighter future," said Dooley in a press release. "Although progress was not reflected in our record, I am proud of the strides we made to strengthen the foundation for future success in all areas of the program."

"When you hire the wrong person, it can take years to get fixed," says former WVLT-TV Sports Anchor Daryl Hobby. "That was the Derek Dooley effect. That hire set the table for things to come."

"We will now move forward in our search process with the goal of securing the best coach we possibly can to come and lead the football program at Tennessee," said Hart in a press conference the afternoon Dooley was fired. "We have tradition, we have history, we have a brand that is still meaningful... but we have a long way to go to get back to where we need to be."

At the end of the press conference, Hart was asked by WNML's Vince Ferrara how he would handle the recommendations he would surely receive from fans and boosters about this hire. "Respectfully, because that's part of the passion," Hart said. "People should have an opinion. But also I know that I've got a job to do. And I have a level of expertise, and I have a level of information that no one else has."

The Vols would now hire their fourth head coach since 2008. Stability that was the benchmark of Tennessee football for more than three decades under Majors and Fulmer was a thing of the past. Tennessee fans hoped the next coach would return the Vols to what they believed to be their rightful place among the elite programs in the SEC, and the nation.

7
Lyle Allen "Butch" Jones Jr.

You might win a few bar bets with this one... Question: "Which head football coach had the highest winning percentage at Tennessee?" Answer: Jim Chaney. He was 1-0 as Tennessee's interim head coach after the 37-17 win over Kentucky in the 2012 season finale. He is officially listed in the record books as the Vols twenty-third head coach.

Chaney was the lone coaching staff constant of the Lane Kiffin and Derek Dooley regimes, but knew that he would be someplace else in 2013. He would soon join Bret Bielema's new staff at Arkansas as offensive coordinator and quarterbacks coach. He enters the 2018 season as offensive coordinator of the defending SEC champion Georgia Bulldogs.

Tennessee athletics director Dave Hart was now embarking on the biggest hire that any AD makes, the hiring of a football coach. Football drives the economic engine. If a college football team is successful, and in turn profitable, that means big things for the entire athletics department. If football is winning, fundraising gets easier. New, shiny buildings get built. The football team doesn't need to be winning conference championships every year, but they need to show that they are on the right track. At the end of the Dooley era, it was obvious they were on the wrong track. Only in the final weeks did apathy really set in with the Tennessee fanbase. A new coach would have to excite the fan base and get them to buy in once again.

First, Hart approached the white whale of Tennessee coaching searches, Jon Gruden. There are a considerable number of coaches with Tennessee ties that have had success in the pro football ranks, but none more so than Gruden. He won Super Bowl XXXVII as the Tampa Bay Buccaneers head coach in 2003. Gruden started his coaching career as a graduate assistant at Tennessee under Johnny Majors in 1986. He met his wife Cindy, a Tennessee cheerleader, at UT. Her family is from East Tennessee. Their son would choose to attend the University of Tennessee. If you ever watched ESPN's Monday Night Football, the odds are you heard him mention the Volunteers. He spent eleven years coaching the Oakland Raiders and the Buccaneers, winning 100 games. Gruden was fired by Tampa Bay less than seven weeks after Lane Kiffin was hired to replace Phillip Fulmer. In 2012, he was four years removed from coaching and seemingly ready to get back in the game.

There were discussions, but eventually Gruden's camp told Tennessee that they weren't interested. A contract was never offered but hey, when is it for a guy who turns down the job? The way Tennessee handled the Gruden situation in 2012 would be repeated five years later. Hart and Tennessee let the rumors, by now affectionately known as "Grumors," take hold for way too long. Vols fans thought Gruden was a real possibility and were saddened when they learned that wasn't the case. Knowing that Gruden was a no go, Hart centered his attention on two coaches. Oklahoma State's Mike Gundy and Louisville's Charlie Strong.

Gundy was only 27-23 in his four seasons at Oklahoma State, but was coming off a nine-win 2008 campaign, the Cowboys' best in twenty years. He was probably best known to Tennessee fans for his memorable, *"Come after me! I'm a man! I'm 40!"* rant at a member of the media in 2007.

Tennessee was all-in on Gundy. It would have meant a substantial raise for Gundy, and a chance for him to test himself in the best football conference in the country. Eventually, the pull to stay in Stillwater was too great. Gundy played his college football at Oklahoma State, and spent only four years of his adult life away from his alma mater. The attention from UT gave Oklahoma State the motivation to ink Gundy to a new seven-year contract worth $15.7 million. Was this just a ploy by agent Jimmy Sexton to get his client a salary bump? No matter how it happened, Tennessee was not having success with their top choices.

Hart's next call was to Charlie Strong, the well-respected former Florida assistant who helped the Gators win national titles in 2006 and 2008. Louisville was 25-14 in his three seasons as head coach and won eleven games in 2012. Hart and Strong reportedly met on Tuesday, December 4 in Knoxville, at which time Strong was offered the Tennessee job. Strong didn't want to make a decision without talking to his team, so that night he flew back to Louisville. That is never a good sign. If the coach doesn't stay in your town, he's probably not coming back.

On Thursday, December 6, Strong told his team that he wasn't going to Tennessee. "It was the toughest decision I've ever had to make in my twenty-nine years of coaching. My enthusiasm and heart is with the University of Louisville," Strong told reporters that same morning. Later that month, Strong received a $1.4 million raise from the University of Louisville, bringing his average salary to $3.7 million. The new contract ran through the year 2020.

But he didn't stick around nearly that long. A year later, he'd bolt for Texas, which proved to be an awful spot for Strong. He's not a big fan of media obligations, and Texas needs a lot of content for its Longhorn Network. Under Strong, Texas most certainly was NOT back. The Longhorns went 16-21 in his three years in Austin before his dismissal at the end of the 2016 season. In 2018, Charlie Strong is entering his second season as the head coach at South Florida.

Hart was learning a valuable lesson the hard way. There was a time when the LSU's, the Michigans and the Tennessees of the world could have their pick of high quality coaches. Their stadiums, their facilities, their pocket books... all gave them an edge over most schools. But thanks in part to massive television contracts, there are more schools than ever that can offer the same type of prizes. Why leave a school you truly enjoy for a few more bucks? For example, why on earth would David Cutcliffe ever depart Duke at this point? He likes the Raleigh area, there is no pressure to win whatsoever as the football coach of the Blue Devils, and he makes $1.7 million per season. In 2017, seventy head football coaches in the FBS made at least $1 million a year. In 2012 the money wasn't quite that high, but coaches weren't exactly standing outside their football complexes with a tin can and a "Will Work For Food" sign either.

Tennessee's nearly depleted reserve fund remained an issue, and they were paying Derek Dooley $102,049 a month to not coach the Vols until December 2016. His total buyout would be $5 million. When all was said and done, the buyouts for Dooley and his staff totaled over $9.3 million.

But the Vols still needed a coach, and Hart's first choices were off the board. The Louisville guy didn't say yes... so Hart looked about 100 miles further to the north to Cincinnati. Their head coach had waited his whole life to get to a place like Tennessee.

Lyle Allen "Butch" Jones Jr. was born in Saugatuck, a tiny city in southern Michigan. His was a coaching career that in its early stages took Jones to college football hotbeds Wilkes University and his alma mater, Ferris State. Central Michigan is where Jones really got the chance to flourish. From 1998-2004 he coached tight ends, wide receivers, running backs and was their offensive coordinator as well. After two seasons on the West Virginia staff, he returned to Mount Pleasant for his first head coaching job when Brian Kelly took off for Cincinnati. It had taken Jones sixteen years as an offensive assistant, but he finally made it.

Under Jones, the Chippewas went 27-13, with two MAC titles from 2007-2009. They were ranked in the top-25 for the first time in program history. This was about as far as Jones could get at Central Michigan. It was time for him to make another career move, and once again his old boss helped make it happen.

Brian Kelly was a red hot name in the coaching world. In 2009, Cincinnati was 12-0 and finished the regular season ranked third in the BCS. Kelly was waiting for his dream job and got it when

Notre Dame came calling after the Charlie Weis "schematic advantage" went haywire. Jones was a finalist for the opening at Marshall, but instead, now for the second time, he would replace Kelly. Butch Jones was heading to Cincinnati.

"It truly is an honor and privilege to be standing before today as the head football coach at the University of Cincinnati," said Jones at his opening press conference on December 16, 2009, six days after Kelly resigned. "I am a teacher of young men and every day is an opportunity to teach. It's not just football, it goes beyond that, champions off the field. Every day we will talk about those core values."

After a 4-8 debut, Jones went a combined 19-6 in the next two seasons. He was named Big East coach of the year in 2011. Following the regular season in 2012, Jones's name had some heat attached to it. He interviewed for the Purdue job on Sunday, December 2. The very next day, he interviewed for the Colorado coaching opening. Jones turned down the Boilermakers. He was more interested in what the Buffaloes had to offer. On Wednesday, December 5, the *Denver Post* reported that the forty-four-year-old Jones would become the Buffaloes next head coach, and that he would be paid $13.5 million over the next five years.

Not bad for a kid from Saugatuck. The same day that news of the Colorado proposition broke, Jones was representing Cincinnati at the Belk Bowl press conference. Later that month the Bearcats would play David Cutcliffe and Duke (the coaching world is a small one, isn't it?). Jones told local reporters that he hadn't made a decision concerning Colorado but expected to make one "pretty soon."

All the while, Jones was keeping an eye on another job that was still open. The Tennessee job. Even with the recent downturn, Tennessee was still a better spot than Purdue or Colorado. Jones wanted the Vols gig and was playing "four corners" with Colorado, delaying the Buffaloes in case the Vols came calling... and they did just that. Hart met with Jones in a Lexington hotel room late in the evening of Thursday, December 6. It was the first time they met in person. For hours Jones sold himself to Hart on what he could bring to Tennessee. The talks lasted until 6am, and after they were done, all that was left was to knock out the fine details.   Butch Jones was coming to Knoxville.

"I didn't know him. I was not part of process at all," said David Blackburn, who had helped save Tennessee from potentially massive NCAA penalties with his oversight of Lane Kiffin's staff in 2009. "I got a call at 6:30 that morning. Dave Hart said to get a suit and tie on for a meeting with Butch. I stayed with him that night until 2am. I helped with him with recruiting. He asked, 'How did they do it here in the '90s?' I think Butch needed someone that knew UT and kept him on task. I maintained that role until I left." Blackburn would work with Jones for a few months before taking the athletics director job at UT-Chattanooga in April 2013.

On December 7, 2012, Butch Jones was officially hired as the twenty-fourth head football coach in Tennessee history. Jones arrived on campus that night with his wife Barb and their three sons. He wore a fresh orange tie for the press conference, and it was obvious that he had done his research on what had been going on at Tennessee in recent years.

Jones spoke to those concerned that he had no SEC experience: "I can assure you that we will put together the best football staff in the country. Not just in the Southeastern Conference, but the entire country."

Jones spoke to the alums: "To our letter winners, you are the foundation. We will have an open door policy with our practices."

Jones spoke about recruiting: "We are going to win first and foremost with the great state of Tennessee. We have tremendous high school coaches in this state. We are the state institution and we will own our state."

"We got a text saying there was a team meeting to meet the new head coach," says former Tennessee defensive lineman Charles Folger. "He seemed to talk the talk. He captivated most of the room with being a player's coach and being a coach who has 'won everywhere he's been.' I was excited for the opportunity for my first spring ball with a clean slate and a fresh opportunity like everyone else."

Folger adds, "I was bought in."

The reaction both locally and nationally was mixed. Some liked his resume. Over the past six years his teams were 50-27 with at least a share of four conference titles. Others asked if he was merely riding Brian Kelly's coattails, and if his offensive system would work in the Southeastern Conference. Some saw him as a coaching mercenary.

Cincinnati Enquirer sports columnist Paul Daugherty didn't pull any punches in his opinion of Jones. For lack of a better word, Daugherty said that the new Tennessee coach was a phony. "He pretended to be committed to Cincinnati," wrote Daugherty. "He made the University look foolish. While [UC Athletics Director] Whit Babcock and [UC President] Santa Ono huddled to find ways to appease Jones, Jones was job hunting. He said how much he loved it here, then spent every available moment looking to leave. Jones was a starlet, batting his eyes all over Hollywood. He is a vacuum salesman, knocking at your door, tipping his cap and throwing dirt on your living room rug."

Jones wasn't Tennessee's first choice, but he brought some much needed energy to Knoxville. That vigor put him on the recruiting trail immediately. He had less than two months to put together his first recruiting class. Jones knew that the Vols needed help at the skill positions. Quarterback Tyler Bray, and wide receivers Justin Hunter and Cordarrelle Patterson had no desire to be part of another rebuild and were going pro early.

In that initial group of twenty-three commitments there were no 5-star recruits, but Jones did shore up the offense. 4-star quarterback Riley Ferguson from Matthews (NC) had committed to Tennessee under Derek Dooley and Jones was able to convince him to stick to his pledge. That was no easy trick, considering that Ferguson had scholarship offers from Alabama, LSU and Clemson, amongst others. "I love everything he's about," Jones noted. "He's a competitor."

But Ferguson wouldn't be the only quarterback in this class. Jones got another highly regarded signal caller in Alpharetta (GA) 4-star quarterback Joshua Dobbs. He flipped from Arizona State to Tennessee on National Signing Day. "To be able to add an individual like that to your recruiting class... he's a 4.0 student,"

Jones gushed. "He wants aeronautical engineering. He's brilliant." This story line would be publicized quite often in the years to come. Dobbs was the epitome of a student-athlete and a fine representative of the University of Tennessee.

Thanks to that haul, Jones would enter fall camp with four scholarship quarterbacks on the roster. Junior Justin Worley, redshirt freshman Nathan Peterman, Ferguson and Dobbs. Worley was the only one, however, that had played in a college football game. At wide receiver, 4-star commit Marquez North would be pressed into duty immediately due to all the attrition at that position. Tennessee couldn't get 5-star linebacker Carl Lawson (he picked Auburn), but 3-star early enrollee Jalen Reeves-Maybin would become a major contributor at linebacker in the years that followed.

A huge miss for the Vols in this class was Vonn Bell. The 5-star defensive back from just across the state line in Rossville (GA) was basically ignored by Dooley and the Vols coaching staff, despite his significant interest in coming to Knoxville. Bell had played his first two years of high school football in Chattanooga. Jones put on a full-court press for Bell, visiting him with several assistant coaches in tow the week before NSD. There just wasn't enough time to build that relationship. Bell picked Ohio State, and helped them win a national championship in 2014.

While they did miss out on that addition for their secondary, they did get in-state 3-star defensive back Malik Foreman to flip from Vanderbilt to Tennessee. Remember, at this time Vanderbilt was on the rise under James Franklin. "I decided to change my mind due to the fact Tennessee was the only school to offer me and my lifelong friend Devaun Swafford," says Foreman of his Kingsport Dobyns-Bennett teammate. "We always dreamt of playing big time college football together." Among the players who Jones kept in the Class of 2013 were two from nearby Christian Academy of Knoxville, wide receiver Josh Smith and offensive lineman Brett Kendrick. Both players were originally offered scholarships when Derek Dooley was head coach.

"Brett did commit under [former UT offensive line coach] Sam Pittman. We are still big fans of his," says Beth Kendrick, Brett's mother. "We spoke to Derek Dooley once, then mostly Pittman. When Dooley was fired we were concerned. Will they honor it? My husband Bryan called Dave Hart's office and asked if they would honor the scholarship or if we should we look around. We didn't hear back from Hart. Brett took a visit to Clemson. When we got back Butch called and said he wanted to meet for dinner at Neyland. It was in a suite and all the commits were there to meet Butch. That was a couple of weeks after Butch got there."

She added, "Butch said he wanted to keep Brett. He needed offensive linemen since Dooley took none the year before. Butch said that he wanted to honor the scholarship. The night I met Butch, I was excited. I'm a praying momma. I'm thinking that he's a nice man and it'll all be good... but things changed once we got to know more about who he was."

247Sports listed Tennessee as having the twenty-fifth ranked class for 2013. The class was also listed as being eleventh-best in the SEC. To be competitive in the conference, future classes would have to be better. Much better. "It wasn't until we got to spring ball that we really noticed that the talent needed to increase greatly for us to have a chance," said Tennessee wide receivers coach Zach Azzanni, who was now on his second stint coaching under Jones. The two had worked together previously at Central Michigan. "It was shocking how the roster had slipped. I don't think people fully grasped what the roster was like, except for that offensive line. But they didn't have anyone around them."

That spring, Butch Jones said that the program rebuild was going to be done "brick by brick," the motto of Tennessee football throughout his tenure. The long and arduous process was just getting started. "Brick by brick" was also the first of a multitude of clichés that produced a variety of reactions from fans and media alike.

One thing Jones had to be concerned about from the jump was Tennessee's academic situation. After the 2011-2012 academic year, the Vols had a score of 909 in the NCAA's Academic Progress Rate (APR). This lowered their four-year average to 924. If the average did not increase above at least 930, Tennessee would face penalties, including a possible postseason ban.

In the middle of August, former Tennessee coach Phillip Fulmer was one of twenty-two former coaches and players at SEC Beachfest in Gulf Shores. He spoke to AL.com about the downturn of Tennessee football since he was fired nearly five years ago. He wouldn't place all the blame on Kiffin and Dooley. Fulmer felt that off the field influences played a major part as well. "What happened to us basically was our leadership. We had four presidents in six years. We ended up with an athletic director [Mike Hamilton] that wasn't prepared for the job. Not a terrible guy or anything like that. He got twisted like a pretzel by the middle management of the university. We lost a lot of the edges that you have to have. Dave Hart's very aware of those."

The 2013 season did start with optimism as Tennessee beat Austin Peay and Western Kentucky by combined scores of 97-20. But the schedule that followed was a vicious one for a young team that had gone through considerable off-season roster attrition yet again. Over the next eight games, the Vols would play seven ranked teams.

The pain started with a trip west to play second-ranked Oregon. Remember back in 2010 when Tennessee bought out the series with North Carolina? That wasn't the series they should have backed away from. The Vols should have sent that cash to Eugene, telling the Ducks, "Thanks but no thanks."

Chip Kelly had turned the Ducks into a powerhouse. Their fast-paced style was exciting for fans and burned out the scoreboard light bulbs. Kelly had gone to the Philadelphia Eagles that offseason and Oregon promoted offensive coordinator Mark Helfrich to replace him. Helfrich smartly saw that little was broken, so why make big changes?

On this afternoon, even the most positive Tennessee fan could see early on that the Ducks were PlayStation 4 while the Vols were Activision. Future Heisman Trophy winner Marcus Mariota threw for 456 yards and four touchdowns as the Ducks raced out to a 38-7 halftime lead. Like Usain Bolt pulling up in a preliminary race, Oregon coasted to a 59-14 victory. They could have scored 75 had they chosen to do so. After the game, the disappointed Vols said what everyone already knew. This was a mismatch of epic proportions.

"We needed to maintain control," said Worley, who threw for only 126 yards before being replaced in the second half by Peterman. "Unfortunately, we couldn't put together drives. Hopefully, next week we'll have more explosive plays."

Worley was already looking towards the second half of a rough back to back. The Vols had to follow up 5,000 miles of flying with a journey to Gainesville seven days later to play nineteenth-ranked Florida. Butch Jones's offensive system requires the quarterback to be mobile, to sometimes make plays happen with his feet. That simply wasn't Justin Worley's game. He was a pocket quarterback. In twenty-four career games at Tennessee, Worley rushed for negative 105 yards. During the Monday press conference before the Florida game, Jones hinted that a change at quarterback was possible.

"You have to earn your spot each and every week. We will see what the freshmen can handle," said Jones. "Nathan Peterman continues to progress along... I think Justin is getting better. It is going to be a week to week process, who can manage the offense the best."

Considering the hostile environment that was Ben Hill Griffin Stadium, it was hard to imagine Riley Ferguson or Joshua Dobbs replacing Worley that week. In fact, Dobbs didn't even make the trip. Nathan Peterman wasn't a much better option either. He was more mobile than Worley, but only had twelve career collegiate pass attempts.

Jones decided to gamble. He felt that he knew what he had with Worley, and that it wouldn't be enough to beat the Gators. With Peterman, there was more upside. This was a game Peterman desperately wanted to win. He grew up in nearby Jacksonville and was not offered a scholarship by the Gators. But things did not go well. In fact, it was the worst quarterbacking debut in Tennessee football history. Peterman completed four of 11 passes for only five yards. He had two interceptions and a fumble. The offense could only muster twelve yards of offense in the first half. The Maginot Line fared better than Nathan Peterman.

Butch Jones had put all his chips on black and the ball landed on red. "This is his first game and a big road game," said Jones. "He kept a level head. He kept scrapping and kept trying. When things were going wrong he still had a level head." Mercifully, Peterman was replaced at halftime by Worley. But it was too late. Florida would win 31-17, extending their domination of the Vols to nine games.

Ironically enough, Worley's game manager talents would have been a better option than Peterman's higher ceiling/lower floor. Florida quarterback Jeff Driskell broke his leg in the first quarter and backup Tyler Murphy had the game of his life. Tennessee's six turnovers to Florida's three giveaways was the difference.

Jones did his best to stress it was a team loss, not Peterman's. "Everyone wants to point to the quarterback, but I don't think we did a good job protecting the quarterback. We had too many third and long situations, and those are situations offensively we can't be in."

In 2017 Nathan Peterman made his first professional start for the Buffalo Bills, and it was deja vu all over again. Against San Diego, Peterman was six of 14 for 66 yards and five interceptions and was benched at halftime. You never forget your first time, but Peterman has two first times he'd like to wipe from his memory.

Peterman took a physical beating in Gainesville. He would need to have surgery on his right hand and wouldn't play again for the Vols in 2013. Two weeks after the Florida drubbing, Tennessee welcomed rival Georgia to Neyland Stadium. Vols fans weren't very confident. The week before they saw their team barely defeat South Alabama. But the sixth-ranked Bulldogs were not looking past the Vols. Even during the Tennessee downturn, they played UGA close quite often. "We knew it would be a tough game," remembers former Georgia linebacker Amarlo Montez Herrera. "We knew that the stadium would be loud, and it was an SEC East game, so we knew we had to come to play."

There was a bit of a spark as the Vols wore their alternate Smokey Gray uniforms for the first time, but they still trailed 17-3 at the half. Things changed in the third quarter. A diving Marquez North touchdown catch was followed by a blocked punt from Jalen

Reeves-Maybin and fifteen-yard return from Devaun Swafford for a score. The game was knotted at 17.

Neyland Stadium was rocking for the first time since the 2012 Florida game. Butch Jones was channeling his inner Les Miles, converting on fourth down on three occasions. "We had a lot of young players playing," Herrera informed me. "They also attacked our weak spots."

The Vols led 31-24, and if they could hold on for another 1:54, they'd have a monumental upset, and the first big win of the Butch Jones era. But Georgia, a team that was decimated by injuries throughout the day, marched 75 yards to tie the game, forcing overtime. That was when a cruel fate was waiting for the Vols. Alton "Pig" Howard was one of Tennessee's best players on this day, with 116 yards from scrimmage. On the Vols' first possession of overtime, he took a hand-off from Worley on a jet sweep. Howard got to the sideline and dove for the pylon. The referee signaled touchdown. Tennessee got their extra point team ready.

Unfortunately, the play would be reviewed. Replay showed Howard diving... and the football leaving his hands at about the half-yard line. The football bounced out of the side of the end zone for a touchback. Marshall Morgan kicked a 42-yard field goal on Georgia's possession, and UGA won the game 34-31. "I love Alton," said Jones. "He's trying to make a play and unfortunately it slipped out of his hands, but we wouldn't be in a situation to win the game without Alton Howard's effort today."

This was the first game of many under Butch Jones that Tennessee could have won, but for whatever reason, couldn't close the deal. It was the Vols' nineteenth straight loss to a nationally ranked opponent. Tennessee fans were saddened, yet encouraged. Except for the 2010 LSU game, the Vols weren't even competitive against good teams during the Dooley era. "The bye week will be something to allow us to look a little more into our opponent," said UT defensive back Justin Coleman. "We will be ready."

Tennessee legend Johnny Majors liked what he saw from the Vols' first-year head coach in that Georgia game, telling WNML, "I doubt that there's ever been a team and a coaching staff that ever did a better job at one game in the entire history of this school, because it was well coached, extremely well coached, with some big decisions made. He's going to get the job done."

All that optimism was rewarded on October 19 when the Vols hosted eleventh-ranked South Carolina on a beautiful fall afternoon in Knoxville. On that day Tennessee was welcoming the man they loved to hate. Gamecocks head coach Steve Spurrier had haunted the Vols for years. He played his high school football in Johnson City, only 100 miles from Knoxville. Spurrier chose to play his college football at Florida in part because in the early 1960s, the Vols were still running the Wing-T offense under Bowden Wyatt and James McDonald. The Gators would give him the chance to throw the football.

Spurrier would win the 1966 Heisman Trophy at Florida. A Tennessee player has never won the Heisman. Spurrier returned to his alma mater in December of 1989 and would win six SEC titles and one national championship over the next twelve years. He went 8-4 against Tennessee's flagship school, reveling in every win and making jokes at the Vols' expense. After a failed two-year run with the Washington Redskins, Spurrier itched to get back to the college game, and took on the challenge of building a winning in Columbia.

With few exceptions, South Carolina had seen a century of mediocre football. Lou Holtz was hired in 1999 and got the Gamecocks moving in the right direction. Steve Spurrier took them to heights not seen before. In 2010 South Carolina won the SEC's Eastern Division for the first time. In 2011 and 2012, they won eleven games. And against Tennessee, Spurrier's Gamecocks were more than competitive. Leading into the 2013 matchup, South Carolina was 5-3 against Tennessee under Steve Spurrier.

It looked like this game would be more of the same. Carolina led 21-20 in the final minutes. The Vols got the ball back at their own 35 with 2:48 left. On third and 10 they needed a big play. What they got was a miraculous one. Worley had to receive an extra half a second from his blockers to allow his receivers to get down field, and he got it. Worley floated a deep ball to Marquez North, who was in double coverage. South Carolina defensive back

Ahmad Christian was holding North's right arm. The pass was perfect, and so was the one-handed catch. North corralled the pigskin, pinning it between his left hand and shoulder pad.

Marlin Lane then got four straight carries, taking the football down to the Carolina two-yard line. The left footed Palardy drilled the chip shot from inside the left hashmark as the clock struck zero, and the Vols finally had a significant victory. Palardy sprinted to the opposite side of the field, where he was mobbed by his teammates at the 15-yard line, right in front of the visiting South Carolina fans. Butch Jones watched the kick go through the uprights while kneeling on the sideline. He gave a sly grin, stood up, and walked to midfield to shake hands with Spurrier. For UT, maybe this was the start of their revival. Jones and Dave Hart celebrated with a chest bump on the field at Neyland Stadium. (Experts put the vertical at a combined two and a quarter inches.) "Great day to be a Vol," a happy Jones said after the game.

The first season for Butch Jones at Tennessee was a rough one as the Vols only won five games... but the fans still showed up at Neyland Stadium. On November 9, 102,455 were there for Tennessee's 55-23 loss to ninth-ranked Auburn.

Reality set back in over the next three weeks, when top-ranked Alabama, tenth-ranked Missouri and ninth-ranked Auburn beat the Vols by a combined score of 131-36. The Vols had to burn

Joshua Dobbs' redshirt after Worley was injured in the Alabama game. He'd have surgery on his right thumb and was done for the season. Tennessee was now down to their third string quarterback. Even with all this adversity, the Vols would make their first bowl game since 2010 if they could beat Vanderbilt and Kentucky. That was easier said than done because in 2013, Commodores head coach James Franklin was doing the unthinkable. Making Vandy a winner.

The Commodores had already beaten Georgia and Florida, and if they could defeat Tennessee, it would be the first time they picked up back-to-back victories over their in-state rivals since 1926. "I think this is good for the state of Tennessee," said Franklin. "I think it is good for our program and UT's program and I think it'll be good for the SEC. We're excited about it and I know people want to call it a rivalry, but I just don't think it is there yet."

Patton Robinette was Vanderbilt's backup quarterback on the depth chart, but he knew that he was going to get some snaps against the Vols. Robinette came to Vanderbilt from the powerhouse Maryville HS program, where he led the Rebels to a 29-1 record and two state championships. Maryville is about a twenty-minute drive down Alcoa Highway from the UT campus, and Robinette had lot of friends and family making the short trip to Neyland Stadium.

Robinette was a recruit for the Class of 2012. At the time Jim Chaney was Tennessee's offensive coordinator. Chaney came to Maryville to see Robinette throw a couple of times, but a scholarship offer never happened. "I was disappointed that UT didn't give me much of a look," recalls Robinette. "I don't think I would have chosen to go there regardless. I was ready to get out of East Tennessee for a while." Robinette would pick the Commodores over North Carolina and Iowa. At the time of this book's writing, Robinette was in his third year of medical school at Vanderbilt.

Points were at a premium on this cold November night, with defenses controlling the action. "There were eleven dogs on defense at all times," said former Vanderbilt outside linebacker/defensive end Kyle Woestmann. "I think our 2013 defense was something special."

Tennessee was in control of the game early in the fourth quarter, leading 10-7. Michael Palardy lined up for a 39-yard field goal on fourth and 19 from the Vandy 22. What happened next was... peculiar. The Vols faked it. Palardy threw the football, and it was intercepted by Vandy's Paris Head. "I knew we needed a touchdown to win the football game," said Jones at his postgame press conference."

There were a lot of questions about that call. That's a lot of yardage to pick up on a fake, while asking your kicker to throw into a cross wind. Plus, Tennessee's defense had only allowed one Vanderbilt score all night to that point. With 21 seconds left, Vanderbilt was in position to steal the game. They had second and goal from the Tennessee 5. Franklin inserted the more mobile Robinette into the game. What followed was one of the biggest plays in Commodores history.

"We set up the play the week before against Kentucky," remembers Robinette. "I ran a jump pass to ice the game. We knew if we came out in that formation, Tennessee would have seen that play on film and be keying on the pass. Sure enough, the whole defense is yelling, 'Jump pass! Jump pass!'" Robinette faked a handoff. On the right side of the formation, two Vols defenders went with Kris Kentera, the 6'4" pass catcher from Colorado Springs. Robinette faked a jump pass to Kentera, which caused Tennessee linebacker A.J. Johnson to leave his feet for a moment in an effort to block a pass attempt that was surely coming. But instead of a pass, Robinette kept the football and took off for the end zone.

"It was a designed run all the way," said Robinette, who was now was free and clear. He jumped over the goal line before the defense could adjust, for what would prove to be the winning score. "I was living in the moment for sure," remembers Woestmann. "I was enamored with the Jumbotron and too scared to watch in person, so I stared at the screen and almost dropped to my knees when Patton made it into the end zone."

"It was an unbelievable feeling. I still remember getting into end zone and screaming, but it was so loud that the only one who could hear me was me," said Robinette. "When you play at Vanderbilt, those Tennessee games matter. Being from Maryville made it even better. When people ask me about that play I say it was the second-best moment of my life, besides my wife saying yes when I proposed."

Vanderbilt 14, Tennessee 10. Robinette and the Commodores raced to where their fans were sitting, and the celebration was on. "It was a hell of a time," says Woestmann. "The atmosphere was always so amazing. I loved playing at Tennessee because they do a great job of creating a hostile playing environment and there's nothing more fun than listening to all the boos and slander as you kick that teams' tail in their own house."

As major as this moment was for the Commodores, it was a historical defeat for the Vols. For the first time in eighty-seven years, Vanderbilt had beaten Tennessee two years in a row. This also ensured another losing season for the Vols. Tennessee hadn't endured four straight losing seasons since 1906. Theodore Roosevelt was President back then and has been credited with saving the sport of football by encouraging reforms for safety. Even Teddy couldn't save the 2013 Vols.

After the game, Jones told Vols supporters that brighter days were ahead. "I see, again, progress... Tennessee football is going to be fine. Right now, we're going through some things, but we have an extremely loyal fan base... a very proud university, and it's a matter of time and we'll be fine."

Year one of the Butch Jones era ended the following week with a win over Kentucky. Jones needed more talented players to get Tennessee out of these doldrums.

Since the final year of the Phillip Fulmer era, the Vols' records were as follows:

- 2008: 5-7, no bowl game
- 2009: 7-6, Chick-fil-A Bowl loss
- 2010: 6-7, Music City Bowl loss
- 2011: 5-7, no bowl game
- 2012: 5-7, no bowl game

- 2013: 5-7, no bowl game

That's a combined record of 33-41.

Tennessee is one of the top ten winningest programs in the history of college football. The Vols had won six national championships and thirteen conference championships. This is the football program of George Cafego and Carl Pickens. Jason Witten and Willie Gault. Shaun Ellis and Andy Kelly. Donte Stallworth and Jamal Lewis. Those six years? That's not what Tennessee fans had grown to expect.

Frustration was mounting. The Class of 2014 would be crucial for the Vols and for the future of Butch Jones at Tennessee as well.

8

JOSHUA DOBBS TAKES CONTROL

BUTCH JONES AND HIS ASSISTANT COACHES hit the recruiting trail hard after the 2013 Kentucky game. They had only two months to go until National Signing Day. Without bowl game preps to take up their time, crootin' was all that mattered. Their hard work paid off. According to 247Sports, the Vols had sixteen 4-star recruits. It was the seventh-best class in the nation and fifth-best in the SEC. This was a marked improvement from recent years. Scout.com listed Tennessee the highest, at fourth in the nation.

The Class of 2014, a robust thirty-two members strong, had a very "Tennessee" feel to it. There was the top-ranked player in the state, Josh Malone from Gallatin. A Mr. Football award winner, he was the fifth-ranked wide receiver in the nation. Tennessee fit the bill in multiple ways for Malone. "It's a great place up there. I enjoy being around the coaches. I know most of the players up there, so I already have bonds with them," Malone told me before he verbally committed. "Butch has an offense where he likes to get the ball in wide receivers' hands, and it is also an opportunity to play early."

"Those were some hard recruiting battles," former Tennessee wide receivers coach Zach Azzanni told me. "Some really long days and nights. I feel like I recruited Josh Malone for two years, but that's what you have to do..."

The second-ranked player in the state was running back Jalen Hurd from Hendersonville. Hurd picked the Vols over Alabama, amongst others in May 2013. That was a game changer for the Class of 2014. "The fact that Butch Jones and his staff could come in and get guys like Jalen Hurd actually surprised me a little bit," says Jesse Smithey, who was the high school sports editor at the *Knoxville News-Sentinel*. "The fact that Tennessee got someone of Hurd's status – someone I had watched run for 394 yards and seven touchdowns in the 2012 Class 5A state title game – helped that class snowball into a top ten class in the country. I knew once he committed, more top players would follow suit."

You also had the third-best player in the state, Todd Kelly Jr., a safety from nearby Webb School. Kelly, like others in this class, served as an extension of the coaching staff in efforts to bring more talent to Knoxville. "It is fun because you feel you have a part in recruiting," Kelly said to me when I interviewed him the previous summer. "I want to play with good players at UT, so I have to recruit as much as I can so that they'll want to go there with me." The fifth-best player in the state was Derek Barnett, a defensive lineman from powerhouse Brentwood Academy. He picked Tennessee as well. Barnett would make the biggest impact on Tennessee football from this class. For all the coach speak about building a wall around the state, Jones and his assistants made it happen. Nine of the top eleven high school football players in Tennessee had committed to their home state school.

Our state.

"I've been recruiting for eighteen years. It's easy to say yes to a team that's on top," Azzanni says. "I understand that. That's the easy choice. It's hard to say yes to a team that is rebuilding because you really are going on faith that they can get it done. The really competitive players look at it as a challenge. Those guys said 'I'm gonna do that,' and thank God they did. They could have gone elsewhere, but they wanted to help us get back to where we wanted to go."

"We had success in recruiting for a number of reasons," says Mark Elder, who was the Vols' tight ends coach from 2013-2015. "First and foremost, Tennessee is a great place. It's easy to sell UT. You got a tradition-rich program, plus the facilities and a support system around players to help them be successful. Now the competition is tough too. You are recruiting against bluebloods like Alabama, Auburn, Georgia, Florida, etc. But this was a group of men that worked hard, a staff of guys that took pride in recruiting and worked their tails off. And Butch Jones was heavily involved. He spent time with recruits and did great job in building relationships. The combination of those things led to our success."

Vols fans took notice, with 68,548 showing up at Neyland Stadium for the annual Orange and White Game. They wanted to see the early enrollees, especially Malone and Hurd. Malone looked like the second coming of Carl Pickens, with six catches for 181 yards and three touchdowns. Hurd had 93 total yards and a score as well.

Now, if they could just figure out who was going to play quarterback. In 2013 the Vols started Justin Worley, Nathan Peterman and Joshua Dobbs at the position, with Riley Ferguson taking a medical redshirt. All four quarterbacks were with the team in the spring. But in late May, Ferguson announced that he was transferring. He ended up at Coffeyville Community College for two seasons. Ferguson then spent two seasons at Memphis, where he threw for nearly 8,000 yards and 70 touchdowns. It was down to Worley, Peterman and Dobbs. The battle was eventually won by Worley. Peterman would be the backup. If the Vols could stay healthy (and the team not go in the tank), Dobbs would get the redshirt season they hoped he'd receive in 2013.

The UT campus remained a place of athletic department controversy during this time. That spring, the shaky era of Cuonzo Martin as Tennessee's men's basketball coach came to an end when Martin resigned to become the head coach at Cal-Berkeley. Martin and Tennessee fans never seemed to mesh. Martin was the opposite of his predecessor, guarded and monotone. His style of play was not visually pleasing to fans that pined for Bruce Pearl to return when his three-year show-cause penalty ended. A petition wanting Tennessee to rehire Pearl received over 40,000 signatures. Hart was slow to publicly back Martin that season, which didn't help matters. Even with all that angst, the Vols went on a late season run in 2014, winning three games in the NCAA tournament, and coming within a bucket of the Elite Eight. Hart would hire Southern Miss head coach Donnie Tyndall to replace Martin.

Once again, a successful football season could help Vols supporters forget about some issues plaguing their beloved athletic program. At SEC Media Days in July, Jones stressed his team's youth. "We're having to replace almost half of our football team," said Jones. In the years that followed, many Tennessee fans saw words like those as excuses Jones was making for failures, either in the past or those they feared were still to come.

Jones brought three players to Hoover for SEC Media Days: Center Mack Crowder, and linebackers A.J. Johnson and Curt Maggitt, who missed all of 2013 with a torn ACL. Johnson had considered going pro but decided to return to Tennessee for his senior season. "We're excited to have A.J. back." Jones told reporters in Hoover. "He means so much to our football team, being our middle linebacker. He's the quarterback of our defense."

An estimated 40,000 fans showed up at Neyland Stadium for an open practice on August 16. Anticipation was building. "To come out with all these fans coming just to watch practice and just to show how important this team is to the community and to Vol Nation, it's just great to see this kind of turnout," said Tennessee freshman linebacker Dillon Bates.

The Vols hosted Utah State in the season opener, but Neyland Stadium was different that night. Long-time public address announcer Bobby Denton had passed away the previous April. He was seventy-three years old. Jeff Jarnigan replaced him and was on the mic for the start of the 2014 season. Tennessee was going to play what looked like a brutal schedule that year, so getting some wins early was crucial. Worley threw three touchdown passes as the Vols dominated the Aggies 38-7 on August 31.

During that game, senior offensive lineman Jacob Gilliam suffered a torn ACL, forcing the Vols to go to the bench. Redshirt freshman Brett Kendrick saw his first collegiate action that night. A week later Kendrick got his first start in the Vols 34-19 win over Bobby Petrino and Arkansas State. "After that game we are standing in the Lauricella Center [inside Neyland Stadium]," recalls Brett's mom, Beth Kendrick. "[Offensive line coach Don] Mahoney gave my husband a high five, says that this is a great start, and that things are looking good and that we are on our way. We are happy and thinking that Brett will really get a chance here."

However, those good feelings didn't last long. "[That night] Brett got a text from Jones with language that Brett wouldn't repeat to his mom and told him that he is not SEC caliber and that his play wouldn't cut it," says Beth Kendrick. "He was very derogatory towards him. Brett graded out as the third-best offensive player overall. They awarded t-shirts to the top three offensive and defensive players after each game. Brett received that recognition and yet was benched the next week. It made no sense, except that Coach Jones had made promises to other players and their parents."

During the Butch Jones era, there were many players who chose to transfer out of the program for a variety of reasons, including expected playing time that didn't come. Brett Kendrick was originally committed under Dooley but chose to stick to with the Vols. "Jones would wait outside the position coaches' room," Beth Kendrick says. "When Brett would come out, he'd get in his face and say that he'd be so happy when Brett was gone. He was trying to run him off. Maybe he needed the scholarship. I didn't know this was going on at the time. I'm proud of my son for fighting through it. He grew in character and learned how to deal with people. He loved his teammates. He is the kind of kid who would bend over backwards for you and do whatever the coach asked. He toughed it out and suffered through it all."

After the Arkansas State win, the Vols were 2-0, but the big games were yet to come. On September 13, Tennessee was pounded at fourth-ranked Oklahoma 34-10. Worley was intercepted twice, sacked five times and completed less than half of his forty-four pass attempts. The Vols were competitive into the second half, but the talent disparity was clear that night in Norman. Two weeks later at twelfth-ranked Georgia, the Vols showed toughness and fight. With 4:32 to go, they only trailed by three points. Backed up at their own goal line, Jalen Hurd fumbled. Georgia recovered in the end zone and the Vols lost 35-32. It was Tennessee's twenty-first straight road defeat to a ranked opponent.

At 2-2, the season was at a crossroads. And now Florida was coming to town. The Vols were a slight favorite in this game for only the second time in over a decade. The expected result had more to do with Florida's struggles than any positive impression of Tennessee. Earlier in the season it took Florida three overtimes to beat traditional conference doormat Kentucky. Vols fans desperately wanted this to be the game that the nine-year losing streak to the Gators would end. A Vols fan named Spencer Barnett edited an orange and white checkerboard pattern into the Neyland Stadium seating grid and posted the picture on social media. Within a couple of weeks, a website (checkerneyland.com) was born. Tennessee's athletics department, which produced something similar for the Kentucky basketball game in 2006, provided its support, as did most of the 102,455 that showed up for the chilly early afternoon kickoff. It was simple, yet beautiful. Fans looked up their section online and wore the appropriate color.

Hundreds of Vols alums "Ran Through the T" with the team. The stadium was rocking just like in the good 'ol days. And defensively, the Vols were controlling the Gators through the first three quarters. They forced four turnovers. And most importantly, the Gators had yet to score a point. But the Vols offense could only produce three short Aaron Medley field goals. In the red zone, the Vols couldn't get the job done.

"They were playing a lot of man coverage. We had our man-beaters," said Jones. "We knew what they were going to be in and we just didn't execute. No matter what you do schematically, football is about matchups. That's football."

Late in the third quarter, the Vols were still in command. They were up 9-0 and had just forced a three and out. Tennessee's Chris Weathered sacked Jeff Driskell and looked at his wrist (where a watch would be). This was an homage to 1992, when Mose Phillips did a similar maneuver following a touchdown in a downpour during a win over Florida.

The Vols were in great shape. The longest drive for the Gators to that point had been a mere 40 yards. Driskell had thrown for only 59 yards and had three interceptions. If the Vols kept playing the field position game, they had a solid chance to win. On first down from the UT 38, Hurd picked up five yards. On second and 5 from their own 43, and less than 25 seconds to go in the third quarter, the Vols could have handed the ball to Hurd once again. They would go into the between quarters timeout leading by two scores, likely with a third down and short to follow. Tennessee's crowd, loud all day, would be ready for the final fifteen minutes.

Instead, Jones and offensive coordinator Mike Bajakian called for a pass. It was a slow developing play which involved the wide receiver executing a double move to the sideline, with a quarterback that was not mobile being protected by a young offensive line. It required the blockers to give Worley extra time to throw, and every Florida defender to be accounted for... but Gators defensive back Jalen Tabor was left alone. As Worley backed up and looked at the receiver to his left, he never saw the blitzing Tabor to his right. Worley was hit before he even started his throwing motion. Tabor recovered the ensuing fumble at the Tennessee 30.

The game changed in an instant. Head coach Will Muschamp inserted freshman Treon Harris into the game for the overmatched Driskell. Harris and running back Treon Harris carried the Gators to the end zone on a short field and it was now a 9-7 game with 13:40 to go. Would Florida have been able to put together a lengthy touchdown drive? Considering how well the Vols defense had played on this day it was unlikely. But now it was anybody's game. The Vols needed to work the clock and take the momentum back. On their next drive they had second and 3 from their own 45. Hurd had been held in check most of the day, but it looked like he was starting to wear down the Gators defensive line, with two straight carries of eleven and seven yards. But instead of feeding their workhorse, the call was for yet another slow developing pass play.

Not surprisingly, Worley was swarmed. Second down and 3 turned into third down and 8 due to the sack, and the Vols would have to give the football back to Florida. After the punt, the Gators traveled 49 yards on their longest drive of the game. Tennessee eventually figured out the Harris-led offense and forced a field goal attempt. Austin Hardin, the Gators long range field goal kicker, lined up for a 49-yard attempt. The play clock hit zero just as the snap went backwards. Hardin nailed the kick. It was his first field goal of the season.

Florida was on top 10-9 with 6:20 to go. All the bad memories from a decade of failures against Florida came roaring back for Vols fans. The questionable Jesse Mahelona penalty that wiped out a pick-six in the 2006 loss. The 39-point beatdown in 2007. The second half collapse in 2012. Peterman's afternoon to forget in 2013. The Vols did have one last chance. On fourth down and 10, Worley hit Pig Howard for a first down at the Florida 48. The clock ticked under a minute, but Tennessee had two timeouts, and only needed about 20 yards to give Medley a punchers chance at the game winner. On the next play, Worley had time to throw as the Gators only rushed three linemen. He went deep for Howard, but the pass sailed on him just a bit. Florida safety Keanu Neal dove for the pigskin and collected it inches from the ground.

Florida 10, Tennessee 9. The streak lived for another year. After the game, Muschamp became a villain in the eyes of Tennessee fans when he spoke with Maria Taylor from the SEC Network. Muschamp sounded like a pro wrestler calling out his foe. "It's a lot of resolve. I'll tell you what, these guys came in here and fought their butts off and it's great to see all these people out here getting disappointed. I love it." It was full NWO Muschamp.

"Everyone at Florida understood what a huge rivalry that was," Muschamp told me in 2018. "That rivalry was built by Phillip Fulmer and Steve Spurrier. That was a game we had to get. We all understood the importance of that game. That was during a tough time at Tennessee. They were going through a lot of changes and going through a lot of things over there."

This game might have turned out differently had the sack of Worley not happened at the end of the third quarter. "Football is a game of momentum swings, but you have to answer the call and that's the way we train," said Jones. "You can't turn the football over... It's a game of inches."

A major criticism of Butch Jones during his Tennessee tenure was how he managed games. The 2014 Florida loss was one of the early signs that his detractors had a point. This was a game the Vols should not have lost. But they did. Once again, Jones was trying to assure Vols fans that the sun would shine on the Big Orange soon. "You guys need to hang in there," said Jones. "We're in it together. We're going to get it together... I promise you we are going to get it right."

A few days before that devastating defeat by the Gators, there were alterations to one of the most recognizable structures on the UT campus. The Jumbotron that towers over the south end zone at Neyland Stadium had three images on the back of it: Condredge Holloway, General Robert Neyland, and Phillip Fulmer, each Tennessee football royalty. But major changes were made that week as Neyland had a new picture, while Holloway and Fulmer were removed. One of their replacements was Reggie White, a member of the college and pro football halls of fame who passed away in 2004. The other substitute was a curious one. Butch Jones. The *Knoxville News-Sentinel* ran a statement they received from UT on the modifications. "The images are changed out by the Vol Network and the athletics department periodically. This is for a variety of reasons, including the opportunity to portray our rich history as well as our current brand."

There was no press release, no unveiling, no petition, and no groundswell of support. But it wasn't like there were protests either. "At the time, we didn't get one complaint about it. And I had inherited the role of 'complaint guy,'" says Brian Rice. He was working as a writer as UTSports.com. "In fact, I got or was forwarded eight or nine emails from people complaining that the General was wearing a baseball jersey in his new photo, but zero about Butch."

Dave Hart was hired as Tennessee's new athletics director on September 5, 2011 and retired on March 31, 2017. His tenure was a controversial 5 ½ years in Knoxville.

This was a Dave Hart call. He wanted the current head coach to be visible to those on campus. David Cobb was a senior sports columnist at UT's *The Daily Beacon* and wrote a column questioning the decision to put Butch Jones on the Jumbotron. "You replace a photo of Phillip Fulmer hoisting the national championship trophy with a photo of the coach who was 7-9 at the time? Huh?" remembers Cobb. "In my column, I equated it to putting a President on Mount Rushmore less than two years into their term. The only reason you would do that is if that President ended poverty or something. The only reason Jones should have been put on the Jumbotron is if he had had a national championship trophy or at least an SEC Championship trophy."

On October 18, the Vols played at third-ranked Ole Miss. The Rebels were nearing the height of the Hugh Freeze era (before the NCAA came calling) and beat the Vols 34-3. The Ole Miss defense flew all over the field, sacking Justin Worley seven times and forcing him to throw three interceptions. How many yards did the Vols rush for against the Rebels? It was the John Blutarsky GPA: zero point zero.

"We still have a lot to play for," Jones said, as if he was trying to convince himself. "We have been through the most difficult schedule in college football. We have to keep that in perspective. Tonight is still unacceptable."

"Our season can't end here in Oxford," said Worley. "All our dreams and goals are still alive." Worley meant well, of course, but unless Tennessee never had a goal of winning its division, there had to be team goals that were no longer attainable. Tennessee was 3-4, and 0-3 in league play. And now, the Vols had to welcome an old friend back to Knoxville.

The last time Lane Kiffin was on the UT campus, the scent of a burned mattress still filled the air. On the late afternoon of October 25, 2014, Lane Kiffin returned, stepping off the Alabama team bus. Kiffin was hired that off season by Nick Saban to become the Crimson Tide's offensive coordinator. Kiffin had his faults but play calling was a strength, and Saban wanted him to change the way the Tide moved the football. Fourth-ranked Alabama was 6-1 and averaging nearly 37 points per game.

It was a tasty story line. The hated former coach, seen by some fans as being responsible for many of the Vols recent struggles, was now on the visitors' sideline representing their biggest rival. "The game means everything to our football program and our fans because it is the University of Alabama not because it is Lane Kiffin," Jones said. Tennessee was downplaying the "Lane Kiffin is back" angle, but that was impossible. Butch Jones might as well have been trying to shove an elephant into a Volkswagen.

When Lane Kiffin walked onto the field for warmups, the boos were as loud as any ever heard for an opposing coach at Neyland Stadium. Steve Spurrier didn't get those kind of boos. Bear Bryant didn't get those kind of boos. In typical Lane Kiffin fashion, he responded only with a left handed two finger point to the west stands. "I was in the student section for the return of Lane Kiffin," says Tennessee student Lucas Panzica, who graduated in May of 2018, and today hosts a show on Fox Sports Knoxville. "I remember there being a campaign to not boo him or anything. I believe it was 'Kill Kiffin with Silence.' That didn't work."

The students chanted "Fuck You Kiffin" multiple times that night, along with other-not-so-kind greetings. As for the game itself, the crowd was quieted a bit after Alabama's first play from scrimmage. The referees allowed a late player substitution from the Crimson Tide. Blake Sims threw a short pass to Amari Cooper, who outraced the Vols defense for an 80-yard score. Kiffin sprinted down the sidelines; nearly stride for stride with Cooper.

Very quickly, it was 6-0. After the game Jones said that officials didn't hold up play to allow Tennessee to substitute as well, and he had a valid gripe. But it didn't matter. The Tide were rolling and jumped out to a 27-0 lead early in the second quarter. As for the Tennessee offense, the Vols announced shortly before kickoff that Justin Worley was out with a shoulder injury. There was no timetable for his return. Worley would never take another snap at Tennessee.

Nathan Peterman would get only his second career start, and the pressure was just as high as in his first start at Florida in 2013. After two series with Peterman accounted for only thirty yards, Jones had seen enough. For the second straight season, they were pulling the redshirt from Joshua Dobbs. Once again, Tennessee was down to their third string quarterback. The Vols needed a quarterback who could make things happen with his feet if necessary. And with an offensive line that still wasn't up to the rigors of the SEC, it was vital.

On this night, the third stringer didn't look like a third stringer. Dobbs threw for 192 yards and two touchdowns and ran for 75 yards on 19 carries. The Vols scored 17 straight points against Alabama, pulling within 10 midway through the third quarter. And Dobbs wasn't the only underclassman making plays for the Vols. Freshman running back Jalen Hurd had 59 yards on the ground. Sophomore Marquez North had four catches for 56 yards. Freshman Josh Malone had a touchdown grab. Freshman defensive back Cam Sutton forced a fumble.

Eventually, Alabama pulled away, winning 34-20. As Lane Kiffin walked off the field and out the south end zone, he gave his trademark visor to a young Tennessee fan. "He's a really good coach and I think why all the people in Tennessee are pissed off at him because they know he's a good coach, and they were upset when he left," said Saban to reporters after the game. Kiffin remained the story nationally. But locally, the story was Dobbs. Yes, it was only one game, but it looked like Tennessee finally found a quarterback who could succeed in that system. "I feel like I played well, of course there is always room for improvement," Dobbs said.

"Josh is a versatile quarterback," said Hurd. "That's really good in this offense." While Dobbs' performance was encouraging, the reality was that Tennessee was now 3-5. They could only afford one more loss to avoid yet another losing season. Going 5-7, or worse, in back to back seasons would do very little for Butch Jones and his recruiting efforts.

The Vols had to get to a bowl game in 2014. Winning the following week at South Carolina was critical to that effort. But they'd be bucking recent history if a victory was to be coming. "During our Wednesday teleconference with Butch Jones, he muses that he doesn't have a single player on the roster who has been part of a win that involved a flight," remembers Tom Hart, who would call the Vols/Gamecocks game on the SEC Network.

"As a coach you are always looking for signs. 'Is team the ready? Are they focused?'" Azzanni says. "On the road you get different vibes. I remember that Saturday we went to the stadium and walked around, just to get out of the hotel. It was cold and nasty, and our guys took off their shirts off and ran around. There was a certain energy, a mentality that the cold doesn't matter. They're ready to play, and we're gonna win."

Tennessee arrived the day before the game. But for some Vols fans, just getting to Columbia was going to be quite the undertaking. On the morning of Saturday, November 1, winter arrived early. Just a few miles over the Tennessee/North Carolina state line, snow and ice led to multiple wrecks, which caused the closure of the interstate for hours.

The road conditions were a serious problem. "The storm was much worse in that area than anyone expected," says Douglas Tarwater, a District Manager for the Tennessee Department of

Transportation. "They got eight inches of snow in the mountains. We were at the I-40 exit at Mile Marker 451 [approximately a mile from the TN/NC state line], turning cars around and telling them the interstate was closed in North Carolina and that they needed to use an alternate route. We got a LOT of dirty looks and comments. I would travel into North Carolina to check on the status and see if we could assist and get stuck motorists out if possible. There were tailgates on the side of I-40. People were having picnics on their cars. I heard 'Rocky Top' blaring from just about every other vehicle. It was definitely the wildest traffic jam I've seen in my career at TDOT."

"My tires were not so great, so decided I was going to rent a car," says Tennessee fan Jason Raby. "By the time I was at the Enterprise dealership, I heard reports of stopped traffic and a wreck around the state line on I-40 East. I've driven in bad weather and had zero desire to do so for this game so decided to stay home." This, of course, was the wisest move. But football fans aren't always rational. Some took the established detour route. Others in Vol Nation found different ways to support their team, no matter how long the trip would take, or what the risks may be.

"So, I was living in La Vergne and had to pick up a buddy in Cookeville," says Tennessee fan Stephen Crutchfield. "I had three college kids with me that had paid $60 a ticket and had never been to a true road game, so at about Crossville we went down Highway 68 to go through Atlanta."

"A four-hour trip turned out to be a seven-hour trip because of the weather," says Panzica. "I believe a semi-truck had flipped over due to the ice as we were going through the mountains. My buddy that I rode with drove a two-door Jeep and would just drive in the emergency lane for miles, skipping all the standstill traffic. We'd dart back into the lane whenever we would see a cop up ahead. There was ice all over the road and we were skidding all over the place. I was terrified."

"I picked up my buddy from his house at 6am and we debated which way to go. The radio weather report said the skies and roads were clear, so we went I-40. Big mistake," remembers Tennessee fan Davis Bodie, who today is a Ph.D. student in Educational

Leadership at UT. "I put my car in park at 8:30am as we came out of one of the tunnels. Finally, around noon, cars started to risk it. This is where we saw the North Carolina Department of Transportation's plan. They were sending cars through about 100 yards at a time and plowing the road. As we made it out of the mountains and stopped outside Columbia for gas and beer we met a couple from Maryville doing the same. Turns out they left at noon, went up I-81 and down I-26. Because of my decision we lost over four hours and almost died."

The treacherous travels meant that the Pride of the Southland Pep Band was nearly an army without the proper artillery. Trumpeter Noah Tuten explains. "We took two buses with the band director and members, and an equipment truck driven by a graduate assistant and an equipment manager. I think they took a more direct route using the highway, which caused them to get delayed by icy roads and traffic accidents. They were able to get in touch with the band directors, so the rest of the pep band took a different route. The band arrived at Williams Brice Stadium an hour or two before kickoff as usual. That's when we realized that our truck filled with half of the band's instruments still hadn't arrived. There was a happy ending though: our truck arrived as South Carolina's band was getting ready to bring all the extra instruments they owned to our buses."

Tennessee student Megan Goetz, a member of the Vols dance team, stayed in Knoxville. "My Dad came up, and my best friend and I went with him to the parents' weekend event," she remembers. "When we got there, we realized there were no TV's, so we turned around and walked out immediately. We went back to my Dad's hotel and started drinking heavily in the lobby."

SEC football isn't supposed to resemble Ann Arbor. In fact, it was the earliest measurable snowfall for the Palmetto State in over a century. While Goetz and others were warm in Knoxville, those in Columbia fought the elements with multiple coats, as well as libations. "We were well prepared, with five layers on, but it still wasn't enough," says three-time Tennessee grad Michael Greene. "I've never been colder at a game. There were also six or seven hours of tailgating in the snow and sleet. Much alcohol flowed.

Much. Too much. I remember shattering my phone on the asphalt on the fairgrounds, trying to check a text and my hands were numb from the cold and booze. I sliced my thumb wide open with an oyster shucker at a USC tailgate. It bled on the table for over a minute before my buddy Jay Ellington called it to my attention. I was too numb to notice."

"I only remember a handful of times I was colder at a football game," says Bodie. "The only thing that helped was the Silver Bullets we ripped in the parking lot and the bottle of Wild Turkey the Tennessee fan in front of us in the stands shared that helped quell the frigid conditions."

"Once the Jack Daniels from tailgating wore off there was no protection from it," recalls Tennessee grad Drew Simmons. "Also, being way up in the stadium in the guest section you had to deal with the brutal winds that chilled you to the bone. I remember thinking 'Is this worth it?'"

"Probably the coldest I have ever been at a football game," Tennessee fan Peyton Lee told me. "I was sitting against the edge of the stadium with the wind blowing right against my face. Multiple times it looked like I had painted half my face red."

While the fans in the stands were ice cold, the offenses for both teams were red hot. The Vols and Gamecocks combined for a ridiculous 1,270 yards. South Carolina wide receiver Pharoh Cooper had a historic night, with 233 yards receiving and two touchdowns, to go along with a rushing touchdown. He even threw for a score. When South Carolina running back Brandon Wilds broke off a 70-yard touchdown run, the Gamecocks were up 42-28. There was only 4:52 to go in the ballgame. The Vols were heading to a sixth loss, with another season out of the bowl picture very likely.

After hours of misery, some Vols fans admittedly had had enough. "There were two or three minutes left, and the hand warmer packets had long since worn out," says Greene. "My sister-in-law and father-in-law left their seats... and we headed back to our truck." Yes, Vols fans had been down this road before. But a funny thing happened on the way to another depression filled Saturday night.

Joshua Dobbs wasn't tired. First there was a 75-yard drive in which he threw or ran for every inch. His third rushing touchdown of the game pulled the Vols within seven points. There was 1:50 left in the clock. An onside kick was unsuccessful (Cooper recovered, naturally), but the Vols still had all three of their timeouts. If the defense could force a stop, Dobbs and the offense would get one more shot. It was third and 4 from the Tennessee 37-yard line. This was the ball game. What happened next was one of the most memorable plays of that 2014 season.

South Carolina quarterback Dylan Thompson rolled to his left but couldn't find an open receiver. Tennessee's Derek Barnett chased him down, grabbed him by the shoulder pads and threw him to the turf. He then gave Thompson an extra spin and toss to the ground. Defensive tackle Danny O'Brien followed that up with a slight shove back to the ground for Thompson when he tried to get up.

Thompson pleaded with officials for a flag, and the partisan home crowd expressed their displeasure. But no penalty was given. By no means were Barnett's and O'Brien's actions any great offense to the sport of football, but considering how often things hadn't gone Tennessee's way in the previous few years, you almost expected the yellow fabric to be thrown. But not on this night. The officials were not going to decide the game. The Vols had a chance. 85 yards to go. 83 seconds left and no timeouts.

That Dobbs kid? He wasn't too bad. Passes to Pig Howard and Jalen Hurd got them in position to tie the game. And when Dobbs found Jason Croom at the goal line, Tennessee had a nine-yard touchdown with 11 seconds left.

"That game was Josh's coming out party," Azzanni remembers. "That was when he really stepped on the scene. As a player, anytime you know you have a quarterback that that makes plays, it ups your game. Guys just play harder for those guys. It gives you more confidence."

Incredibly, the game would go to overtime. "[After the onside kick] we left the stadium and were walking past all the tailgates and I was just bummed," says Panzica. "Then we walked past a tailgate with a TV and I watched Dobbs throw a touchdown to a wide-open Jason Croom to send it to overtime. We sprinted a good half-mile to get back to the stadium and they let us back in."

In overtime Aaron Medley kicked a field goal to give the Vols the lead. Tennessee's defense, which struggled most of the night, was now rejuvenated. They blitzed Thompson on first down, as Curt Maggitt got the sack. On second down the more conventional four-man rush led to a Derek Barnett sack. South Carolina lost 15 yards on those two plays. Nothing happened on third down, so Spurrier had two choices: Go for it on fourth and 25 or send Elliott Fry onto the field for a 58-yard field goal attempt, 13 yards longer than he'd ever made in a college game. Spurrier chose to kick. "The ball was spotted on the black 'C' at midfield," recalls Hart. "The ball comes off Fry's foot like his club face was closed. It hit the turf around the 5. It wasn't even close."

Tennessee 45, South Carolina 42. The field was flooded with celebrating white jerseys. "It feels good anytime you win, but I feel great for Vol Nation," said Jones. "We've been on the other side of things, so we're going to enjoy the night."

"Butch was always referring to the style of play," Azzanni told me. "The kids believed in it. We played hard and were able to get a win on the road."

Tennessee fans were already partying like it was, well, 1998. They made the trek in dangerous circumstances and were rewarded with perhaps Tennessee's most important win in years. "I was obnoxiously jumping and screaming as we were leaving the stadium, now the second time," says Panzica. "I was definitely getting some dirty looks from the USC fans around me, but I didn't care. It was my freshman year of college and the first good win I got to see as a student."

One Vols fan in Columbia had a parting gift for Gamecocks fans. "On our way out of town we stopped at Waffle House for breakfast," said Bodie. "We were wearing Tennessee gear, so we naturally got some smack talk from South Carolina fans there. I went to the juke box and noticed that somebody put $20 in and only played one song. So, I picked a Foo Fighters song. Then I picked 'Rocky Top' to play fourteen times in a row. We hightailed it out of there as the first notes started playing. I wish I could have been there as it played thirteen times more that morning."

The sweetest story I came across related to this game was from two-time Tennessee grad Doug Brooks. His family has had season tickets since 1991. "I'm a retail pharmacist at Walgreen's and I had to work that weekend," Brooks remembers. "Otherwise I would've considered making the trip. I watched the entire game after work on Saturday and went in the next day to open the pharmacy. One of our regular patients was already shopping in the store. He was a kind, friendly man (he has since passed) who always brought us mints when he came in the store and always liked to talk Tennessee football. I said hi to him and he asked what I thought of the game. I started saying how I was impressed with the way Dobbs led the comeback. He said, 'Wait, did we win? I went to bed in the third quarter.' I said, 'Yeah, in overtime.' He had this trademark laugh and started cackling so loud the whole store could hear him. He said, 'You just made my day! You get extra candy for that!' and then proceeded to give me a whole handful of mints. He then stayed for ten minutes and talked to the other patients in line about the game now that he had found out the result. Rest in peace, Mr. Campbell."

The Vols needed to win two of their three remaining games to get to the postseason. A 50-16 victory over Kentucky was followed up with a 29-21 loss at nineteenth-ranked Missouri. It came down to the Vanderbilt game. On paper the 5-6 Vols were certainly better than the 3-7 Commodores. It was Derek Mason's first season as head coach, replacing James Franklin. Vanderbilt looked like, well, Vanderbilt once again. They were 0-7 in league play, losing all their SEC games by double digits. But rivalry games matter and the Commodores wanted nothing more than to spoil the Vols' postseason plans.

It was an especially emotional game for Tennessee's Evan and Eric Berry. Earlier that week, it was revealed that their big brother, Vol legend Eric Berry, had been diagnosed with what was believed to be Lymphoma. Testing in the weeks that followed confirmed it. After nine months of treatment, he was declared cancer free, and returned to play for the Kansas City Chiefs in 2015. Tennessee fans chanted Eric Berry's name throughout the evening.

They watched the Vols jump out to a 10-0 lead in the first quarter. But nothing was coming easy for the Vols, even in Nashville. Jalen Hurd missed most of the game with what was called at the time an "upper body injury." Wide receiver Marquez North was absent due to injury as well. The Vols were very limited on offense. The fourth quarter was one of survival for Tennessee. At the start of the quarter UT and VU swapped turnovers.

Tennessee was clinging to a 24-17 lead. The entirety of their offense was now as follows:

- Snap the football to Josh Dobbs.
- Watch him hand the football off or keep it and run.
- Pray he doesn't get killed.

The clock couldn't tick fast enough the Vols. In the final minute, Vanderbilt faced fourth and 10 just inside Tennessee territory. Patton Robinette, the hero of the Commodores 2013 victory, tried to get his team back to the end zone. But his pass intended for Trey Wilkins fell incomplete. Josh Dobbs threw for 92 yards, but his 91 rushing yards and two scores were critical. The Vols offense picked up a total of 262 yards of offense.

It wasn't pretty, but Tennessee was bowl bound. "This game summarized our season with adversity, great resiliency and we found a way to win the football game," said an exhausted yet enthusiastic Jones after the game. "I'm just proud of everyone. We found a way to get it done. This is a stepping-stone to this program and it's definitely an exciting time."

The Vols would be playing in the postseason for the first time since 2010. For decades, trips to the postseason were an afterthought for Tennessee fans. They saved their money all year to go to New Orleans or Miami or Tempe or wherever the Vols were headed. After that absence they were going to make this one count.

A week later, Tennessee accepted a bid to play Iowa in the TaxSlayer Bowl (the artist formerly known as the Gator Bowl) in Jacksonville on January 2. "Playing in a New Year's bowl game is a tremendous reward for our coaching staff, players, alumni and fans," said Tennessee athletics director Dave Hart. "We are looking forward to the game," said Jones. "And I am sure that Vol Nation will be well represented in Jacksonville."

The day after the bowl news broke, Tennessee announced that Butch Jones had received a contract extension through the year 2020. "We have the right man leading our football program at the University of Tennessee," said Hart. "Butch Jones has clearly re-energized our fan base; he is an outstanding ambassador for our University which transcends his role as head football coach... Butch Jones is our coach and will be our coach for a very long time."

At the TaxSlayer Bowl, Iowa never knew what hit them. The Vol Walk into the stadium drew a sea of orange, as EverBank Field became a de facto Neyland. Jalen Hurd ran for 122 yards and two scores. Josh Dobbs had a combined 205 yards of offense and three touchdowns. Midway through the third quarter it was 42-7. For the first time since Erik Ainge led Tennessee to a victory over Wisconsin in the 2008 Outback Bowl, the Vols got a postseason win.

Tennessee 45, Iowa 28. At 7-6, the Vols had a winning season for the first time since Lane Kiffin was coach in 2009. The bandwagon was ready to roll. "This is the start of a foundation for something big going on in Tennessee," said Dobbs, who was named the TaxSlayer Bowl MVP. "It shows that we're here to compete and you better watch us for us because we're coming," boasted Hurd. "We're coming, for real."

Not one player on the 2014 roster would be selected in the NFL draft, but that was going to change in the years to come. Tennessee fans had an improving team to root for, with young, talented athletes on both sides of the ball.

2015 just might be their year.

9
GAME MANAGEMENT

BUTCH JONES TOOK THE MOMENTUM from the 2014 season and filled the Class of 2015. Once again, he and his coaching staff pulled off a quality grouping. The Vols needed a quarterback in this class as they didn't take one in 2014. They got 4-star quarterback Quinten Dormady from Boerne (TX). 5-star wide receiver Preston Williams from Hampton (GA) was a tremendous athlete and his state's long jump champion.

The Vol legacy connections continued with 5-star defensive lineman Kahlil McKenzie from California. Kahlil's father Reggie played eight seasons in the NFL and is currently the general manager of the Oakland Raiders. His Uncle Raleigh played in the NFL for sixteen seasons. Both were standouts for the Vols and Kahlil was expected to be as well.

Tennessee kept building the wall around the state too. 5-star defensive lineman Kyle Phillips was from Nashville. 4-star receiver Jauan Jennings and 4-star offensive lineman Jack Jones were from Murfreesboro. 4-star offensive lineman Drew Richmond was from Memphis and chose the Vols over Ole Miss on National Signing Day. The player in this class who had the biggest impact would be 5-star JUCO running back Alvin Kamara. He came to Tennessee from Alabama, with a one year stopover at Hutchinson Community

College. Kamara's talents and positive nature made him a fan favorite.

"I think we have proven that Tennessee is a national brand," said Jones. "I think we have proven that we have the respect around the country of what we're building here at Tennessee... I think this just adds a whole other element to our current team."

Tennessee's twenty-nine commit Class of 2015 was tabbed as the fourth-best in the nation, and second-best in the SEC by 247Sports. The days of Derek Dooley's recruiting indifference were long gone.

The most significant off-season change in the football program came when offensive coordinator Mike Bajakian left Tennessee for a job on the Tampa Bay Buccaneers staff. The timing was not great as Bajakian bolted two weeks before National Signing Day. Jones didn't have a new OC in place before NSD but said that had no impact on the class.

Two days after NSD, Jones replaced Bajakian with his old boss at Central Michigan, Mike DeBord. "First of all, the Tennessee name speaks for itself," DeBord told me. "Plus, I had a relationship with Butch Jones in the past. I was out of coaching at the time and had come from five years in the NFL. I had an offer to go to an NFL team, but decided to go to Tennessee. I wanted to be a coordinator again."

DeBord brought three decades of coaching experience to Knoxville. However, he had spent the most recent three years as the sport administrator with the department's Olympic sports teams at Michigan and hadn't been an offensive coordinator since 2007. This move was most of all about a comfort level. The Vols were bringing back ten starters to an offense that really clicked over the final few weeks of the 2014 season, and Jones didn't want to rock the boat.

"We've been able to walk in and really the terminology has basically stayed the same," Jones said to Bleacher Report's Brad Shepard soon after DeBord's hiring. "That has really helped the overall learning curve. We can go out there and Coach DeBord already knows how to speak the language, and that's critical from a trust standpoint and a communication standpoint as well."

Not to say that DeBord wasn't working on what he felt Tennessee needed to do to improve. "I saw things I felt that I could change," says DeBord. "I thought Josh [Dobbs], when I got there, was still in development as a quarterback. We had resources and talent and work to do."

From a purely football standpoint, Tennessee was on the rise, night and day in terms of talent from when Jones and his staff arrived in December 2012. "They kept getting better," said Bruce Feldman, a writer for TheAthletic.com and best-selling author. "When I went to visit Tennessee that first spring (2013), they had the worst skill guys for a Power 5 school I had ever seen." In 2015 Jones now had basically three recruiting classes of his guys in place. The SEC East was slumping. The timing was nearly perfect for the Vols to make a run at Atlanta. But off the field, some news was not positive.

Tennessee football players A.J. Johnson and Michael Williams had been suspended the previous November from all team-related activities after allegations of the sexual assault of a Tennessee female athlete became known publicly. Johnson was a team captain and the leader of the Vols defense. Less than two weeks after National Signing Day 2015, Johnson and Williams were booked on charges of aggravated rape. They have maintained their innocence, and a trial date was scheduled for July 16, 2018. Previous alleged incidents involving Vols players were getting more publicity as well. In April of 2013, the *Tennessean* newspaper reported that the suspension of running back Marlin Lane occurred a few days after he was accused of sexual assault. Lane was never charged or arrested in that case and he played that season. In September of 2014, Jones dismissed running back Treyvon Paulk after he allegedly punched an ex-girlfriend.

These stories were played out across the media in Knoxville. "The feeling from outside was, 'Ok, we have this not so good stuff happening, but we are winning and that's most important,'" says former WATE-TV Sports Director Michael Spencer. "Some fans lost a sense of what was right and important. This was tough to cover, and the bad stuff directly involved some of the biggest names in the program. And as bad as it sounds, to some, winning cured all."

In the months that followed, Tennessee was under fire for a move that did not reflect kindly on how the athletics department was seen as treating women's sports. On November 10, 2014, Tennessee announced that the 2014-2015 season would be the last in which the historic Lady Vols name and logo would be used for all sports. The only sport for which it would remain was basketball. "I initially had found out from a fellow teammate and was completely floored. We all were." says Leslie Cikra, a Lady Vols volleyball player from 2009-2013. "It seemed as though the University was discrediting the work every Lady Vol put in to help win championships and build the Lady Vol name. I hadn't heard any rumors that this was being discussed beforehand."

The University of Tennessee said that they were making this move to coincide with the switch from Adidas to Nike, as well as its own "One Tennessee" campaign, which was making the "Power T" the primary mark for the UT-Knoxville campus and its athletics. "Brand consistency across the university is critical as we strive to become a top-25 research university," said UT Chancellor Jimmy Cheek. "It is important that we take advantage of all the successes across this great campus, both in academics and athletics."

"Following significant branding studies by both our University and the department of athletics, as well as conversations with head coaches and student-athletes, we will implement the related changes that resulted from this collaboration on July 1, 2015," said Tennessee athletics director Dave Hart.

The reaction was immediate, and not pleasant for the Tennessee athletics department, or University of Tennessee itself. In the months leading up to the name change there were multiple protests against the move on the UT campus. "The powers that be leaned on Nike's rebranding program to explain the change," says Cikra. "But we received a letter from Nike that explained they were just doing what they were told, and they had not suggested Tennessee get rid of the [Lady Vols] name."

Cikra started bringbacktheladyvols.com, which became a go to resource for Lady Vols fans. Tens of thousands signed petitions against the name change. "No one in the upper administration believed that there would be any significant blowback," said Brian

Rice, who at this time was a writer at UTSports.com. "They were almost incredulous when I would bring up the negative reaction that was coming."

"We got calls and emails every day," says Spencer. "People wanted us to cover the story more often. We covered the protests and they still wanted more coverage. They felt that if we continued to talk about it and get the narrative out, it would change the decision..."

Forty-five state legislators signed a letter asking the Board of Trustees to talk about this topic in their June 2015 meeting. Instead, UT President Joe DiPietro responded with an email. "We understand and respect your opinion and that of your colleagues, but we continue to hold that the decision in this matter rests with the Knoxville campus administration."

Perhaps the most important question was this. How could it be "One Tennessee" when the women's basketball team was going to be allowed to use the name "Lady Vols," but the women's track team, the softball team, the rowing team, etc. were forced to switch to "Vols?" All eighteen Tennessee teams should have the same name if it is "One Tennessee," right? Cheek gave an answer to that question when he wrote a letter to the *Knoxville News-Sentinel* on June 21, 2015. "For those who have questioned our decision to stay with the Lady Vol logo for women's basketball, the answer is quite clear. It is a tribute to Pat Summitt, her eight national titles and her national legacy."

Many openly questioned if this move would even be happening if Summitt hadn't fallen ill. Hers was a towering presence on the UT campus. She was the person most responsible for the building of the Lady Vol brand. It's hard to imagine that she would've been supportive of this decision.

Dave Hart spoke about the topic during an April 2015 appearance on "The Nation," the statewide Vol Network radio program. Hart said, "It will be good. I can assure you. It will be good when all is said and done. When we're in the transition with Nike, when all the new uniforms begin to roll out, it will be good for all parties concerned and we will not forget, and we will continue to honor the tradition of Lady Vols."

But this was hogwash. It was not going to be good for all parties. "The Lady Vols stuff was ridiculous," said former Tennessee wide receiver Jayson Swain. "Don't piss on my leg and tell me it's raining. 'One Tennessee' but you keep one team named Lady Vols made no sense. Fans are not stupid."

Amongst those Tennessee fans there was either passionate disapproval or complete indifference at the decision to take away the Lady Vols name. Frankly, those fans that only care about the men's sports could give a darn what the women's sports decide to do. "At one point it was strongly suggested that there should be no formal announcement, and that they should just unveil the uniforms on July 1," says Rice. "As long as the Lady Vols logo appeared on the basketball uniforms, no one would notice that the rest of the teams had transitioned away from it until months later when they started playing. But Hart was insistent that there be a big announcement, which was a huge mistake. It empowered months of protests that did nothing but give a black eye to UT, and ultimately cost him the support and trust of the average fan."

"The AD asked for feedback from the current Lady Vols at the time, and said that the students supported their decision," says Cikra. "We later found out that the majority of female athletes in school did not agree with the change."

Rice added, "In the meetings when they told the teams, there was no discussion. It was just, 'Here's what's happening.' There was no feedback. Members of two different teams left those meetings in tears. Never heard about that publicly... it was a happy face put on the whole thing."

Dave Hart had a reputation as being a "likes to fight" guy before he showed up in Knoxville and the past four years did nothing to change that. Hart was going to run the Tennessee athletics department his way, though the heavens may fall. In this case, Hart and the UT administration were on the same page, but it would be Hart who had to take almost all the criticism.

January 27, 2015

Knoxville, TN 37917

Dear Mr. & Mrs. █████

First, thank you for conacting Nike and Mark Parker. Your letter was reviewed and forwarded to me for response on Mark's behalf.

We appreciate that you took the time to let us know your thoughts regarding the University of Tennessee and the Lady Volunteers.

Please know, while we support all University of Tennessee athletics, Nike has no decision making capabilities whatsoever regarding the University's choice to phase out the Lady Volunteers nickname for all women's sports. This is completely and solely a Univesity decision. All feedback and concerns regarding this decision would be best directed to the Universities Athletic Department.

However, your feedback is highly valued and has been forwarded to the proper departments within Nike. We share consumer feedback with our business partners on a daily basis.

Again, thank you for writing.

Sincerely,

Kelly
Nike Consumer Affairs

NIKE, INC   ONE BOWERMAN DRIVE   BEAVERTON, OREGON 97005 6453   T: 530.671.6453   F: 503.671.6300   NIKE.COM

Tennessee eliminated the Lady Vols nickname and logo for all sports with the exception of women's basketball. The move was met with immediate and nearly universal criticism from Tennessee fans. This change coincided with the transition from Adidas to Nike, part of what UT Chancellor Jimmy Cheek called "brand consistency." In the above letter, the Oregon based apparel provider denied playing any part that controversial decision.
(Courtesy: Leslie Cikra)

"The Lady Vols transition was a microcosm of the entire Dave Hart era," explains Rice. "Once he made a decision, he would stick by it and defend it, even if it was obvious in the long run that it was the wrong decision. He lost the goodwill and support of the common fan over a fight that was not necessary to pick. Instead, he doubled down on it."

"I think Dave was a good AD, but there was a disconnect with the fans," says David Blackburn, the former senior athletic director for administration at Tennessee. "I think that goes to not having people that knew Tennessee history in positions to have an influence. That's where you saw it be a problem. They didn't know. That's not their fault, but they should have had Tennessee folks around him. East Tennessee people are warm, friendly and want to be heard. You have to give them a voice. Most of the time they are right."

Dave Hart was seen by some as not being a backer of women's athletics. But his supporters believe that is patently unfair. Hart had a large role in the planning and fundraising for the Pat Summitt Plaza, which was dedicated on November 22, 2013. Her statue was built and placed at the corner of Lake Loudoun Boulevard and Phillip Fulmer Way, across the street from Thompson-Boling Arena. "It's a goosebumps day on Rocky Top," Hart said at the unveiling.

Hart also hired Beth Alford-Sullivan as Tennessee's director of track and field and cross-country. This put Sullivan in charge not only of the female, but of the male student-athletes as well. Sullivan was the first woman to coach men in the SEC in any sport.

The hiring of Dave Hart was perhaps the last piece needed for the University of Tennessee's goal of remaking the athletic department. Tennessee was one of the final holdouts in terms of split departments and needed someone like Hart to serve, at times, as the hitman when the departments were put under the same umbrella. "For too long, the University of Tennessee had been fumbling the merger," says Gridiron Now's John Brice. "Hart was more of a businessman than an outsider. He had a vision and a plan for fiscal responsibility and improvement."

Dave Hart had few previous relationships with those at Tennessee and didn't shy away from making changes with those he didn't feel shared his vision. Bud Ford had spent forty-five years working in the Tennessee Sports Information Department and retired at the end of 2011. He was set to take over for the late Haywood Harris in the role of Vol Historian. Terms were exchanged between university representatives and Ford in the spring of 2011. But later that year, Hart took over for Mike Hamilton as athletics director. Shortly before Ford's retirement, Hart told Ford that the position of Vol Historian would no longer be part of the athletic department. Ford filed a breach of contract claim against the University of Tennessee. But the Tennessee Claims Commission dismissed Ford's action that summer, saying that Ford fell short of producing a valid contract.

It wasn't the only time Hart went toe to toe with a long-time Tennessee sports information department employee. Debby Jennings spent thirty-five years at Tennessee, serving as the Lady Vols Sports Information Director. Following the 2011-2012 basketball season, Pat Summitt's last as head coach, Hart reportedly gave Jennings four hours to retire or be fired for "insubordination." Jennings sued the University of Tennessee and Dave Hart, alleging that age and sex discrimination led to her forced retirement. Both sides would eventually reach a $320,000 settlement in October 2014. "I am hopeful my lawsuit has cast some light on some of the inequities that I and others experienced in the combined UT athletics department," said Jennings in a statement.

Yet another discrimination lawsuit against Tennessee was working its way through the courts starting that same year. Former Tennessee sports medicine director Jenny Moshak and ex-Lady Vols strength coaches Heather Mason and Collin Schlosser said that they received less compensation for the same jobs due to their gender or association with women's teams. That lawsuit was settled in January of 2016. The lawsuit cost the University of Tennessee's athletics department over $1 million.

During Hart's tenure, there was a lot of turnover in Tennessee's athletics department. Some were dismissed, some left for other opportunities. Brian Davis was a two-time Tennessee grad, the first in his family to go to college. He spent thirteen years working in sports information for the Lady Vols and says that he was forced out the door in the summer of 2012. Today, Davis is the associate director in charge of soccer and softball on the athletics communications staff at Texas.

Davis admits that there are still hard feelings towards Hart and his associates. "It was a family. A bunch of people I spent so much time with... I spent more time with them than my own family and friends," says Davis. "We had each other's backs. It became cut throat, like a true business and none of us were prepared for that. We loved what we were doing. It was all about the student-athletes first. But under those guys, it was about the money. How can we get more money and make more money and build facilities."

In 2015, Hart was under fire for another situation that didn't come as much of a surprise. Donnie Tyndall, who was hired by Hart to be Tennessee's men's basketball coach in April 2014, was dismissed in March 2015 after serious NCAA violations came to light during Tyndall's time at Southern Miss. Tyndall's resume was already stocked with NCAA issues from his time at Morehead State. Hart knew about those past transgressions, but hired him anyway. He said that Tennessee also did its due diligence in this matter. "I think we vetted that very well," Hart maintained after firing Tyndall. Former Texas coach Rick Barnes was hired to replace Tyndall.

So, as was now a yearly tradition for the Tennessee athletics department, a rough off season was the lead-in to football. College football teams never have full rosters during spring workouts due to off season surgeries or nagging injuries. But Tennessee had as many absences as any team in the country. Key guys like defensive end Derek Barnett, linebackers Curt Maggitt and Darrin Kirkland Jr., and defensive tackle Danny O'Brien had to skip all of spring practice. Football is a tough sport. The human body was never meant to play something so fast paced and physical within close quarters. Injuries are going to happen. But Jones felt that winter workouts went well and said that there were no issues with regards to the strength and conditioning program.

"We thought that we made great strides," said Jones at his pre-spring practice press conference. "Dave Lawson and Michael Szerszen, everyone on our strength and conditioning staff did a tremendous job in preparing our players."

Former Vol Peyton Manning has supported each coach that followed Phillip Fulmer at Tennessee, including Butch Jones. This picture comes from the Orange & White Game on April 25, 2015. The Manning name alone has given Vols coaches a boost in their recruiting efforts.

Still, sixteen Vols missed the Orange & White Game due to injury. But fans were fired up from the solid end to 2014 and 63,016 came out to Neyland Stadium on April 25. It was the third-highest attended spring scrimmage all-time at Tennessee. "Before the season my wife and I had decided to take the plunge and purchase season tickets because we genuinely believed in Butch what was doing and the direction he had the program headed," says Troy Elliott, a Tennessee fan since 1985.

"My thoughts were already planning and starting to save money for Atlanta and a chance to attend my first SEC Championship game," Tennessee fan Sherry Walker says. "I really expected the Vols to dominate the season. The talent was there, and it was year three under Butch Jones, the year everything was to fall into place."

The Vols arrived at SEC Media Days in as good a position, in terms of the football program's direction, since perhaps 2007. But

Jones didn't want the hype train to get rolling. "64% of our roster has played one year of college football or less," Jones told the horde of reporters in Hoover. The players though? They knew what this roster was capable of achieving. "We're excited for this upcoming season," Tennessee cornerback Cam Sutton told reporters. "We're happy to be here. We're the men of Tennessee. This is what we come to Tennessee for, to play football."

The Vols opened the 2015 season with a neutral site game against Bowling Green in Nashville. Tennessee was ranked twenty-fifth in the country, the first time they were in the national rankings since September 2012. Tennessee pulled away in the second half, winning 59-30. Mike DeBord's offense racked up 604 yards. Jalen Hurd rushed for 123 yards and three first half touchdowns in front of friends and family in his return to the mid-state. Newcomer Alvin Kamara had 144 combined yards and two scores. Dobbs accounted for nearly 300 yards of offense and three combined touchdowns. Yes, this was against a MAC team and the defense had some work to do, but Tennessee was serving notice to the nation that they'd be no pushover.

The true test was still a week away.

Tennessee fans had been waiting for the Oklahoma game. The boats and RV's arrived in Knoxville more than a week in advance. This game had been sold out for months and scalpers were making a mint. Tennessee was twenty-third and Oklahoma was nineteenth. The game was scheduled for a 6pm kickoff, giving fans lots of time to tailgate.

Neyland Stadium was amped. "We went out for warmups and the students were already there and everyone was yelling," former Oklahoma center Ty Darlington told me. "We ate that up. We always enjoyed the back and forth with students, and they were already rowdy way before kickoff."

It was 72 degrees at kickoff, partly cloudy with a light breeze. This is what the sport is supposed to be. These were two historical powers, playing on campus, in one of college football's cathedrals. This wasn't a generic, neutral site experience. For the second time,

"Checker Neyland" was enacted, and Vols fans were wearing their Saturday best.

I've been going to games at Neyland Stadium since 1994, and the 2015 game is the loudest one I ever experienced. I was not at the 1998 Florida "Pandemonium Reigns" game, but according to people I've talked to that were at both contests, the 2015 Oklahoma game is on the short list that compares in terms of consistent noise in Tennessee history. I was on the sidelines, shooting the game on Saturday, September 12, and made sure to pause a few times and just look around.

It was madness. And it stayed that way for four straight hours. "There is no other game close to having the sustained enthusiasm, excitement, and volume that the Oklahoma game had," remembers Stephen Callis, a Vols fan who has been going to Tennessee games since he was five years old. "I think it was a perfect storm of high expectations. A high-quality opponent with a coach [Bob Stoops] with a public disdain for SEC football."

"Our seats for the Oklahoma game were in Section Q, top row, which is under cover and of course reverberates the sound," says Elliott. "The best way for me to describe the level of sound from that game was that my ears literally rang for the next week."

"I was there in 2004 when James Wilhoit went from goat to hero against Florida, standing in the student section D, row 20," recalls Kim Jeffries, a Tennessee grad and season ticket holder since 2008. "The whole student section was jam-packed, and my feet didn't touch the floor for a good five minutes since everyone was jumping around and screaming in jubilation. Parts of that game were LOUD, but Oklahoma was the loudest and most sustaining loud environment ever at Neyland Stadium."

On Oklahoma's first possession, Texas Tech transfer quarterback Baker Mayfield was picked off by Tennessee sophomore safety Todd Kelly Jr., who would play one of the best games of his college career that night. He had eight tackles and two interceptions. "We were experimenting with a new cadence with clapping," Darlington says. "We were assured that we would have no problem hearing it. On the first play I was obviously at center and I was waiting for the clapping and hadn't heard anything... I look back between my legs and Baker is clapping furiously. We couldn't hear it. We go back to the sideline and say, 'Ok they'll calm down. This won't be an issue.' Well, it was an issue all game. The sheer volume was incredible."

The Vols offense then drove down the field, leading to one of the most talked about moments of the Butch Jones era at Tennessee. On second and goal from the 6, Dobbs threw to tight end Ethan Wolf, who was brought down short of the pylon. But there was a video review, giving Jones and DeBord extra time to come up with a play call from the Sooners one-yard line. On third down, Josh Dobbs lined up center, and handed the football to Alvin Kamara. He ran straight into the middle of the line and was stopped about eighteen inches from the end zone.

Butch Jones immediately sent out the field goal unit. There was no wavering. The crowd barely got a chance to yell "Go For It" before Aaron Medley trotted on the field. The chip shot was good, and Tennessee had an early 3-0 lead. In the stands, in the press box, in the bars and in the homes of Tennessee fans, the questions were asked. Why wasn't Jalen Hurd in the game? Hurd was the Vols 6'4", 240-pound battering ram. This seemed to be the perfect place for him on third and goal. If you can't pick up thirty-six inches on two carries with Hurd, maybe you don't deserve to win anyway.

"We're looking for points," said Jones after the final whistle. "We knew it was going to be this type of game. Football's a game of momentum and you create your own momentum. You don't want all or nothing plays at the beginning of the game. We just felt we needed to get on the board, get some confidence, and get some points."

But what message are you sending by not going for it? Yes, there could be a fumble and a run back (and something similar did happen a few weeks later against Georgia), but the most likely outcome would have been that if you get stopped on fourth down, Oklahoma would have to snap the football from their own one-yard line with 102,455 screaming at them.

"It was definitely a WTF moment," says Walker. "I looked at my cousin and said, 'We're gonna play this game safe to not to lose and end up losing.' I mean dang! We just had an awesome drive and we settled for a field goal." Tennessee's defense was doing their part. They forced three straight three and outs and the crowd was getting more hyped with each stop. Later in the first quarter, Dobbs threw to Josh Malone in the end zone for a touchdown, making it 10-0. In the second quarter Dobbs scrambled for a touchdown of his own, and it was 17-0 Vols. Neyland Stadium was a terrordome of sound.

With 34 seconds left in the third quarter and the Vols up 17-3, Kelly picked off Mayfield again, this time at the Oklahoma 29-yard line. It was a golden opportunity to put the game away. If they could get a bit closer for a Medley field goal (he missed a 48 yard attempt to start the third quarter), the Vols would be up by three scores, which would have made an Oklahoma comeback very difficult. But a Hurd fumble (that he somehow recovered) stalled the drive, and Tennessee punted from their own 40. The Trevor Daniel boot went into the end zone, and the Sooners had new life.

On the ensuing drive, the Vols defense showed signs of tiring. Multiple penalties on third downs kept the chains moving. Mayfield was getting beat up, but still scrambling and keeping plays alive, showing the form that would earn him the Heisman Trophy two years later. With 8:20 to go, a Mayfield touchdown pass brought the Sooners within seven points. For the first time all night, Neyland Stadium was no longer bedlam. It was nervous.

The Vols offense had to move the ball a bit when they got the ball back, if for no other reason to give the defense some rest. They had just been on the field for fourteen plays. Instead, two Hurd runs that went nowhere were followed by a false start penalty and a short pass on third and 15. The Vols had to punt. The momentum they had for most of the night was waning. And things got worse from there. Mayfield broke multiple tackles on one third down conversion. Then Tennessee's Malik Foreman was called for pass interference on a throw that almost hit the back wall behind the end zone. Even if the wide receiver was Manute Bol the pass was uncatchable, but the officials didn't see it that way. The Sooners were marching closer to the Vols end zone.

"The first thing that went through my mind was, 'Is this really happening?'" recalls Foreman. "It was very frustrating but that's the game. Sometimes you aren't going to get the calls and that is just part of it. After the flag was thrown the only thing I could do was get ready for the next play." Officials also missed a false start on the Oklahoma offensive line on third down inside the 10. Even with Oklahoma rallying, the noise never waned. In fact, it got even more intense. "On those third downs I could feel the sound on my skin," says Darlington. "I never felt sound before. It was incredible. Even when we were losing I was in awe of the experience."

The Vols had opportunities throughout the night to put the game away. But when Mayfield lobbed the football to Sterling Shepard for a spectacular five-yard touchdown on third and goal, the game was suddenly tied with 40 seconds to go and overtime was imminent.

The Tennessee offense was stagnant throughout the second half but responded in overtime with a Jalen Hurd touchdown run. He had 109 rushing yards on the night. Mayfield responded with a one-yard touchdown keeper on fourth and goal. Another Mayfield to Shepherd touchdown pass gave OU a 31-24 lead in the second overtime. The pressure was really on the Vols offense, and they couldn't respond. After two short runs and a false start, Dobbs was intercepted on third and 12.

A wild night at Neyland Stadium was over. Oklahoma's players celebrated with their fans that made the trip from Norman. Sooners' linebacker Eric Striker screamed expletives at Vols fans. It was a devastating end for Tennessee, on what was an incredible evening of football. "We have a group of kids that take great pride in their performance. They give us everything that they have, and I love them," said Jones. "I'm proud of them. We came up short, but they laid it on the line."

"We were beating Oklahoma bad. That game was just a great lesson that in any sport with any team, you have to keep the gas pedal down," says former Tennessee wide receivers coach Zach Azzanni. "You can't give a team like that more opportunities. At the end of the day we gave them life and we paid for it. Baker Mayfield was like Houdini that night. I think of players that take over games. He took that game over. We couldn't tackle him."

"We found a way to win, on the road, in that environment... it was special for us," says Darlington. "That spurred us on to the rest of season. We went to the playoff in 2015 and I think that set us up for our run the last couple of years too. If we don't beat Tennessee, I don't know how rest of these seasons go."

As rough as the loss to the Sooners might have been, in the grand scheme of things it meant very little for the Vols. No one expected the Vols to compete for a spot in the college football playoff. Winning the SEC East was the top priority. Two weeks later, the Vols would play at Gainesville, hoping to end a decade of frustration. Jones tried to downplay the significance of the Florida matchup. "It is the most important game in terms of it's the next game, and that is the way it is." At the same time, he was yet again stressing his team's youth. "Twenty-nine individuals will board the first plane for an SEC road trip for the first time in their careers."

If the Vols were nervous at the start against the Gators, they didn't look that way. A beautifully designed trick play tied the game at seven in the first quarter. A lateral to receiver Jauan Jennings (who played quarterback in high school) was followed by a throwback to Josh Dobbs. He had a convoy and ran untouched 58 yards to the end zone.

Tennessee was dominating, leading 20-7 midway into the third quarter. The Vols defense was hounding freshman quarterback Will Grier constantly. But the game started to turn. A Dobbs fumble gave Florida great field position. The Tennessee defense held and was forcing a 42-yard field goal attempt on fourth and 6. This was a situation in which if you are the Vols, you have won the battle. You play it safe on special teams. If they make the field goal, you are now up by 10 points and still have control of the game. Instead, Jones called timeout. "We thought they were going to do a fake field goal so that is the one time that we did it," Jones said after the game. "Another time is making sure we had the right personnel on the field in some different things we had seen from scouting."

But what this also did was give new Florida coach Jim McElwain time to realize the error of his ways as the CBS broadcast went to commercial. His kicker, Jorge Powell, had never tried a field goal in a college game. The pressure of the moment made that kick no gimmie. So McElwain changed his mind and went for it. Grier hit Brandon Powell for a big gain to the Tennessee 4, and Kelvin Taylor scored on the next play.

Florida was back in it, pulling within six points. Late in the third quarter, Tennessee embarked on a tough minded 16-play, 70-yard drive that ate up nearly seven and a half minutes of clock. The drive was mostly runs by Dobbs, Hurd and Kamara. They converted on five straight third down attempts. On third and goal from the 10, knowing a field goal would put them up two scores, Tennessee was not going to throw the ball. They'd take their chances on the ground. It worked better than Mike DeBord could have dreamed. Hurd ran through a gaping hole on the left side of the line, and high stepped into the end zone.

With 10:19 to go, the Vols now led 26-14. They had the Gators right where they wanted them. But despite the limited time remaining, Jones called for an extra point instead of a two-point conversion attempt. If Tennessee had missed on the two-point conversion (barring an unlikely two-point return by the Florida defense), they would still be up 12 points. The difference between 12 and 13 is pretty much nothing when the other team needs two touchdowns to win. But if you go up 14, the likely worst-case scenario is that if the Gators score two touchdowns, you would go to overtime.

After the game, the first question from reporters to Jones was about the decision not to go for two. "Well a number of reasons and we were discussing that prior to the drive. If we did score whether we go for one or two, we have a chart that is pretty standard in football first of all and maps it all. We just felt like at that stage in the game that we had great confidence in our defense of getting off the football field and allowing them to push the ball down the field, so we felt very comfortable with the decision."

This made no sense. At all. "I think the Florida game was when I started to question Jones's abilities as an in-game coach," says Spencer. "Partly because of those the answers after the game. Butch talked about his chart. What chart are you looking at? No chart says you don't go for two. That's when you felt that something was not connecting."

Florida's offense had been held in check most of the day, but they still had time. The Gators marched 86 yards on 17 plays, converting on a fourth and 7 and a fourth and 8 along the way. A Grier to Powell touchdown pass brought them within 6 points once again, with just over four minutes to go.

"Impending doom would be a good way to describe it," says Tennessee student Nick Yeo, who was at Ben Hill Griffin Stadium that afternoon. "As they started to drive and get those fourth down conversions, you could feel The Swamp come alive. The crowd wasn't great throughout the game but down the stretch when the game tightened up they definitely started to play a larger and larger role."

Yeo was right. The place got loud. But if the Vols could pick up a couple of first downs, the game would still be theirs. Two short Hurd runs led to a third and 6 from the Florida 19. Josh Dobbs led the Vols in passing, rushing and even receiving on this day against Florida. He was the best player on the field. DeBord was going to put the game in his hands. Instead of a run/pass option, Dobbs headed to the short side of the field, a run play all the way. Florida had seven defenders and Tennessee had six blockers. Dobbs never had a chance, losing four yards, and the Vols had to punt.

"Tennessee fans started to shrink," remembers Yeo. "We started to get a helpless feeling. Coming off the Oklahoma game, which was an equally devastating loss, it was almost like watching the ending of that game on replay."

But there was still hope that Tennessee's defense could win the game. Jalen Reeves-Maybin blew up a screen pass for a four-yard loss and Derek Barnett put pressure on Grier, nearly for a sack. Eventually, Florida had fourth and 14 from their own 37. This was it. Make a stop and the game was over.

Tennessee defensive coordinator John Jancek called for a three-man rush, with linebacker Chris Weatherd serving as a spy in case Grier decided to run for it. Thanks to the limited pressure,

Grier had all day to throw. He zipped a pass to Antonio Callaway at the Tennessee 46. But the damage was not done. Callaway then turned to the sideline, got a block, and ran all the way for the touchdown.

With 1:26 to go, Florida led 28-27. The decision not to rush at least four men was an odd one by Jancek. Grier was a mobile quarterback, but it was doubtful he'd make it past midfield on a scramble. After he crossed the line of scrimmage the Tennessee defense would have converged. Weatherd would have been better served rushing the passer. His sitting at the line of scrimmage did the Vols no favors.

The Gators were five for five on fourth downs against Tennessee. The only good news for the Vols was that they still had 86 seconds to play with, plus two timeouts. The Vols were out of sorts on this drive, with precious seconds ticking away before plays began. The officials were slow in their decisions as well, and Tennessee had two penalties.

It would come down to a 55-yard field goal attempt by Aaron Medley with three seconds left. The last time Tennessee won this game was in 2004, when James Wilhoit kicked a 50-yard field goal in the final seconds. The Vols needed Medley to be just as clutch. Medley stood on the Gators midfield logo and lined up inside the right hashmark. He swung his right foot forward and missed the kick badly. But McElwain, in a moment of overcoaching, had called timeout before the snap to ice the kicker. This gave Medley one more opportunity. On his second attempt, Medley struck it well. The kick had the distance to be good from 60. The ball began to hook towards the target. On the Vol Network, Bob Kesling and Tim Priest had the call:

Kesling: "Snap down, kick on the way, kick spinning for the upright the kick is…

Priest: "GOOD!!!!!!"

Kesling: "No, no good."

Priest: "Oh no."

Kesling: "Apparently off to the right."

The kick did indeed look like it was going to be a game winner. Jones, along with some Vols players, ran onto the field thinking it was true. But the football that was heading towards sunshine fell in darkness. It just... stopped... drifting. The football passed the right goalpost about six inches the wrong way.

Florida 30, Tennessee 28. The streak was still alive. To that point of the 2015 season, only six games had been lost in the FBS when a team was leading in the fourth quarter by double digits. The Vols were on the losing end of two of them. "I remember thinking, 'I told ya they needed another year. They're not ready to win,'" says Jillian Mahen, a sports reporter/anchor at WATE-TV in Knoxville from 2013-2016. "It felt like the whole city was punched in the gut."

A week after the Florida loss, over 100,000 fans saw the Vols lose yet another close game, 24-20 to Arkansas. Back in 1994, I worked as one of the film guys for Tennessee's football team. They started that season winning only one of their first four games. It felt like the sky was falling in the city of Knoxville. But inside the football complex, it was business as usual when practice got underway the Monday after a loss. Twenty-one years later, the response in that building was the same. Everyone just went back to work..

"As a player or a coach, every week is its own season, so you start over," Azzanni told me. "You get back into game planning and get that hangover done quickly. It doesn't resonate long. Same with winning. The players go outside and hear it from everyone, but when they come back in, it's full speed ahead. You don't have time to cry."

"That game is over and it doesn't matter anymore," says former Tennessee tight ends coach Mark Elder. "You have to make adjustments and corrections. Whether you won by 50 or lost by 50, if you want to be a championship caliber team, you have to turn the page. You have to move on."

Tennessee was 2-3 and could just have easily been at least 4-1. The season was on the brink of true disaster with nineteenth-ranked Georgia coming to town. The Vols hadn't beaten the Bulldogs since Lane Kiffin was patrolling the Neyland Stadium sidelines, and through the first 28 minutes, it looked like that losing streak was going to reach six games.

The first insult came when Georgia's Leonard Floyd recovered a Jalen Hurd fumble on first and goal from the half yard line. He ran it back all the way, 96 yards for a touchdown. Later in the half, Reggie Davis misplayed a punt and collected it on the bounce. The uncertainty actually led to open running lanes and a 70-yard return for a touchdown. It was 24-3 Georgia, and Neyland Stadium was filled with boos. Tennessee fans expected the worst. But just when it seemed that the Vols were heading towards a 2-4 record, the breaks started to go their way.

On fourth and 4 from midfield, the conservative Jones understood that they needed to change the game's momentum and went for it. With just over two minutes to go in the half, Dobbs threw to his left, where wide receiver Von Pearson was open. Pearson slipped, but still caught the pass for a first down. Four plays later, Tennessee faced fourth and 9 from the Georgia 39. Too far for a field goal, Jones went for it again. Dobbs threw behind his intended receiver, but Josh Smith came up with a spectacular play. He adjusted his body in midair to make the catch, then ran the remaining 27 yards for the touchdown.

"When wide receiver recruits got on campus I showed them that play," Azzanni says. "I show the TV version copy because it was so good. I'd pause the play. 'See the score?' We were getting our butts kicked. 'See the down and distance?' Then I go through the route and the technique of every guy, and why that was important. I show the drills we worked on all the time. All that drill work we did a thousand times came to life."

Sony Michel fumbled the ensuing kickoff, which led to an Alvin Kamara touchdown catch. Georgia was a minute and change from getting to the locker room up 24-3. Now it was anyone's game at 24-17. Tennessee kept the momentum going in the second half, leading 38-31 with under four minutes remaining. On third and 9 from their own 44, Georgia's Greyson Lambert was under pressure and bought some time. Just before he was going to be sacked by LaTroy Lewis, Lambert spotted Reggie Davis breaking away from Vols defensive back Emmanuel Moseley. Lambert threw as good a pass as possible. It hit Davis in stride at the Tennessee 5. The game was going to be tied and...

Davis dropped the ball.

And there was one more moment of good fortune still to come for the Vols. They'd punt the football away from their own 44. Trevor Daniel launched one that fell at the Georgia 6, took a hop towards the end zone, then turned to the sideline, and crossed the boundary inside the one-yard line. "I was going to go out there and punt the best I could," Daniel said after the game in the most punter quote ever. If Georgia was going to send the game to overtime, they'd have to go 99 ½ yards to do it. With six seconds left, Georgia would have time for one more play from the Tennessee 27. Lambert heaved it to Malcolm Mitchell near the goal line, but Brian Randolph batted it away. The game was over.

Tennessee finally had a big win. "It means everything because of our kids," Jones told CBS sideline reporter Allie LaForce during the postgame celebration. "Our kids showed great resiliency. They were not gonna be denied tonight... This is the first of many."

"It was a great feeling because of how the season was going and the way we were losing close, big games," says Foreman. "Great confidence booster and I think that helped us get over some of those tough losses."

A video posted on Twitter by @TheVerboss showed a Tennessee fan standing in the end zone seats. He was crying and screaming "Thank You God!" after the game. It's been viewed over 5.6 million times.

It was becoming clear with each passing week that Josh Dobbs was special, and a savior for the Tennessee offense. Against Georgia, Dobbs had 430 yards of offense, with three passing touchdowns and two rushing scores. Tennessee's offensive performance was even more impressive against what was a really good UGA defense, whose coordinator would one day become a part of the Vols family. "That was at the time the most yards [519] and points [38] given up by a Jeremy Pruitt defense," Azzanni remembers. "I was proud of that."

Two weeks later the Vols played at eighth-ranked Alabama, and took a 14-13 lead on a Jalen Hurd touchdown run with less than six minutes to go. But the Vols defense ran out of gas as Derrick Henry ran it in from 14 yards away. The Tide escaped with a 19-14 win, Tennessee's ninth straight loss to the Crimson Tide. But it was also UT's final defeat of the season. In their final six games, the Vols averaged more than 36 points per contest. On New Year's Day, Big Orange Country showed up in droves in Tampa for the Outback Bowl.

Northwestern might have been the higher ranked team in this matchup (they were somehow twelfth in the country at that point), but it was Tennessee that played like a team worthy of national attention. The Vols destroyed the Wildcats 45-6. For the second straight year, Tennessee beat up a Big Ten opponent in the postseason. Dobbs, Hurd, Kamara and a freshman named John Kelly ran wild, combining for five touchdowns and 235 rushing yards. Hurd was injured during bowl week preparation but recovered to run for 130 yards and was named the Outback Bowl's Most Valuable Player. John Jancek's defense intercepted four passes. The final tally came on a 100-yard interception return by Evan Berry. There might have been eight seconds left on the clock, but the Vols didn't care, with many players on the sideline running to the end zone to celebrate with Berry.

On October 10, 2015, UT upset nineteenth-ranked Georgia 38-31 at home. Defensive lineman LaTroy Lewis celebrated with fans. The win snapped Tennessee's five game losing streak to their Athens rivals.

"The road to success is always under construction, and we need to continue to recruit and develop and continue to grow and elevate our football program," said Jones. "But where we've come in three short years is amazing, and I owe it to all of our players, our staff, our support staff, and our seniors. They've really taken the charge."

2016 wasn't even a day old, but the Tennessee Vols were already thinking about the season to come. "To come out today and compete like we did, hold them to the points we did, and do what we did on offense, that was great," said Dobbs. "The sky's the limit. We just need to put in the work this offseason to reach our potential."

Tennessee had won nine games for the first time since 2007, when they won ten games under Phillip Fulmer. They won five conference games and finished second in the East. The SEC West remained a minefield, but the Eastern Division was once again going to be ripe for the taking. The Vols would return a veteran quarterback (Dobbs), one of the best running back tandems in the nation (Hurd/Kamara), a solid one-two punch at receiver (Malone/Jennings), and dominant pass rusher (Barnett).

Josh Dobbs was right. The sky was the limit for the Vols in 2016.

10

2016 GETS UNDERWAY

ONCE THE OUTBACK BOWL WAS OVER, Tennessee's coaches were set to go on the recruiting trail. But not all of them. Tight ends coach/special teams coordinator Mark Elder had accepted the head coaching job at Eastern Kentucky on December 8, and left after the win over Northwestern. "It was a long-time aspiration of mine to be a head coach," Elder told me in January 2018. "I wanted to be a head coach at a place that had all the ingredients. A place you could win, a place where football was important, that had history and tradition, and that all fit here. And it was a good fit geographically too. EKU is just outside of Lexington. I was born in Cincinnati, and I've recruited a ton around here... I wouldn't have left Tennessee for just anything. It had to be the right fit."

Elder had spent nine years working on Butch Jones's coaching staff. He was with Jones at Central Michigan, Cincinnati and Tennessee, but now would venture out to run his own program. Elder's replacement would be Larry Scott, who had been at Miami in the same position.

On January 6, a rumored move became a reality. Butch Jones and his longtime assistant, defensive coordinator John Jancek, had mutually agreed to part ways. "I want to thank Coach Jancek for his contributions to the University of Tennessee football program the past three years," said Jones. "We feel strongly about the direction our program is headed and will work diligently to find the best person available to lead our defense."

Three days later, Tennessee announced that Penn State's Bob Shoop (the former Vandy DC) had agreed to become the next Tennessee defensive coordinator. "This was not an easy decision and one that I didn't take lightly," said Shoop in a Tennessee press release. "I had an opportunity to meet with Coach Jones and his staff. It became evident to me that he is building a great program, a program on the rise and certainly one that will compete for an SEC Championship."

The hire was applauded by most both inside and outside the program and seen as a significant upgrade at a key position on the coaching staff. Shoop's defenses had been ranked in the top-25 nationally the past five seasons. He helped the Vols secure the Class of 2016, and that first week in February was one of the best weeks in years for Tennessee. First, on National Signing Day (February 3), the Vols brought in another very good class. While it didn't reach the heights of 2015, it was still ranked fourteenth in the nation by 247Sports. The class had yet another legacy in 4-star safety Nigel Warrior, from Sewanee (GA). Warrior's Dad is Dale Carter, one of Tennessee's top players in the 1990s. There was Jarrett Guarantano, a 4-star dual threat quarterback from Bergen Catholic in New Jersey. Tennessee also got another late pull when 4-star JUCO defensive end Jonathan Kongbo picked the Vols over Ole Miss, bringing back memories of Drew Richmond's recruitment the previous year. 4-star linebacker Daniel Bituli from Nashville was the Vols' top in-state commitment.

Tennessee was in good shape in terms of starters. This class was supposed to help give them the depth necessary to win the SEC East. "We have a recruiting profile, and it is about finding a right fit here at Tennessee," said Jones. "We had some very specific needs in our program this year. We thought we needed to bring in as much speed and athleticism as we could, bring in players that can play multiple positions and give us flexibility whether it's on the offensive side of the ball, defensive side of the ball or special teams."

Four days later, Tennessee alum Peyton Manning was the Denver Broncos' quarterback in Super Bowl 50 as they beat Carolina 24-10. Former Vols Malik Jackson and Britton Colquitt played on that Broncos team as well. Jackson even recovered a fumble for a touchdown. But the story was Manning. This was his second Super Bowl title in what would be the final game of his Hall of Fame career.

But events outside the arenas of competition yet again cast a shadow over the athletic department. On February 9, six women filed a Title IX lawsuit against the University of Tennessee. The federal lawsuit alleged that Tennessee created a hostile environment for female students by showing "deliberate indifference and a clearly unreasonable response after a sexual assault that causes a student to endure additional harassment."

The lawsuit singled out UT Chancellor Jimmy Cheek, Athletics Director Dave Hart and football coach Butch Jones, saying that they "had actual notice of previous sexual assaults and rapes by football players, yet acted with deliberate indifference to the serious risks of sexual assaults and failed to take corrective actions."

The University of Tennessee released a statement through legal counsel, which said in part, "Any assertion that we do not take sexual assault seriously enough is simply not true. To claim that we have allowed a culture to exist contrary to our institutional commitment to providing a safe environment for our students or that we do not support those who report sexual assault is just false."

For the next couple of weeks, UT was raked over the coals locally, regionally and nationally by sports and news media outlets. Making matters even worse, a week after the lawsuit was filed, two Tennessee football players, one current and one former, were in the news. Defensive lineman Alexis Johnson, a JUCO transfer from Atlanta, was arrested on charges of aggravated assault and false imprisonment. He was immediately suspended by Butch Jones. Ex-Tennessee offensive lineman Mack Crowder, who played for the

Vols from 2011-2015, was arrested in a child sex sting in Florida. Crowder represented the Vols at the 2014 SEC Media Days.

It felt like each day was going to bring forth another negative story about UT athletics. On February 23, the University of Tennessee responded by holding a joint press conference in which all sixteen varsity coaches sat on stage at the same time. "Most bizarre thing I'd ever seen," a former UT athletic department administrator told me. The coaches didn't speak directly about the Title IX lawsuit. Instead, they spent an hour basically saying that all the teams loved each other, that Tennessee was a great place and that everything was fine.

"If I had a daughter, I would not hesitate one bit for her to come on campus," said Lady Vols basketball coach Holly Warlick.

"The culture here is the best it's ever been, and those stories aren't being told," Tennessee softball co-head coach Karen Weekly told reporters. "The image that's being displayed of our culture is unfair, and that's why we're here today because we want people to hear the positives."

"We just came back from Chattanooga this weekend," Tennessee baseball coach Dave Serrano stated. "One of the hotel attendants grabbed us and said, 'I just want you to know, this might be one of the best, well-mannered teams that has ever come through our facility.' That's what going on here at the University of Tennessee."

Pretty much every comment shared this common theme. While all the varsity teams were represented on that stage, issues surrounding the football program were the biggest reason the press conference was happening. Butch Jones did his best to express concern for those involved.

"Everything is about the alleged victims, and we take that very, very seriously," said Jones. "We feel for them. We hurt for them. It's not who we are. We have great players in our football program. We have great individuals in this entire athletic department. We have a very good culture in place. That's why I said we're going to defend our culture. We have good people. We're embarrassed by it. We're upset by it. It's not who we are."

But there was one glaring absence at that press conference. Reporters were told that Dave Hart was traveling and not able to attend. Hart had already been at the center of multiple lawsuits filed against him and the Tennessee athletics department since he took the AD job in 2011.

The perception amongst some Tennessee fans and media members was that Hart left his coaches out to dry at a time the AD should have been out in front of a very serious situation. Two days later, Hart held his own press conference, and explained that he wasn't there at the media availability on request of the coaches. Hart said they sought to use that time on their own. Hart also had a message for his detractors.

"I assure you, had I been there, some of the same people that have been critical that I wasn't, would have said, 'Well, he's putting pressure on them. What's he doing there?' So, I'm not offended by those thoughts, but this was our coaches wanting to express themselves." It was an interesting choice of words. I've been told by multiple sources within the athletic department that some of those coaches weren't on board with having the press conference but didn't want to leave their fellow coaches hanging. It also allowed them to stay in Hart's good graces.

Dave Hart hired Butch Jones in December 2012 and wanted to make sure that reporters knew where he stood with regards to his football coach. "I believe very, very strongly in what we're doing here in the athletics program at the University of Tennessee, and I trust Butch Jones implicitly. I know who he is. I know what his work ethic is. I know what he's meant to this university well beyond the department of athletics, and I know how he's represented the university."

In July 2016, with the most anticipated football season in years a couple of months away, UT would settle the Title IX lawsuit for $2.48 million. This put an end to perhaps the most damaging recent chapter at the University of Tennessee and ensured that another "Bruce Pearl timeline" type graphic wouldn't be a fixture on Tennessee football game broadcasts. Dave Hart was not happy with the settling of the Title IX lawsuit, or the settling of the Debby Jennings lawsuit, or the settling of the lawsuit involving three former Tennessee trainers. Hart felt that he and Tennessee were in the right in these cases, so why not have their day in court and defend themselves? To Hart, just because they were facing PR hits didn't mean Tennessee should pay a dime.

Once spring practice got underway in mid-March, attention of the fans turned to the possibility of a return to Atlanta for the first time in nine years. Tennessee went through the spring with more than twenty players missing some or all those workouts due to injury. That didn't stop 67,027 fans from sitting in Neyland Stadium on April 16 for the third-highest attended Orange & White Game, over four thousand more than the year before.

Tennessee defensive lineman Kahlil McKenzie spoke of the hard work still to be done. "We can't just talk about winning the title because that doesn't happen if starting on Tuesday we don't have a great transition into our summer program... we have to have a great summer, great camp and all of the rest will take care of itself."

A week after the Orange & White Game, strength and conditioning coach Dave Lawson and Tennessee parted ways due to "philosophical differences." Former Vol Jayson Swain, host of "The Swain Event" sports talk radio show, was among those who reported Lawson had his football duties taken away all the way back in January.

This was a huge moment for Jones, and one that may have eventually helped seal his fate in Knoxville. "Very thankful and grateful for Dave Lawson," Jones said in an interview with WNML. "We've been through so many, many things together for a long period of time... when you're in a leadership position, you're forced to make some hard choices." Jones didn't hire a replacement for Lawson. Instead, associate director of strength and conditioning Michael Szerszen would now also oversee the football team's strength and conditioning program.

Later that year, Tennessee lost part of its soul. On the morning of June 28, 2016, former Lady Vols head coach Pat Summitt passed away, five years after she was diagnosed with early onset dementia in the form of Alzheimer's. Thousands of family, friends and fans, including Phillip Fulmer and Peyton Manning, attended a service celebrating her life a few days later at Thompson-Boling Arena. Summitt's presence will be felt on the UT campus forever. She was sixty-four years old.

Pat Summitt was not only the best coach, but the best person I covered in all my years as a sportscaster.

At SEC Media Days in July, Tennessee was the media's pick to win the SEC East. This was not a surprise. Among the contenders, the Vols were the only team bringing back an experienced quarterback. Josh Dobbs entered his senior season as one of nine Vols picked to an all-SEC preseason team. There was not one player in the league more important to their team than Dobbs. In 2015, Dobbs accounted for more than three thousand yards of offense and 27 touchdowns. He started every game while playing in an offense in which the quarterback often took a beating. Dobbs had an ability to make things happen when a play broke down, which really helped with what was still a young offensive line. He was probably worth a couple of wins a season. There's no way the Vols finish 9-4 if Josh Dobbs wasn't their quarterback.

Off the field, he was the definition of student-athlete, majoring in aerospace engineering at Tennessee. "I can't say enough about Joshua Dobbs," Jones told reporters in Hoover. "You look at his curriculum. You look at the time demands that are placed on him from an academic workload and then being the starting quarterback at the University of Tennessee, that's a global position, and he's done a great job."

His friendship with a child in Knoxville made national news. A.J. Cucksey was battling brain tumors, and Dobbs treated him like a little brother. "Every time you visit him, he's high energy, he always wants to do something different, something exciting," Dobbs said. "He puts a smile on my face every time I see him. It puts things in perspective when things get tough because here's a six-year-old kid going through something that I can't even imagine. I'm thankful for him and all of the other kids that we have the opportunity to talk to."

"To know Josh is to love him," says DeBord. "And I love him. He speaks volumes for what the term student-athlete means. He's the best."

Dobbs had the respect of his teammates and coaches. Tennessee couldn't have had a better representative for its, at times, embattled football program. "Josh is a phenomenal human being. He doesn't know it yet, but he is gonna marry my four-month-old. It'll be an arranged marriage," says Elder (I only think he was half kidding). "Just an awesome young man. Positive, fun, intelligent. And the kindest of hearts. Here I am, as an adult, wishing I could be as well rounded as Josh. I couldn't say enough good things about him."

The hype train that Butch Jones tried so hard to curtail was a runaway locomotive heading into the season opener on September 1 against Appalachian State. The Vols brought back nineteen starters and were ranked ninth in the nation in the preseason AP poll, just below Stanford and right above Notre Dame. It was their highest preseason ranking since 2005. "As we all know, first games are the games of the unknown, from tendencies to new players," Jones said before the Mountaineers came to Knoxville. "There may be new schemes that you haven't seen or haven't prepared for. You have to rely on your training and your communication. It's going to be a good test for our football team."

Boy was Butch Jones right. Appalachian State has struck fear in the hearts of major football powers ever since they upset fifth-ranked Michigan to open the 2007 season. At the time, the Mountaineers were an established FCS power. In 2016, Appalachian State was now in the FBS, and put a similar scare into the Vols. Tennessee was playing on a Thursday night for the first time since 1991. The move caused a change on campus, as the University canceled all classes that day to accommodate the traffic, parking, and security measures that you'd have on your average game day. You can't have Katie looking for a parking spot as she heads to chemistry lab while fans are in the same garage, playing cornhole and pounding Bud Light tallboys.

Wait, I forgot. Tennessee is a dry campus (*wink wink*).

Moving the game up accommodated television (it aired on the SEC Network). But it was obvious early on that the Vols could have used a couple of extra days of preparation. The normally reliable Cam Sutton fumbled a punt, giving the Mountaineers a short field after they went three and out on their first possession. They then drove 36 yards for a score and led 7-0. A 33-yard touchdown pass from Taylor Lamb to Marcus Cox put Appalachian State up 13-3 midway through the second quarter, and the fans who made the short trip from Boone were daring to dream yet again. They missed the extra point, the first in a series of breaks that fell the Vols way.

In the opening minutes of the fourth quarter, Tennessee finally broke through. Dobbs saw that Josh Malone had single coverage and sent the football far down the field. Malone adjusted to the football slightly, shed his defender after making the grab, and completed a 67-yard touchdown. "That spring, that summer, that camp... Dobbs spent a lot of hours behind the scenes working, and he became the best deep ball thrower in the SEC," says Azzanni.

The game was tied at 13 with 10:30 to go. Remember, had that extra point by the Mountaineers been good, the Vols would have had to go for two.

Well, if the chart said so, of course.

With 5:30 to go, Mountaineers kicker Michael Rubino had a chance to make up for his error with a 42-yard field goal attempt. Neyland Stadium got very loud for one of the few times all night.

Cam Sutton, perhaps hoping to make up for an earlier mistake of his own that cost the Vols seven points in the first quarter, waved and yelled at Rubino throughout a timeout leading up to the kick.

Did the gamesmanship work? There's no way to know for sure, but Rubino's kick was wide to the right, and the game stayed even at 13. Appalachian State was driving again in the final seconds when Lamb ran out of bounds at the Tennessee 30, less than a second after the clock struck zero, costing them a chance at a game winning field goal attempt.

In overtime, more good luck for the Big Orange. It was third and goal from the two-yard line for Tennessee. Dobbs looked to throw, but with everyone covered, he took off for the goal line. As he leapt for the end zone, he got drilled in the chest by defensive back Desmond Franklin, who proceeded to slam him into the turf, WCW Goldberg style. The ball popped loose, falling onto the ground in the checkerboard. It went through the legs of both Tennessee's Eli Wolf and Appalachian State's Devan Stringer. Fortunately for the Vols, Jalen Hurd was there as well. He dove on the football in the end zone for a touchdown, giving Tennessee a 20-13 lead. And when Micah Abernathy broke up a pass on fourth down, the Vols had survived. "I've never been part of a frustrating win. A win is a win," said Jones, who was trying to bring positivity to a game that should not have been this close.

Starting the season early did give the Vols two extra days to prepare for the biggest college football game of all-time. Literally. For decades there was gossip that a college football game was going to be played on the infield at Bristol Motor Speedway. The historic NASCAR track was located on the orange side of the Tennessee/Virginia state line. It's a city split down the middle. Bristol, Tennessee and Bristol, Virginia. It seemed like a natural fit for Tennessee and Virginia Tech to meet there. 236 miles separates Knoxville and Blacksburg, and Bristol is basically right smack dab in the middle. But for years the money wasn't right, or the schedules didn't mesh. Finally, it all worked out.

On October 14, 2013, the "Battle at Bristol" was announced. The Vols and Hokies would play a college football game at BMS on September 10, 2016. "There has always been a desire by fans to see a football game at our historic Speedway," said Bruton Smith, chairman and CEO of Speedway Motorsports. "We couldn't be more excited to turn this long-time rumor into a reality and to provide sports fans with an unforgettable, once in a lifetime opportunity..."

In years that followed, football fans from across the country planned their pilgrimages to Upper East Tennessee, including 2001 UT grad Janna Abraham. "I made the trip from Los Angeles for the Battle at Bristol," says Abraham. "This isn't an easy flight path. It took a very long day of travel but there was no way I was missing it."

It was the kind of spectacle that Butch Jones loved. This was a recruiting tool, and a chance to put Tennessee on a different level. Had Ohio State ever won a game in front of 150,000 fans? Had Alabama? No, but Tennessee could. The winner got a trophy too, and yes that did matter to Jones. He enjoyed saying that Tennessee was the TaxSlayer Bowl or the Outback Bowl champion. Some Vols fans weren't happy with that way of thinking.

Butch Jones was feeling immense pressure leading up to Bristol. This would have no bearing on the SEC standings, but after the tight win over Appalachian State, the Vols fell eight spots in the latest AP poll. That was the second largest drop ever for a team coming off a victory. Losing to the Hokies could knock them out of the rankings before league play even began. 156,990 fans filed into Bristol Motor Speedway on a late summer night. The game would be broadcast on ABC starting at 8pm.

ESPN's College GameDay program was broadcasting from Bristol that morning, with guest picker Dale Earnhardt Jr. (of course it was "Little E") picking Virginia Tech to upset Tennessee. Fans were camping out around the track for days and days, just like the two times a year BMS hosts NASCAR events. "We got there Thursday at 2am, pulled our RV into the lot and Vols fans were still up and active," recalls Joe Kinsey from BustedCoverage.com. "I had never been to Bristol. We see the gigantic stadium. This is unbelievable. The buildup on game day was insane. We were tailgating, and it was just people after people after people..."

Kinsey had a pregame credential that he received from Natural Light, the sponsor of their RV trip, and he certainly made the most of it. "The security guy says, 'Watch out.' I look behind me and here come the Tennessee players. I don't know why but I thought, let's open the phone and see if I can get any footage." Eventually, redshirt freshman Tennessee defensive end Darrell Taylor walked by...

Kinsey to Taylor: "What's gonna happen tonight?"

Taylor to Kinsey: "We're gonna whup their fuckin' ass."

But as the game got underway, the only whupping being done was by the Hokies. The Vols appeared nervous and trailed 14-0 after the first quarter. Was the stage too big for them? In years past this might have been a moment of panic for Tennessee. But finally, they had experienced players across the board. There was plenty of time left and no reason to worry just yet.

In the second quarter, Tennessee gave their fans a ton to crow about, scoring 24 straight points. Josh Dobbs had two touchdown passes and a touchdown run as well. Two Hokie fumbles led to ten of those points, and the Vols were up 24-14 at the break. Tennessee would force five turnovers that night, with Abernathy recovering three fumbles. In the third quarter, Alvin Kamara, who only got six offensive touches the entire night, scored on a 23-yard touchdown reception. The Vols coasted to a 45-24 victory. "I think we woke up a little bit and this team has learned how to have intensity for 60 minutes," said Jones in his postgame interview with ESPN's Sam Ponder.

Dobbs only had 91 yards passing but did have three touchdown passes to go along with 106 rushing yards. Jalen Hurd collected 99 yards on the ground. Tennessee's players wore "Battle at Bristol Champions" hats and Butch Jones held the winner's trophy up high. Vols fans were hoping for a few more championship moments later in the season.

As for Darrell Taylor, he had two tackles in what was his first college football game. But his pregame quote was much more memorable than the stats. It was a moment made for Twitter. "We knew phone access was not easy to get out of there, so I just ignored the video," recalls Kinsey. "The game was so big I didn't even think about video until the next day. I see the video and think, 'Wow, I've gotta put it online.'" The Vine alone received over one million views.

#WGWTFA became a thing. "The now infamous video of Darrell Taylor started making the social media rounds while I was on the drive from Bristol to middle Tennessee," says Abraham. "I was with a bunch of good hometown friends and we must've watched the video two dozen times. We couldn't get enough."

Abraham thought this would present an opportunity to combine her passion for Tennessee athletics with her business acumen. "I was having so much fun with it myself that I wanted to keep it going and make it the mantra of the season," says Abraham. "It was just gritty enough, just pushing the boundaries enough, that it would be supported by a large audience. I truly thought it was the rallying cry that would give the proverbial middle finger to the Vol curse and would change the course of the football program."

Abraham started wgwtfa.com, which gave Tennessee fans a platform to purchase t-shirts and tank tops with the simple yet spectacular "#WGWTFA" in orange letters on the front. Head to a game at Neyland Stadium and you'll see a few of these shirts even today. "The response was insane," says Abraham. Most importantly, the Vols looked to be over the Appalachian State hangover. "It [The Battle at Bristol] lived up to every bit of the hype that I had created in my mind," Abraham says.

"After that game, I was certain the Vols would go on to win the SEC East."

11

FLORIDA-GEORGIA LINE

THE FOLLOWING WEEK, THE VOLS WERE A BANGED UP GROUP before and during the Ohio game, but they did enough to beat the Bobcats 28-19. Tennessee was 3-0. But now the season really began. It was a difficult stretch of games upcoming for the Vols. In the next four weeks, they'd host Florida, play at Georgia and at Texas A&M, and then host Alabama. Most fans would have taken a 2-2 split and been happy with it. That might be good enough to win the East, as the Vols schedule got much easier after the Alabama game. The previous two years Tennessee was better than Florida everywhere but the scoreboard. The win streak for the hated Gators over the Vols was at 11 games. "I'd be lying to you if I said we didn't think about it," said Tennessee defensive lineman Kendal Vickers. "Every day we're just trying to be a better team and when we come into this week we know it's Florida. We know we're rivals and we know we pretty much don't like each other."

Florida didn't seem to take Tennessee seriously. During game week preparations, Gators cornerback Quincy Wilson told Gainesville reporters, "Nobody has ever seen a duck pull a truck. Florida Gators are going to win, simple as that."

For the second time in three weeks, the ESPN College GameDay crew set up before a Vols game. In a mild surprise it wasn't Kenny Chesney this time. Instead, the guest pickers were Steve Spurrier and Phillip Fulmer, guys that knew this rivalry better than just about anyone. Of course, Spurrier picked Florida and Fulmer picked Tennessee. 102,455 filled Neyland Stadium on a steamy 91-degree Knoxville afternoon to watch two nationally ranked foes (Florida was nineteenth and Tennessee was fourteenth).

A new, unwanted tradition for Tennessee was emerging. Slow starts. They had rallied for wins over Appalachian State and Virginia Tech, but Florida was a better team than the Mountaineers and Hokies. A comeback would be more difficult should they fall behind. Tennessee trailed 7-0 in the first quarter, but got a huge break when Florida's Antonio Callaway, the hero of the 2015 game, fumbled a punt on his own two-yard line. Dillon Bates recovered, and the Vols were in great position to tie the game. But could the Vols capitalize? Jalen Hurd gained a yard, then Jason Croom dropped a sure touchdown. On third and goal Hurd was stuffed at the line, setting up fourth and goal. Perhaps sensing a riot if he sent the field goal unit on the field (as he did a year before against Oklahoma), this time Jones went for it. DeBord called for one of Tennessee's bread and butter plays close to the goal line, with Kamara going out into the flat from left to right. The Gators snuffed out the pass, and Tennessee was cooked.

The second quarter was rough for the Vols. A 93-yard Gators touchdown drive was followed by a Dobbs interception in the end zone. Then, Florida marched down the field on an 80-yard touchdown drive. The absence of Cam Sutton, who wouldn't play for weeks after he injured his right ankle during the Ohio game, was glaring in that first half. Austin Appleby, who was subbing for the injured Luke Del Rio, had two touchdown passes. It looked like the Vols history of backup quarterbacks beating them in big games was going to have a new chapter.

It was 21-3 at the half. Zach Azzanni remembers that there was no panic in the locker room. "As an offensive staff we talked about how the plays were there, but we were dropping balls. They weren't doing much to stop us. We were stopping ourselves. We just had to calm down and didn't really need to tweak a bunch. We just challenged the guys. It's time. Enough is enough in losing to these guys."

The third quarter started with Dobbs throwing his second interception of the day, this time by Jalen Tabor. During the week, Tabor got noticed by Tennessee fans after his comment, "I feel like they haven't really played anybody of our caliber yet, so they've probably just been kind of slacking around most likely." 32 minutes into the game, Tabor looked to be accurate. There was no reason to believe that the Vols were going to rally and give their fans a moment in the sun for the first time since George W. Bush's first term in office.

But rallies often start with seemingly the smallest of plays. On third and inches from their own 19, Florida handed the football to Jordan Scarlett. They were averaging nearly five yards a carry at that point, so a first down seemed very likely. Tennessee defensive back Emmanuel Moseley was cheating a bit, came around the right side of the Florida line, and hit Scarlett. At nearly the same moment, linebacker Colton Jumper, who was subbing for the injured Darrin Kirkland Jr., shed a block and hit Scarlett from the front side. There was no gain, and Florida had to punt.

There was still a lot of time remaining, but the Vols needed to keep the momentum going. On their ensuing drive, Mike DeBord called a beauty: Jalen Hurd on the wheel route for a 23-yard score. Suddenly it was 21-10, and now Bob Shoop's defense was taking over. Dimarya Mixon blew up a screen pass on third down, and then the Gators special teams was guilty of a false start. The 102,455 "Checker Neyland" crowd was awake once again.

Late in the third quarter, Dobbs tossed a lob down the middle of the field. He was popped by two Florida defensive linemen but heard the cheers while lying on the Shields-Watkins turf. Tight end Ethan Wolf made a fingertip catch in the end zone to bring the Vols within four. "Anytime anyone second guesses Dobbs, show that Ethan Wolf touchdown when he got shellacked and still threw a perfect pass to Ethan," says Azzanni.

Derek Barnett was unblockable. He stopped Scarlett for a two-yard loss and then sacked Appleby on Florida's next drive. This was the dominant level of play that would make him a first round draft pick of the Philadelphia Eagles the following spring. Neyland was bedlam. Looking back, you'd think the final result was inevitable. The Vols were soaring and the Gators were playing scared. However, Tennessee had seen too many dreams squashed in devastating ways in this series over the past eleven years.

But the knockout punch was coming. Early in the fourth quarter, Tennessee sophomore Jauan Jennings was matched up against Florida's Jalen Tabor. Jennings made a move on Tabor so nasty that it's been banned in seventeen states, as well as the District of Columbia. Jennings took two steps to his left, and then crossed over to his right like Allen Iverson. Tabor's ankles were broken.

Jennings was all alone near the sideline while Tabor was picking himself off the ground. The pass went over his right shoulder. Jennings juggled the football, corraled it with his right hand and secured the reception, all while tiptoeing the boundary. He raced to the end zone for a 67-yard touchdown, and Tennessee led 24-21. In the Vol Network booth, color commentator Tim Priest spoke for Vol Nation. *"Get ya some of that, Jalen Tabor!"*

Yes, Jauan Jennings was a driven player who just threw a haymaker. "All of the things that they [Florida] were talking about before the game," said Jennings. "They said that we were the worst receiver group that they'd faced. We just took that personal because right here is the original Wide Receiver U, and we felt like we had to bring that back and we did."

"What Jalen Tabor said, that was motivation for our receivers," says Azzanni. "They wanted to get after their secondary. They blocked tails off. We got after them so bad we decided to put Jennings all by himself and just let him go. We didn't do that just throwing a dart at the playbook. We saw him beating Tabor all game on run plays. We knew that could happen. Jennings made an unbelievable, electric play. That was one of best games to be ever part of as a coach."

Things got even better on the first play of Florida's next drive after the Jennings score. Appleby was running for his life as the Tennessee defensive line converged in the Gators backfield. He threw a pass that he never should have and was picked off by Todd Kelly Jr. at the Florida 42. Three plays later, another spectacular pitch and catch from the Vols shook Neyland Stadium. Dobbs hit a streaking Josh Malone in stride for a 42-yard score. It was a play in which Malone started in the backfield, then raced past Florida's Duke Dawson like he was standing still. The Vols were now up ten points with 11:46 left and showed no sign of slowing down. Offense, defense and special teams... it was a complete team effort.

Here's what Florida did offensively on their first six possessions of the second half:

- 3 and out.
- 3 and out.
- 3 and out.
- 3 and out.
- Interception on first play of drive.
- 3 and out.

They had sixteen offensive snaps. Counting penalties, the Gators picked up negative nine yards. Was this stretch of complete control worth the eleven years of pain for Tennessee? No. Of course not. But it sure felt good.

But not everyone was there to see it. Brian Sisk made the ten hour round trip with three other Vols fans from west Tennessee. "We are lifelong diehard fans and at the same time a little jaded, so our expectations were low going into the game," says Sisk. "Needless to say, that first half was awful, and we had a few libations before the game, so we decided to cut our losses and go tailgate. Our parking pass is in G10, the garage right next to Neyland Stadium. We are tailgating and listening to the game on the radio at the same time. Every time the crowd roared, five seconds later the radio would tell us the great play. And every time we'd score, four idiots in the G10 parking garage would watch the fireworks explode in the sky over the river. All while knowing we could be in the stadium watching. After a few more beers we made a pact to never EVER tell anyone we left the game at halftime. And to this day no one knows. Until now."

Sisk, who says he went into debt to follow the Vols to the 1998 BCS title game in Tempe, had never left a game early before the 2016 Florida game, or since that September afternoon. He didn't see Dobbs complete Tennessee's scoring on a five-yard touchdown run, in which he and the offensive line barreled over Florida's defense. It was 38-21. You ever watch the 1988 classic *Bloodsport*, starring the great Jean-Claude Van Damme? The Vols made the Gators say *"Matei."* They had tapped out.

It was a monster game for Dobbs. 319 of his 399 total yards came through the air. "As the quarterback goes, so goes the offense," DeBord told me. "We were able to do more in our second year in the throw game. Josh made the jump in his development that made us able to throw more. We had great success because of the work he put in. All that work he put in, the film study, the drill work... he made that thing happen."

With 2:19 to go, Appleby's pass fell incomplete on fourth down deep in their own end of the field. The competitive portion of the football game was complete. Verne Lundquist was on the microphone in the CBS booth as the clock struck zero. He said it basic and said it best.

"It's over. The streak... has ended."

Butch Jones gave multiple fist pumps on his way to shake hands with Florida coach Jim McElwain as Tennessee players jumped into the student section. It was the first game for freshman linebacker Daniel Bituli. He had one tackle and made the most of the celebration, standing on the top of the wall and raising his hands to his fellow students. Todd Kelly Jr. was among the many players who ran around the field, giving high fives to the fans. The party was in full swing across Big Orange Country. The bars on the Cumberland Strip did a brisk business that night.

Tennessee was back.

At this moment, Butch Jones was one of the most popular people in the state. You'd figure the post-game press conference would be a joyous one. And for the most part it was. But there was a comment that stood out to reporters when Jones addressed them in the media room. "I hope you guys understand the resolve and the resiliency of this football team, and the local media should understand that," Jones said from the podium. "We have something special here. Must win, all that... that is not the case. We are building something special here with character and competitiveness."

"You're talking about probably the greatest moment in Tennessee football in at least a decade, and Butch used that platform to put a dig in at the media," says Bleacher Report's Brad Shepard. "I remember looking over at [247Sports writer] Wes Rucker with this funny look. I mean, why then? It just seemed like a cuss word in a gospel song at that very moment. Butch was thin-skinned and always wanted to control his message, but this was not the time or the place. The media is the direct line between a coach and the fan, so having an 'I told you so' moment then did not resonate."

On September 24, 2016, Tennessee snapped an 11 game losing streak to Florida with a 38-28 victory over the hated Gators.

Like coaches in Tuscaloosa or Baton Rouge or Tallahassee, Butch Jones had moments when he was distrustful of the media. And he was still getting used to all the attention. Mt. Pleasant, Michigan didn't have lots of reporters waiting for Jones after every Chippewas practice. Cincinnati is a pro sports town, so his Bearcats were well behind the NFL's Bengals and MLB's Reds in terms of fan interest. Plus, a considerable number of the college football fans there care more about what goes on 106 miles to the north at Ohio State. But there is large media contingent in Knoxville that covers Tennessee football on a daily basis. Television, radio, websites... it's not going to be "Cocktails and Dreams" all the time. Jones was letting the folks on the Vols beat know he wasn't happy with them, at a time that he should have been nothing but pleased with his professional life.

Tennessee was well aware of the fact that 1-0 in the SEC could easily be 1-1 if they didn't play well at Georgia in seven days' time. Incredibly, that game would prove to be even more dramatic than the Florida contest. "Everyone had the same thought," says Zack Peddicord, a UT grad from Rockwood. "We've FINALLY gotten over the Florida hump. We can beat anyone now. We just need to go out and do it."

Even during the dark days of the Derek Dooley era, the Vols and Dawgs played close football games. Since 2011, the margin of victory averaged less than six points per game, with every result a one possession contest. "We are expecting a dogfight coming into this weekend, especially on the road," said Alpharetta, Georgia native Josh Dobbs. "Anytime you go on the road in the SEC, you have to be ready to play a full 60-minute game and we will be ready to do that."

Tennessee fans Matt and Kelsey Osborne would not be at the game. They had something else planned for that afternoon: their wedding. "We know all the social etiquette tied to SEC football and fall weddings," emphasizes Matt. But to accommodate family, schedules, and not wanting to push the wedding into December or even later into 2018, they picked the first road game weekend of 2017. "Kelsey may be more of a football fan than me," Matt informed me. "She wanted the wedding to be like a fancy tailgate where everyone could come, hang out, and watch the game together. We told the guests to wear orange and let them know they wouldn't have to watch the game on their phones." The couple gambled that Tennessee/Georgia would be the CBS game of the week and they were correct. The game was shown on a projector at their reception.

The Tennessee/Georgia rivalry started in 1899, but the two teams only played twenty-one times in the first ninety years. When the SEC expanded to twelve teams in 1992, it became an annual matchup. The yearly games, their competitive nature (Tennessee leads 23-22-2 going into the 2018 season), the recruiting battles and the fact that the two states border each other has turned this into one of the SEC's best competitions. Plus, Georgia lawmakers want access to water from the Tennessee River, citing a "faulty" survey from two hundred years ago. (Yes, this is really a thing.)

For the fans, it is an important game and... well... can be a source of lifelong memories. "You can imagine the Georgia rivalry is special for me," says two-time Tennessee grad Brian Kaplan. "My sister went to Georgia, and so did a majority of my good friends and coworkers." He adds, "I lost my virginity the night of Heath Shuler's amazing game in Athens (a 34-31 win in 1992)."

But in 2016, the Georgia Bulldogs were the only ones scoring in the early stages. In the second quarter, UT was down 10-0 when Dobbs found a wide-open Hurd in the middle of the field. Hurd eased up on his way to the goal line while looking at Georgia's Aaron Davis over his right shoulder. He didn't see Georgia's Deandre Baker giving chase over his left shoulder. Baker blasted Hurd at the one-yard line, causing a fumble that Davis recovered in the end zone for a touchback. On the sideline, an incensed Butch Jones screamed at running backs coach Robert Gillespie, and then yelled, "What are you doing!" towards Hurd.

It took a spectacular four-yard scramble for a touchdown by Dobbs to get the Vols some points in the final seconds of the half. Tennessee was down 17-7, but had finally done something on offense. They doubled that up with a Hurd touchdown reception to start the third quarter and it was "game on" in Athens. Late in the fourth, Georgia was ahead 24-21 and had a chance to put the game away with a couple of first downs. But thanks to a terrific punt by Trevor Daniel and downfield coverage by Riley Lovingood, the Bulldogs were backed up at their own six-yard line.

The tag team duo of Derek Barnett and Cortez McDowell was about to change the game. They busted through the line and met at freshman quarterback Jacob Eason. Barnett got there first and McDowell was just a quarter step behind. Eason took the hit but couldn't hang onto the football and it popped free in the end zone. Tennessee's Corey Vereen fell on the gift, and with 2:56 to go, UT was up 28-24. Vols fans who made the trip to Sanford Stadium were bellowing screams of joy. It was their first lead of the day. "When Vereen recovered that fumble in the end zone, it was complete pandemonium," says Tennessee fan Matt Allen, who watched the game from the third deck at Sanford Stadium. "Lots of hugging sweaty, orange clad strangers."

The cheers kept coming when on Georgia's next possession, Malik Foreman picked off Eason. "We were in man coverage and once I saw the receiver turn around and look for the ball I just tried beating him to the spot," recalls Foreman. "We were near the sideline, so I knew that I had to make sure I got both feet down."

"It seemed like the game was over," says Tennessee fan Michael Burgess. "People started talking about the SEC championship, who we may face and if we had any national championship hopes."

There was still time remaining, but the Vols had the game on their terms. Tennessee though, was shorthanded on offense. Hurd would normally get some carries in this kind of situation, but he hadn't played for most of the second half. Speculation was that Hurd had been benched by Butch Jones for the fumble that cost Tennessee a touchdown in the second quarter. But after the game, Jones said Hurd was out due to a a "lower extremity injury." Instead, Tennessee gave the ball to Kamara three times in a row. He gained only four yards. There would be no gambling, no chance-taking of any kind. Tennessee would count on their defense to win the game. "I was furious," says Tennessee fan Matthew Chambers. His family has had season tickets to Vols games since the 1970s. "All we needed was a first down and Butch pulled the exact stunt that he did in Gainesville the previous year."

Tennessee had only allowed seven points in the second half and forced turnovers during the past two drives, so you could see the logic behind the conservative play calling. The Bulldogs would have to go 81 yards in 67 seconds, with only one timeout. Incredibly, they did just that. Eason took the snap at the Tennessee 47 with 19 seconds left. The Vols rushed four men, but they couldn't get to the Georgia quarterback. He had time to throw, and sent it deep. Malik Foreman was running down the sideline with Georgia's Riley Ridley. He had help from safety Micah Abernathy on that side of the field as well. But Foreman got a step behind, and Abernathy was a step too close to the center of the field. Eason threaded the needle. Riley caught the football at the 1 and walked over the goal line.

"On the play I got beat we were in man coverage," says Foreman. "I simply lost the ball in the lights and didn't know he threw the ball until I saw the receiver speed up... just a crazy play." Back in 2001, the Bulldogs scored a touchdown in the final seconds to beat Tennessee. Legendary Georgia play-by-play announcer Larry Munson yelled, *"We just stepped on their face with a hobnail boot and broke their nose! We just crushed their face."*

Fifteen years later, it looked like this was going to be "Hobnail Boot 2." The mood in the Tennessee sections, as you can imagine, was not good. "When the throw went up, I gasped. I'm confident everyone in my section did," says Richard Collins, a Tennessee alum from Sweetwater. He's had season tickets since 2008. "I instantly felt sick as I saw the separation on the receiver, the ball land perfectly in his hands, and the arms of the Georgia fans go victoriously in the sky. I saw the Tennessee heads dip down. The same kind of slump we were so used to seeing."

"The doubts we were having as UT fans had proven correct. It was a gut punch," says Peddicord.

"I was in the stands for the 2013 Georgia game, the 2014 Florida game, the 2015 Oklahoma game, along with many other heartbreaks," says Burgess, a teenager who has few memories of Volunteers success. "I wanted to leave, but I had left at halftime of the Florida game the week before, so I wasn't gonna let another moment slip through my fingers, no matter the improbability of it happening. No part of me believed Tennessee would win."

"I knew the game was over and that our season was ruined," recalls Tennessee fan Lee Arnold. "But I stayed because I wanted to see the whole thing through."

"100 times out of 100, I would normally just leave at that point," said Kaplan. "But I had driven two friends and knew I was going to have to wait for them regardless. So, I waited."

"Immediately my roommates all decided to leave and head back to Knoxville," says Tennessee student Nick Yeo. "I tried to protest, still holding out a sliver of hope that something could happen, but ultimately they decided to leave, leaving me alone and potentially without a ride back to Knoxville. I started to get nervous that I was going to get left in Athens, so I decided to move to the concourse so that I could run out of the gate and try to catch up in case we lost."

"I know we probably shouldn't have left, but I just couldn't take another loss," admits Chambers. "As we get out of the stadium my girlfriend Hannah and I are walking on the street, not saying a word. Out of nowhere a Georgia frat boy walks up, gives us the double bird and yells 'F--- the Vols.' I was already mad and went after him. Thankfully, Hannah stopped me, and we carried on. We had no idea what was going on in the game at this point. We thought it was over."

"Georgia students started to crowd towards the sidelines with anticipation of rushing the field," said Peddicord.

Jackson Smith, a Tennessee student, had decided to go to Athens with friends in the early morning hours. They watched the game at Southern Standard, an Athens bar. It looked like they would have a long trip home. "Once Eason threw that touchdown pass we were devastated at the possibility of losing our first game and early season momentum," says Smith. "The bartenders all had bottles of champagne prepared and popped them after the score."

You could excuse those bartenders for the premature popping. There were only ten seconds left in the game. It would take a miracle for the Vols to win. "I was heartbroken," says

Christopher Foster. His Dad played high school football with Vol legend Carl Pickens in Murphy, North Carolina, so it wasn't a surprise that Christopher became a Tennessee fan. "I left my section and rode the escalator to a large concourse outside the stadium but still in the gates. I knew they had to kick to us and that Evan Berry would likely be getting the rock directly or with a lateral so I stepped back in on the lower level directly behind the Georgia student section."

Georgia's kickoff came from their own 20 following an excessive celebration penalty. Berry was one of the best return men in the country, so the Vols had a chance (as slim as it might be) if he could only get his hands on the ball. The Bulldogs didn't kick it deep, but they didn't squib it either. Berry ran forward, caught the football at his own 32, and brought it into Dawgs territory, using up only six seconds. Georgia was offside on the play, giving the Vols five more yards. Josh Dobbs was warming up on the sideline. He'd have one chance to steal a win, one opportunity from the Georgia 43. "Before the play, I kept thinking to myself – 'Don't get sacked, give somebody a chance to make a play - throw it high and far," says Peddicord.

Tennessee lined up with Jason Croom, Josh Malone and Josh Smith to the left side and Jauan Jennings on the right. Wide receivers coach and passing game coordinator Zach Azzanni didn't like what he saw. "We had a timeout in our pocket and I told Coach Jones to call timeout. He's like, 'Why?' I said, 'Trust me.' He said 'ok.' I worked with him for a long time and he trusted me. So, I switched everyone up." Azzanni now put Jennings, Croom, and Smith to the left of Dobbs and Malone to his right. Why did he want to make the changes?

"Jennings has a better high point and Malone is faster," Azzanni explained. The pass was going to be thrown to that left side, putting Jennings in better position to make the catch. Malone would hopefully get there right about the time the football would be dropping to the receivers, putting him in place to grab a possible tipped pass. Jennings had a message for his coach before he ran back onto the field. "Jauan looks at me," Azzanni remembers. "He said, 'I'm gonna catch it. I love you and I'm gonna make it right.'"

Dobbs had his five-man offensive line and running back Alvin Kamara there for protection. Georgia defensive coordinator Mel Tucker only rushed three linemen, which helped give Dobbs the time he needed to allow for his receivers to sprint to the end zone. The Tennessee quarterback launched the football into the Athens night. "As Dobbs released the ball and it began to fall in to the pile, I thought there was no chance anyone could come away with it," recalls Burgess.

Most of the Georgia defensive players were about four yards deep in the end zone. Jennings was three yards deep. Jennings jumped into the air, leaning slightly to his left, but kept his hands slightly to the right. The Bulldogs defenders were basically boxed out as the football dropped to Jennings. He then fell directly onto his back on top of the "E" in the word GEORGIA. It was the kind of fall that would keep a normal human in traction for a month. Instead, the catch gave Tennessee a 34-31 victory.

Oh, to be young and athletic...

WVLT-TV Anchor/Reporter Casey Wheeless was assisting with the sports department that day, shot that play from her phone and had the perfect angle. She was near that end zone, less than 10 yards from where Jennings caught the ball. "I was thinking, 'No way,'" says Wheeless. "When I saw the catch and time run out, I knew I could get on the field to get close to the celebration. I saw a sea of white rushing over from the sideline. Since I didn't have a shoulder camera it was easier for me to get in the middle of it. I remember Dobbs on top of Jennings just hugging him and shaking him. From there the players raised Dobbs and Jennings up and basically carried them off the field."

The video Wheeless shot was a unique look at the catch and became a favorite among Vols fans. The clip would be posted to social media shortly after the game and has gotten over 260,000 views. While Vols players ran to the end zone dogpile, Tennessee head coach Butch Jones sprinted onto the field as well and leaped in the air. He then fell to his knees, overcome by the emotion of the moment. "I told our kids in the huddle that we were going to come

183 | MARK NAGI

down with it... we're going to find a way," said Jones after the game. "And Josh threw the best ball he's thrown in his career. And what can I say about Jauan Jennings. He wasn't going to be denied."

"It was just an awesome feeling, it was unbelievable," said Jennings. "I will never forget it for the rest of my life."

"We have the most competitive team in the nation, I feel like," a joyful Dobbs told reporters. "There's no quit from this team."

"The only thing I felt was relieved and blessed," says Foreman. "God and Jauan Jennings had my back and I was glad we got out of there with a win. We deserved to win that game."

Tennessee fans in Athens experienced an unlikely combination of happiness, sorrow and finally ecstasy, all within about fifteen minutes.

In 2001, it was the "Hobnail Boot."

In 2016, it was the "Dobbsnail Boot."

"It's literally one of the greatest moments of my life," says Arnold. "I cannot put into words what went through my head. All I can say is that when Jauan came down with the ball, I lost my damn mind."

"My brother heard the bells ring in Athens that signaled a win," says Burgess. "Then he heard a lady yelling, 'Stop the bells, we lost.'"

"My girlfriend tells me I let out a screech that she had never heard before," admits Kaplan.

"We are about 400 yards from the stadium where Georgia fans were watching the game at their tailgates," says Chambers. "I couldn't see the play happen, but I saw a group of about twenty Georgia fans groan and put their hands over their heads. At this point a random Tennessee fan grabs me and proclaims, 'WE WON!'"

The party kept going inside enemy territory for a while. "I thought I was experiencing the rise of Tennessee football," says Wheeless.

"There was a young boy nearby crying into his father's shoulder because of the outcome," said Arnold. "I have a photo of me, arms thrown to the sky, final score on the board behind me.

You can see the crying boy in the corner and the blanket of red behind me as I'm yelping for joy. I wasn't holding anything back."

"A teenage girl sitting in front of me and walking out of the stadium told me to 'Shut the f--- up', so that was fun," remembers Kaplan. "But there was no killing my smile."

"As soon as he caught it, the student section just dropped," remembers Foster. "Folks started filing out and for some reason I looked at a girl wearing a [former UGA running back] Todd Gurley jersey and just said 'I'm sorry.' Then I ran out to beat the crowd and started notifying Tennessee fans who had left early."

"I immediately jumped straight up in the air, screaming hysterically," recalls Michael Mubarak, a UT football and men's basketball season ticket holder. "I accidentally kicked a Georgia fan's child in the chest in my leap of excitement. As I was being cursed out by the child's mother, I was looking for a flag. I knew the football gods would not allow something like this to happen to us. No flags!! I still revel in the sight of watching the Georgia fans exit the stadium."

"There were a handful of Tennessee fans standing around where I was and we all immediately went berserk," says Yeo. "Instinctively me and another fan jumped up and hugged each other like we had known each other for years. I guess that's what years and years of being beaten down as a fanbase does to you. As soon as we let go of each other, a middle-aged Georgia fan came up and started to cuss me out. We started going back and forth and he punched me in the face. For a second, I thought about swinging back but I saw several cops standing just a few feet away and prison sounds like too much of a buzzkill. So instead, I just told him to go fuck himself."

As for the newly married Matt and Kelsey Osborne back in Knoxville? Their special day was now even more memorable. "As they lined up for that Hail Mary, the room was still. Jennings comes down with that ball and the entire place goes insane," says the groom. "I shoved through the room to find Kelsey and hug her as they replayed the catch. The emotion was beyond description. A chant broke out. 'Best Wedding Ever.' The father of one of the bridesmaids came up to me and said, 'I may not remember your name, but I'll always remember this wedding.'"

Courtesy: Matt and Kelsey Osborne   Pictures taken by Saul Young

For as long as people are playing football, Tennessee fans will consider the Jennings catch to be one of the biggest in Vols history. "I'm happy about that," says Azzanni. "As a coach you always try to leave your mark on a program. I'm happy to be a part of it. That's a tough place to coach and win and it is nice to have such positive moments. It makes it all worthwhile."

Tennessee was 5-0. They now had the tiebreaker against their two biggest division rivals. They won the first two games of their brutal four game stretch. Dating back to 2015, the Vols had won eleven games in a row, something they hadn't done since the magical 1998 season. They were now the overwhelming favorite to win the Eastern Division for the first time since 2007. The nation was taking notice. The Tennessee Volunteers were a force to be reckoned with. Tennessee fans were very confident. "The reaction was everyone thought we are going to Atlanta," said Mubarak. "Nothing would stop us. No way we beat Florida and Georgia and don't go to Atlanta."

But no one could have known that the next two months were waiting with cruel intentions.

12

THE COLLAPSE

TENNESSEE STARTED THE SEASON RANKED NINTH in the country. Five games into the 2016 season, the Vols were 5-0. They had wins over two nationally ranked conference rivals. So, what was Tennessee ranked now? Ninth in the country.

They beat Appalachian State in overtime in the season opener, but the Vols looked ill-prepared and were knocked down eight spots. They had been fighting their way back up the charts ever since. On Saturday, October 8, Tennessee would make their first ever trip to College Station to play eighth-ranked Texas A&M. Both teams were undefeated. Depending on how the rest of the season went, this could end up being a preview of the SEC title game in December. For many Tennessee fans, the game was going to be a special occasion, even before the terrific start to the 2016 season.

"This was a 'circle the calendar' trip for me," says Charles West, a 1996 Tennessee grad. "I've seen the Vols play in every SEC stadium except Lexington and had really been looking forward to this trip, since we don't rotate as much as we did before the recent SEC expansion."

Tennessee fans love new football experiences and travel well, no matter where the Vols play. College Station might now be SEC country, but it was a new world for Vols fans to witness up close.

"A&M is like a time machine back to 'Ozzie and Harriet,'" says West. "Everyone is so nice. Their fans seemed to go so far out of their way to be welcoming and try and give you directions or invite you to their tailgate parties. It reminded me of that old Chevy Chase movie, *Funny Farm*, where he pays the townspeople to act nice so he can sell his home to some out-of-town buyers... it was that over the top. I kept thinking their campus culture is such a juxtaposition to Knoxville where we've recently had administrators updating pronouns and canceling Christmas."

"I've been to a lot of college football stadiums around the country, and I can say that Kyle Field is without a doubt the nicest one I have ever been to," says Wyeth Wilson, who is currently a student at the University of Tennessee. In 2016 he was a senior at nearby Bearden High School. "As soon as I knew that Tennessee was going to be playing in College Station, I started mentioning the idea to my Dad, who wanted to go just as badly as I did."

As tough as Florida and Georgia might have been, Texas A&M was expected to be an even bigger test for the Vols. "It's going to be a physical football game for us," said Butch Jones during his Monday press conference. "It's going to be a great challenge, again, going on the road in this conference."

ESPN's College GameDay show would be at the Vols game for the third time in five weeks. After years of irrelevance, Tennessee was back on the national stage. But even with all the attention and the positive spirits about the direction of the football program, there were concerns about where Tennessee really stood at this point. Yes, the Vols might have won all five games they had played, but they also had trailed by double digits in four of those contests. The Vols were getting off to awful starts, and the fear was that eventually, they'd run out of time when trying to make a comeback.

Another worry was Tennessee's injury issues. It wasn't just that the Vols had some guys banged up. They had hugely important players missing significant game time. Linebacker Jalen Reeves-Maybin was out for the Aggies matchup with a shoulder injury. He hadn't played against Georgia and had missed most of the Florida game. Linebacker Darrin Kirkland Jr. was missing his fourth straight game with a high ankle injury. Cornerback Cam Sutton was still out as well.

And then there was the Jalen Hurd situation. Hurd was only a junior, but already closing in on Travis Henry's career rushing record at Tennessee. He had missed almost the entire second half of the Georgia game with what Jones called at the time a "lower extremity injury." Early in the week, Jones said that Hurd would practice and play in College Station. Later, he changed his tune, and termed Hurd's status "day to day."

The day before the game, Tennessee announced that Hurd didn't make the trip to Texas and would not play against the Aggies. That made it Alvin Kamara time. In 2015, Kamara got 10.8 offensive touches a game, despite averaging 6.5 yards per carry and 8.6 yards per reception. So far in 2016, he was getting slightly fewer opportunities at exactly 10 per game. He simply wasn't getting the football enough when you look at the production that he was giving the team.

Was that because there were so many other playmakers that needed their touches? Dobbs, Hurd, Malone, Jennings... they each played massive roles in that offense. No matter the reason, with Hurd out Tennessee would need a big day from Kamara to have a chance. The Vols were sloppy against A&M. Really sloppy. Josh Dobbs had two interceptions and two fumbles. As a team the Vols lost three other fumbles. If you turn the football over seven times you aren't going to win many football games. They also had 12 penalties for 84 yards. UT trailed by 21 points midway through the third quarter. It appeared that their run of good luck was finally over.

Yet again, the Vols battled back. Behind the arm of Dobbs and the feet of Kamara, Tennessee had made it a 35-28 game with 2:07 to go. The Vols were a tough football team to put away. They believed that if there was time on the clock, they could still win. This wasn't an inexperienced team. This was a veteran group, with leaders who had played a lot of minutes over the past couple of years.

But on second down from their own 27, the Aggies gave the football to Treyveon Williams. He broke a couple of tackles at the line of scrimmage and was off to the races. Williams was clutching the football in his right arm with the sideline on his left side. Tennessee's players were giving chase. Defensive back Malik Foreman was closing in. "I just remembered the guy running and seeing how he was carrying the ball," says Foreman. "We practiced drills like that all the time, where we would come up from behind and strip the ball. I know that if he scored then the game was pretty much over, so I felt like I owed it to my teammates to at least try to keep us in the game."

Foreman fought through a block and was about six yards behind Williams at midfield. But he got within arm's distance at about the 5. At the 2, Foreman swung his left arm in an upper cut motion, like southpaw Iron Mike Tyson back in the day. The timing was perfect. The ball was punched out and went through the side of the end zone. It was a touchback and the Vols were still alive. "That's a never say die attitude. That's a never quit attitude," said Jones about his senior leader. "He could have quit, he could have given up. That was a character play."

"God willing, I was able to make a play and keep us in it," says Foreman. "Probably one of the most fun games I've ever played in, besides the Georgia game the previous week." With 1:49 left, Tennessee had 80 yards to go. They had two timeouts. Over the past quarter and a half, the Vols offense was dominating the Aggies defense. They were gassed, and it showed on a 43-yard pass from Dobbs to true freshman Tyler Byrd. Later in the drive, Dobbs checked down to Kamara. He was all alone in the middle of the field. Kamara made the catch, turned and ran into three defenders near the end zone. He bulled his way through them for an 18-yard score.

Incredibly, with 41 seconds left, the Vols had tied the game. "I was honestly in disbelief," says Wilson. "How many ridiculous comebacks can a team have in a three-week stretch? I distinctly remember turning to my Dad and saying, 'team of destiny.'"

As it turned out, the Aggies had enough time left to drive down the field themselves. Sophomore Daniel LaCamera had a 38-yard attempt for the win. But with college kickers, nothing is assured. LaCamera hooked it badly left. The Vols sideline was energized, and the 106,248 at Kyle Field were in shock. The game was going to overtime.

"I remember feeling confident," says Wilson. "But I also remember the crowd reaching a noise level I had only ever heard in Neyland Stadium and thinking that Texas A&M wasn't going to lie down." In the first overtime, the two teams exchanged short field goals. In the second overtime, the Aggies got a short touchdown run from Knight. On the first play of Tennessee's possession, the Vols good fortune finally ran out. Dobbs was looking for tight end Ethan Wolf down the middle of the field. His pass went over Wolf's head, and into the arms of Texas A&M defensive back Armani Watts. And just like that, it was over.

Texas A&M 45, Tennessee 38. "The pixie dust evaporated," said CBS play-by-play announcer Verne Lundquist. "But boy they gave it a run, didn't they?"

Alvin Kamara had an absurd afternoon. He got 18 carries for 127 yards and two touchdowns. He caught eight passes for 161 yards and a touchdown. He was the best player on the field. Finally, Kamara was the focus, and he delivered. "Alvin Kamara, what he brought to the table, not only rushing but catching," said Jones in his opening remarks after the game. "We asked a lot of him and he really stepped up... [it was] his grittiest performance probably of his career."

"I prepare the same every week and I prepare like I'm the number one guy," said Kamara. "Of course, we miss Jalen, but we have a next man up mentality."

Even with the four turnovers, Dobbs had 398 yards passing and 57 yards rushing. Sophomore John Kelly had a breakout game with 89 rushing yards and a score. In all, Tennessee's offense put up 684 yards. But the seven giveaways were killers and kept the Vols from remaining undefeated. "I couldn't help but feel deflated," says Wilson. "But I remember telling my friends after the game that it's the best I've ever felt after a loss."

During the game, Tennessee defensive tackle Danny O'Brien had been taken off the field on a stretcher and was sent to a local hospital for precautionary reasons. Reporters asked for an update on his condition. Jones wasn't happy to hear these questions and provided no information. "From here on out, there will be no more talk of injuries. Done deal," Jones snapped.

At least eight Vols that played against Texas A&M missed parts of the game due to injury. Whether this was an issue with the strength and conditioning program, or just the results of playing a sport that wasn't kind to your physical well-being, something was wrong in this area. Tennessee had become one of the most injury-prone teams in the nation. Jones's decision to fire strength and conditioning coach Dave Lawson in the early part of 2016 was openly questioned both inside and outside the football complex. Lawson had not been replaced with a full-time coach, and the Vols' depth was now a serious problem, with half the schedule yet to be played.

The odd way the rankings worked out continued the following week. Despite the loss, Tennessee stayed at number nine for their game against top-ranked Alabama. This would be the fourth straight time the Vols would be on the 3:30pm CBS Game of the Week, something no school had ever accomplished before. Even during the Tim Tebow years, when CBS basically opened a Gainesville bureau, Florida didn't have a streak like that one. The happiest people in Knoxville due to this scheduling rarity? Likely the sales staff at WVLT-TV, Knoxville's CBS affiliate.

The previous year, Tennessee got Alabama at a great time on the schedule. The Vols were coming off a bye week. They were well-rested while the eighth-ranked Crimson Tide were banged up, playing their last of eight straight games. Thanks in part to those factors, the Vols nearly pulled the upset. But leading up to the 2016 matchup, Tennessee was running on fumes. They had a much needed week off on the schedule after hosting Alabama, but it couldn't come soon enough. It felt like every game was a battle. Five of their six contests had final margins of ten points or less.

And the injuries. Oh, the injuries. Linebacker Elliott Berry, defensive back Baylen Buchanan and defensive tackle Kahlil McKenzie each got their first career start against the Crimson Tide. This wasn't a reward. This was a necessity. Yes, Jalen Hurd would return to the Tennessee backfield after missing the Texas A&M

game due to what was now being called an "undisclosed" injury, but too many key guys were staying in the training room. In addition to the continued Kirkland/Sutton/Reeves-Maybin absences, linebacker Cortez McDowell and offensive lineman Dylan Wiesman missed the Bama game with concussions.

Alabama was steamrolling pretty much everyone at this point in the season, and Tennessee was forced to throw what looked like their JV squad on the field. The Neyland Stadium atmosphere was electric at kickoff, but most Vols fans realized just staying competitive with the Tide was going to be a tall order. The Tide romped 49-10, and it could have been much worse. They only allowed 163 yards of Tennessee offense, while Lane Kiffin's group racked up nearly 600 yards.

And it kept getting worse. Against Alabama, McKenzie tore a pectoral muscle and was done for the season. Alvin Kamara hurt his knee and would miss the next two games. After the loss, Jones was frustrated. The injury factor was out of control. "What can I say? The next man goes in," said Jones. "These kids are warriors. I believe in them. They are going to be alright... These kids have had great resiliency and will continue to do that."

"We have to stay together," said Dobbs. "We can't let this game divide us, but we've got a lot of work to do." Dobbs had his critics throughout his time at Tennessee with regards to accuracy. But his toughness never should be questioned. While his teammates were dropping left and right, Dobbs would start the final thirty-one games of his college career.

Tennessee was now a game behind Florida in the SEC East, but the Gators schedule was much tougher the rest of the way. They were not expected to run the table. If the Vols won their remaining games, they'd most likely win the division. "We did not overlook Alabama. They outplayed us and deserved to win," says former Tennessee defensive lineman Charles Folger. "However, there was almost a sigh of relief in the locker room because we could collect ourselves during the bye week and prepare for South Carolina."

The Vols got some good news leading up to that game when it was announced that linebacker Darrin Kirkland Jr. would play for the first time in seven weeks. On the Wednesday of the bye week, Jones surprised his team by canceling practice. Instead, the Vols went to the movies.

"I thought it was a very productive open week," said Jones. "Now, what did we do with it? We had a lot of individuals gain physical reps. Some gained mental reps… the goal does not change. We're looking to be 1-0 each and every week and it starts with today looking to be 1-0 today."

"Mental reps" had many fans shaking their heads. The "brick by brick" type slogans that were rallying points early in Jones's Tennessee tenure were now met with groans by fans.

The Tennessee defense would face Gamecocks freshman quarterback Jake Bentley. He skipped his senior year of high school to play at Columbia early, and now would be making his second career start. South Carolina was not a very good football team at this time. They were 3-4, with close wins over Vanderbilt, East Carolina and the week before against UMass with Bentley under center. But first-year head coach Will Muschamp had Tennessee's number while at Florida, winning all four of the games he coached against UT.

Tennessee was a two touchdown favorite on a warm, clear evening in Columbia. But there were few moments in this game when they looked like the better squad. Late in the first quarter Jalen Hurd ran it in from a yard out to tie the game at seven. But Hurd only got a total of eight carries on the night for 16 yards. He wouldn't play in the second half due to another "undisclosed injury."

That score would turn out to be the twentieth and final rushing touchdown of Hurd's Tennessee career. With Kamara still on the shelf due to injury, sophomore John Kelly picked up the slack on the ground, collecting 94 rushing yards. Evan Berry returned a kickoff for a touchdown in the second half, his fourth at Tennessee. Overall though, the Vols were struggling. This was a game they shouldn't lose, no matter the circumstances. But three of their four captains didn't even dress for the game. Josh Dobbs was the only player from Tennessee who went to midfield for the opening coin toss.

Dobbs was the most reliable of the Volunteers, but against the Gamecocks, he played perhaps the worst game of his college career. He threw for 161 yards and a touchdown, to go with three turnovers. He completed less than 50% of his passes. On the other sideline, Jake Bentley was the one who looked like an experienced signal caller, completing 75% of his passes for 167 yards and two touchdowns. Most importantly, he had no turnovers. "We had made a change at quarterback and caught lightning in a bottle with Jake," remembers Muschamp. "He showed great leadership and he was positive. We saw how confident he was versus UMass and saw how well that he performed. He really provided a spark and gave us an identity."

In the final seconds, Tennessee drove into South Carolina territory, trailing by three points. Jones had a choice. Send Medley out for a 58-yard field goal attempt or try a Hail Mary. Four weeks earlier, Jauan Jennings caught a Hail Mary pass to beat Georgia. However, that was a different Tennessee team than this one. Jones took his chances with Medley, who was 0-4 all-time when attempting a field goal over 50 yards or longer. Neither team had a timeout remaining so there would be no icing Medley. 58 yards is a long way to boot a football. Medley's kick was on line, but about seven yards short.

South Carolina 24, Tennessee 21. It would be the Gamecocks most important win of the year and helped them finish the regular season at 6-6, earning them a spot in the Birmingham Bowl. "UT had gone through as rough a stretch in the league as I had ever seen." Muschamp told me. "Florida, Georgia, Texas A&M, Alabama. I know they had a bye week but that's a tough run against some quality teams. I think they were ripe to give us that opportunity to win."

Muschamp would add, "We played really well, and they didn't have Alvin Kamara."

As for Tennessee, there were so many questions about how this loss could have possibly taken place, knowing how much there was to play for. "That loss is one where I think we all felt like we had some pressure on us," remembers Folger.

"I don't know what happened," said Tennessee defensive tackle Kendal Vickers. This echoed the sentiment of Vols fans everywhere. Only a few weeks before fans were expecting a December trip to Atlanta. Now they were two games off the pace in the East.

"It starts with me. I'll sit up here and I'll tell you, I'm responsible for everything," said a somber Butch Jones after the game. "But everyone has to take ownership in it. We've got to own it. We've got to own it."

There were glaring parallels to another devastating stretch for the Tennessee football program. This was 1992 all over again. Twenty-four years ago, Tennessee had beaten Florida and Georgia early in the season, only to lose three straight league games that knocked them off the inside track to the SEC Championship Game. In 1992, the Vols third loss in a row was also at South Carolina. Back then, it was another freshman quarterback leading the 24-23 upset. Steve Tanneyhill gave the Vols fits, just like Jake Bentley did. In 2014, Tennessee's win at South Carolina started them on the road to once again becoming relevant in the SEC. In 2016, Tennessee's loss at South Carolina started them on the road back to mediocrity.

Two days after the loss to the Gamecocks, the Jalen Hurd saga came to an end. "I met with Jalen Hurd this morning," said Butch Jones during his Monday presser. "We have a great relationship, but we had a conversation and Jalen informed me that he intends to transfer. I support him on that. I am thankful for everything he has done for our football program."

Hurd never played another snap for the Vols. He departed with 2,638 rushing yards, 440 yards shy of Travis Henry's single season rushing mark of 3,078 yards that he set in 2000. On November 7, Hurd broke his silence with a Twitter post. "Transferring was completely my decision. It was not an easy decision made rashly but one I have been thinking about for quite some time. I came to Tennessee to help turn around a program that had stalled for years and create something special..."

Hurd then confirmed what had been rumored. "I have suffered multiple injuries this year that were not and should not have been disclosed including a concussion that sidelined me from the A&M game."

Even with all his on-field success, Hurd wasn't necessarily the best fit for Butch Jones's offensive system. He addressed that issue and expressed frustration. "While I hoped for scheme adjustments to suit my strengths, this did not happen on a consistent enough basis. This did have a factor in my decision as I want to play in an offensive scheme that highlights my abilities to run but also expands to allow me to show my abilities to catch the ball and be a mismatch for defenses."

In April 2017, Hurd announced that he was transferring to Baylor, where he is listed on their roster at wide receiver. Multiple requests to interview Hurd for this book were denied by Baylor. While Hurd is the highest profile player to transfer from Tennessee during the Butch Jones era, he was by no means the only one. There was quarterback Riley Ferguson, defensive end Dewayne Hendrix, wide receivers Vic Wharton and Preston Williams, offensive tackle Ray Raulerson...

Rocky Top Insider did the math. 22 of the 62 players from the classes of 2014 and 2015 transferred, a startling 35.5%. That isn't counting players kicked off the team or those who were academically ineligible. Transfers happen in every program, but that is a very high percentage of attrition. Expectations not met (or not kept) certainly led to some of those departures. "I don't know about other positions, but even some of the other offensive line parents I'm close with, other parents were promised starting deals," says Beth Kendrick, mother of UT offensive lineman Brett Kendrick. "It was really bold. They'd put a kid out too soon. Butch would do whatever to stick with his promise. I know other parents felt they had the freedom to call and fuss at Butch when they were upset with their sons playing time, but that's not us."

Not having more experienced players ready to go became an issue for this team for the rest of 2016 and into 2017.

The week after the South Carolina loss, the Vols took out their frustrations on Tennessee Tech, winning 55-0 on Homecoming Weekend at UT. At the end of the first half the Vols were up 35-0 and had the football on the Golden Eagles one-yard line with eight seconds left. Quinten Dormady (in the game for Dobbs as it was already in hand) threw an incomplete pass, leaving time for one more play. Jones elected to kick a field goal. This prompted a chorus of boos from the crowd. They had seen this movie before and didn't like it when it was originally in theaters.

I'm no lip reader, but the SEC Network cameras caught an angry Jones mouthing something that sure looked like an expletive in response to the crowd. Many fans saw the same thing and immediately shared the video in question on social media. After the game, Jones addressed that moment. "I was animated there because I wanted to score a touchdown," he said. "I didn't want to kick a field goal."

This was an example of why sometimes, the Tennessee stage was too much to handle for Jones. He said that he didn't want to kick a field goal. Well, he didn't have to kick a field goal. He's the head coach and that decision lies with him. Plus, whether they scored a touchdown or not, Tennessee Tech had no chance of rallying for victory in this game. But Jones chose the sure three points, got criticized by the folks paying his huge salary (he made $4.11 million in 2016), then appeared to lash out at those same people.

Yes, it was still a much needed win for the Vols in Knoxville, but the key game for their SEC dreams was in Fayetteville. The Gators got pounded by Arkansas, which gave the Vols some hope. If UT could run the table and Florida drop one of their remaining SEC games, Tennessee would still get to Atlanta. On November 12, the Vols outraced Kentucky 49-36 while Florida beat South Carolina 20-7. The Gators only had one SEC game left to play, and the buildup made it one of the most controversial SEC affairs in recent memory.

Back on October 8, Florida was scheduled to host LSU, but the game was postponed due to Hurricane Matthew. LSU had offered to play the game that week in Baton Rouge, as they had done in

2015 for South Carolina when flooding in the Columbia area made playing a game at Williams-Brice Stadium a logistical impossibility. But Florida refused. LSU reportedly offered to play the game at a neutral site, like New Orleans or Nashville. But Florida refused that option as well.

Skeptics looked at this as a case of Florida not wanting to play LSU that week. Other games, like the one between Georgia and South Carolina, had simply been moved back a day because of the impending weather. The Gators had looked lousy the week before in a 13-6 win at Vandy. Also, not playing LSU gave Florida what amounted to an extra bye week in the middle of the SEC schedule. Florida fans pointed to LSU's refusal to buyout a non-conference game later in the season. LSU didn't want to give up that home game and the revenue it brought to Baton Rouge.

For Tennessee fans, it was the ultimate nightmare. If the game was not rescheduled, Florida could win the East after losing to the Vols, playing only seven conference contests, and skipping one of their toughest matchups. This entire situation was an embarrassment for the SEC. New commissioner Greg Sankey had been on the job for more than a year, replacing the well-respected Mike Slive. Sankey was trying to make everyone happy, while Slive would have taken a firmer stance.

Sankey finally had enough of the nice guy routine. ESPN's Brett McMurphy reported that Sankey told both sides they wouldn't be eligible to play for the SEC title if they didn't complete their full allotment of league games. Things moved quickly from that point forward. After a week of bad PR, the SEC announced that the LSU/Florida game would be played on November 19. Both teams would buy out non-conference games previously scheduled for that day. The 2016 LSU/Florida game would be played in Baton Rouge, while the 2017 and 2018 meetings would be played in Gainesville.

LSU/Florida would kickoff at 1pm ET (12pm CT). This was a sticking point during negotiations for the Gators. No way they were going to play this game in Death Valley at night. Tigers fans having ten hours of tailgating would have made things even tougher on the Gators. LSU begrudgingly agreed to the early game time stipulation.

Tennessee/Missouri would kickoff later that afternoon. Back in the day the only way UT fans at Neyland Stadium would find out what was going in the SEC and the nation was when Bobby Denton would announce "scores of interest." In 2016, Vols fans would have one eye on Shields-Watkins Field and one eye on their phones.

Four games into the 2016 season, LSU fired head coach Les Miles and replaced him with interim coach Ed Orgeron. They had won four of five games under Coach O, leading to speculation that if Orgeron could finish strong, he would get the job on a permanent basis. Florida was banged up, missing multiple starters. I mean, they weren't "Tennessee" kind of injured, but they certainly were not at their peak. The 2016 LSU/Florida game video will never be sent into space so that someday alien lifeforms will see the sport of college football played at its finest level. But the ending was dramatic.

With under a minute to go, LSU trailed 16-10, but had first and goal at the 7. After two plays, they were at the Florida 1. A touchdown in Baton Rouge would mean that Tennessee was once again in control of their own destiny in the East. If the Tigers didn't score, Florida would win the Division. LSU was stuffed on third down. It came down to one play, with three seconds left, from the one-yard line.

Les Miles lost his job in part because the Tigers struggled to get their offense in line. Too many games were lost because of inept play on that side of the ball, no matter how much NFL talent they had. But now, if Orgeron could coax a mere thirty-six inches out of his offense, he just might be sending Tennessee to Atlanta. Ed Orgeron, the guy who called Tennessee's early enrollees and told them not to go to class nearly seven years before, could help his former school end a long division title drought. The pitch to running back Darrius Guice was off a bit. He adjusted and jumped into the middle of the line. He stretched for the end zone... but never got there. Florida had won the game, and the East. Afterwards, Gators coach Jim McElwain had all sorts of things to say about LSU. "The way I look at it, they got what they deserved – and it should have been worse."

On three occasions against Florida, LSU moved inside the ten-yard line and didn't come away with points of any kind. It was the kind of incompetence that should have meant Orgeron, as Cajun as a Po' boy sandwich, lost the gig he wanted more than any other. But LSU finished the year a win over Texas A&M and a Citrus Bowl victory over Louisville. Then, Houston's Tom Herman used the leverage of an LSU offer to get the job he really desired at Texas. LSU had no yearning to get burned again and gave the job to Orgeron.

It worked out for Florida. For the second straight year, the Gators won a division title. It worked out for Ed Orgeron. He got his dream job. It didn't work out for Tennessee. Despite having the most talented team in the division, they once again failed to win the SEC East. Nathanael Rutherford is the managing editor at Rocky Top Insider, and like the other reporters at Neyland Stadium that day, knew that the real story was taking place at Tiger Stadium. "It was on just about every TV in the press box that didn't have the Vols game or the stats feed," Rutherford says. "I remember watching that final play and immediately checking Twitter. The meltdown was phenomenal, and not in a good way."

The Vols and Missouri were still playing in the first half when the clock struck zero at LSU. Cell phone service can be spotty at Neyland Stadium, but word spread quickly amongst Tennessee fans that the game they were watching was now insignificant in the SEC race. The Vols trashed Missouri 63-37 on Senior Day, but lost their SEC title shot at same time. "Of course we were aware of what was going on, but at the end of the day the only thing we were worried about was beating Mizzou," says Foreman. "That's the only thing we had control over and we took care of business."

"There's still a lot to play for," Dobbs told reporters after the game. "Our legacy is on the line, how we want to leave Tennessee."

On the Monday after the Missouri game, Jones talked about his seniors, a group that helped get the program out of the depths of the Dooley era, but never won a division or conference title. "These individuals mean a lot to me personally and they mean a lot to our football program," said Jones. "When we talked about winning championships, they're a champion. They've won the biggest championship and that's the championship of life."

Immediately, Butch Jones was ripped pretty much universally for this statement. Chad Withrow, host of Midday 180 on 104.5 The Zone in Nashville tweeted, "Has Butch Jones officially lost his mind with this 'champions of life' comment?" Dan Wolken from *USA Today* tweeted, "Alabama hears Butch Jones quote, attempts to tabulate how many Life Championships they can claim."

Someone updated Butch Jones's Wikipedia page. The "Accomplishments and honors" section was as follows:

Championships
2 MAC (2007, 2009)
2 Big East (2011, 2012)
1 Of Life (2016)

At that point the Vols were 29-20 under Butch Jones, with two bowl game wins, plus recent victories over two of their three biggest rivals. But it was now eighteen years since the Vols had won a national or conference championship, and nine years had passed since their last division title. For a program like Tennessee's, those were droughts of biblical proportions. Fans had bought in with Butch Jones, just as they had done with Lane Kiffin and Derek Dooley, only to be disappointed yet again. They wore the "Butch, Please" t-shirts and sold out Neyland Stadium, yet would have to cancel their Atlanta hotel reservations one more time.

That year in the SEC, it was Alabama and everyone else. The Vols were 8-3 and still an attractive option for bowl committees. With one week to go in the regular season, Tennessee couldn't win the SEC East. But they could give their fans a nice consolation prize: the Sugar Bowl.

The traditional tie-in with the SEC, the Sugar Bowl has hosted the Vols seven times. But Tennessee hadn't played there since New Year's Day 1991. The Vols had a glorious run in the mid-late 1990s, but in the postseason they ended up in Miami or Tempe or

Orlando, not New Orleans. This was a generational absence, one that looked ready to end after more than a quarter century. If the Vols could finish the regular season with a win at Vanderbilt, it was believed by most in the college football world that the Sugar Bowl would call Tennessee. Vols fans would buy as many tickets as were available and guzzle all the hurricanes on Bourbon Street.

While Tennessee was playing for a trip to "The Big Easy," Vanderbilt would be playing for a chance to, well, keep playing. They were 5-6 under third-year head coach Derek Mason and hadn't been to a bowl game since James Franklin left for State College. For a while on November 26, it looked like a typical UT/VU game. Josh Dobbs was putting up big numbers (31 of 34 for 340 yards and two touchdowns), as was Alvin Kamara (141 yards from scrimmage and three touchdowns). The Vols led by 10 late in the third quarter.

But Tennessee's defense was leaking oil like a 1987 Yugo. A week before, the Vols allowed a program-worst 740 yards in their blowout win over Missouri. Yes, even more than when Sal Sunseri's defense gave up 721 yards to Troy in 2012. The defensive line and linebacking corps were decimated by injury, and it showed. "We were killing Vandy, and then they found that we had only two scholarship defensive tackles make that trip," Azzanni laments. "Give credit to Vandy because they started running the ball down our throat."

The Commodores collected 192 yards and four touchdowns on the ground against the Vols. Also on this night, Vanderbilt freshman quarterback Kyle Shurmur threw for 416 yards, as the Commodores had their highest score in an SEC game in more than forty-five years. Tennessee's defense gave up 608 yards of offense to a Commodores team that was getting better on offense, but not exactly reminding anyone of the 1999 St. Louis Rams. A Dobbs fumble was sandwiched between the first and second of three straight touchdowns for the Commodores. For the third time in five years, the Commodores won this in-state rivalry.

Vanderbilt 45, Tennessee 34. After the game, while most of the reporters on the Vols beat were still finding their way to the small visitors' media room, Butch Jones was already at the podium.

"Plenty of media kept working in the press box until the game was over," remembers WNML's Vince Ferrara, one of only a few media members who was in attendance for Butch Jones's media opportunity. "That usually still gives them plenty of time to get to the media room of most stadiums since coaches usually aren't in a hurry to meet us. Butch did get there much quicker than most."

Jones answered questions for less than four minutes before getting a fast hook from the Tennessee Sports Information Department. "[Senior Associate Athletics Director for Communications] Ryan Robinson did ask if there were any more questions, but it was a quick wrap of less than one second after the question," says Ferrara. "With all things considered, I thought they wanted to get in and out and limit the negative questioning. Whether that was instructed by Butch or it was Ryan trying to protect Butch, I'm not sure. I liked Ryan, never had any problems with him and in some ways can understand his position, but that move triggered even more criticism when the intent was to limit it. In some ways, that summarized the Butch Jones era. Fall short, wrong approach in reacting and serious venom from a proud, frustrated fan base followed."

In the short time that Jones did talk to the media, he addressed an odd end-of-game situation. Tennessee was down 11 points but driving. Eventually, they'd face fourth and 4 from the Vandy 13 with less than two minutes remaining. They needed two touchdowns to win, or a touchdown, a two-point conversion and a field goal to send the game to overtime. If they kicked the field goal, they could go for an onside kick. Even if they didn't recover, the Vols still had hope. With two timeouts left they'd get the ball back with a defensive stop.

But instead of an Aaron Medley chip shot, Jones elected to go for it. A Dobbs to Kamara pass picked up only one yard, and the game was pretty much over. So, did Jones think about kicking a field goal in this situation? Jones answered, "I did but I just felt we needed at that point in time to be able to score, go for two and try an onside kick."

"We actually left the stands with twelve minutes to go," remembers Tennessee fan Terrance Pryor. "After the Dobbs fumble and ensuing touchdown drive from Vandy, I told my wife that I wasn't sitting here to watch us lose to Vanderbilt. I remember listening to Bob Kesling and Tim Priest on I-65 North and they were both truly shocked by the outcome."

In this game, Tennessee's outstanding defensive end Derek Barnett had tied the late, great Reggie White for UT's career sacks record with 32. That didn't mean much to the Nashville native. Considering his draft stock, it was expected that Barnett would pass up his senior season for the pros. This loss meant he'd finish his college career without a conference title or playing in a "New Year's Six" bowl game.

"It's unacceptable and I'm embarrassed," a clearly frustrated Barnett said after the Vandy loss. "I don't play this game for records. I play this game to get victories with my teammates."

The Vols finished the regular season at 8-4, 4-4 in conference play. They tied Georgia and Kentucky for second place in the SEC East, a brutal result to a season in which everything was supposed to fall into place. "We needed to get to Atlanta in 2016," says Azzanni. "We had the makeup and the talent to get it done. But coming up short in the South Carolina game killed us. That's the one I remember the most. That and the Vandy game. I'll never forget those games."

Former Tennessee assistant Mark Elder had left after the 2015 season to take the head coaching at Eastern Kentucky. If their game was done early in the day and the Vols game took place at night, he'd watch his former team on TV. "I looked at those injuries they had, and it was devastating," says Elder. "They just didn't have the depth to sustain their excellence because of the injuries. My heart breaks because I would have loved to have seen 2016 to go differently. I'm seeing guys that were on the scout team earlier that year playing on critical downs because no one else was there."

The Vols played Nebraska in the Music City Bowl. Derek Barnett recorded one sack, moving him past Reggie White for the all-time Tennessee career sacks record at 33. Josh Dobbs finished his college career in style, throwing for 291 yards and a touchdown, while rushing 118 yards and three scores. This completed a record breaking season for the Vols offense under coordinator Mike DeBord. They averaged 36.4 points per game, a high mark in the history of UT football.

Tennessee beat Nebraska 38-24, their third straight bowl game victory, something the Vols hadn't done since 1996. Dobbs and Barnett conducted the Pride of the Southland Marching Band one last time.

Butch Jones had gone 18-8 over the past two seasons, but with so many of his best players about to head to the NFL, it felt like the end of the road for this era of Tennessee football.

13

A SEASON ON THE BRINK

FOR BUTCH JONES, 2017 was shaping up to be a make-or-break year. And Jones went into that season without his biggest ally. Back on August 18, 2016, Tennessee athletics director Dave Hart had announced that he'd be stepping down the following summer. Jones was getting a new boss. A few weeks earlier, UT Chancellor Jimmy Cheek said that he was stepping back to work in the faculty. Before Tennessee could hire a new AD, they had to hire a new Chancellor. Tennessee dragged its feet on those hires for months. The AD situation hung over the football program throughout the 2016 season. It also brought two names to the forefront in terms of who was going to replace Hart.

David Blackburn was the people's choice. A Tennessee guy who knew the inner workings of that athletics department, he had gained valuable experience in running a department since 2013 as the AD at UT-Chattanooga. And he wanted the job. Beverly Davenport had been hired to replace Jimmy Cheek as UT Chancellor in December 2016. Her first official day on campus was February 15, 2017. Two days later, Blackburn went on "The Erik Ainge Show" on WNML and wasn't holding anything back.

"That's my school, that's where I went and I worked there," said Blackburn. "If asked to be a part of this process officially in terms of an interview, I would love to. And it would mean the world to me to be able to lead that institution that led me."

Phillip Fulmer also let it be known publicly that he was interested in the job as well. ESPN's Chris Low reported that Fulmer was a prime candidate. In January 2017 Fulmer told Low, "Since I was eighteen years old, UT's best interests have always been my interest. I want what is best for UT. Dr. Davenport has laid out a clear process, and we have to respect the time and her vision to complete that process."

Having a former football coach as AD isn't a foreign concept at Tennessee. General Robert Neyland stayed on as Tennessee's athletics director for ten years after his coaching career was done in 1952. Doug Dickey was the Vols football coach from 1964-1969, then came back as AD from 1985-2002. But in 2017, the world of collegiate athletics is as complicated as it has ever been, and you wondered if Tennessee would give the AD job to someone with no experience running a department.

The overwhelming majority of Vols fans would have been happy with either Blackburn or Fulmer as the choice to replace Hart. They were both well respected on the UT campus and had decades of service to the University. But two weeks after Davenport was officially on the job, she hired a different candidate, one that also had Tennessee ties.

John Currie had worked in a variety of positions in the Tennessee athletics department from 1997-2009, and was a key advisor for athletics director Mike Hamilton. He had the experience that Davenport coveted in running a Power 5 Conference athletic department. Currie was the AD at Kansas State for the past eight years and like Hamilton, had success in fundraising and in the building of facilities. Kansas State teams won nine NCAA championships and fifty Big 12 titles during his time in Manhattan.

"This is truly an exciting day for the University of Tennessee and our athletics department," said Davenport. "We were looking for the best candidate, and we feel strongly that we have him in John Currie... he is a man of high integrity, strong values, a progressive thinker, he fully understands the importance of being compliant in everything we do, and he is a leader who will put the well-being of our student-athletes above everything."

"As a graduate of the University of Tennessee, I know how much UT athletics means to the people in the state," Currie said. "I look forward to serving all of the Big Orange Nation, its wonderful coaches, staff and student-athletes, for many years to come. We are excited to return to Rocky Top."

If there was a red flag for Currie, it was his relationship with coaches. At Kansas State, he and men's basketball coach Frank Martin butted heads often. Currie's perceived lack of support led to Martin leaving Manhattan for the South Carolina job in 2012. Five years later, Martin led the Gamecocks to the Final Four. Currie hired Bruce Weber to replace Martin, and Wildcats fans were not pleased to say the least. The Wildcats did advance to the Elite Eight under Weber in 2018.

In football, ESPN's Brett McMurphy reported that Currie wanted to hire Jim Leavitt as the "coach in waiting" to replace head coach Bill Snyder. That plan blew up, in part because Snyder wanted his son Sean to succeed him. In Manhattan, working with the legendary Bill Snyder is a delicate dance. He built that football program from scratch over twenty-six years on two separate tours of duty, and has won 210 games and two Big 12 titles. Fair or not, it appeared to some that Currie was trying to force out Snyder.

Currie had returned to Knoxville without a football coach hiring on his resume. The last thing he wanted to do was hire someone to replace Butch Jones during his first year as Tennessee's AD, and he'd give Jones every opportunity in 2017 to keep his job. As for the Tennessee guys who didn't get hired, it was tough for them to take. "UT never talked to me. I don't know what went on there," Blackburn said in our interview. "No one ever explained why, and I never yearned for an answer. I'd been left out."

Blackburn paused a few seconds, and then continued... "I think there are a lot of agendas out there... those agendas came through, but I don't know why. There's not much closure for me. UT doesn't have to give it to me. There are still a lot of questions I have that I will never ask. I don't deserve answers... but there are hurt feelings for not getting any real consideration for the job. I think it was confusing to me given what I had done at UT-Chattanooga. I had a good track record. I think UT felt I like was campaigning for the job. I can't help what the media and the public thinks. I think my popularity hurt me. I think they felt that I'd be a little hard to deal with, but my track record never showed I would be. I'm at peace with everything, but it is confusing."

For Fulmer and his supporters, the hiring of Currie was also hard to swallow. Currie was one of Hamilton's top lieutenants when the decision was made to fire Fulmer in 2008. In June 2017, Fulmer was named as a special advisor to UT President Joe DiPietro for community, athletics and university relations. Was this an olive branch being extended to Fulmer after he wasn't given the AD job? Fulmer said no, and that this was something being discussed between him and UT even before Hart announced that he was retiring.

"It's really difficult to win and be champions in anything, even if things are going really well," said Fulmer at the time. "But when things are not pulling in the same direction, it's impossible. We've had such dysfunction in the last few years with coaches and all that... and it's been difficult. Everybody has to pull in the same direction and I can help that."

"Coach Fulmer never stopped trying to help the University of Tennessee," Currie told the *Knoxville News-Sentinel*. "He has always cared, loved and sacrificed for the university, so this furthers the example of leadership that he provides for the athletics program, the university and the state... This is a very special day for the university."

As for Dave Hart, his controversial tenure was over. Hart was supposed to leave on June 30, but since a hire was made, his final day was March 31. He was still under contract when he retired and was sent on his way with $645,454.

The results in athletic competitions were not what anyone on The Hill had expected. Tennessee never finished in the top-30 in the Directors' Cup all-sports standings while Hart was in charge. One of the issues that Hart faced was that some fans didn't believe he was truly invested in Tennessee. His critics called him "Bama

Dave," and they got louder as the trophy cases gathered dust. Furthermore, there were numerous well-publicized PR issues and multiple lawsuits filed against Tennessee during Hart's tenure.

That said, Tennessee's financial situation greatly improved under Hart. Yes, there was an assist from the new SEC Network's cash infusion, but that alone didn't solve all of UT's previous financial problems. "Everyone had their hand in the cookie jar," one former Tennessee athletic department official told me.

"The UTAD had been treated as an unending revenue stream for too many years," says Gridiron Now's John Brice. "It was expected to pay for anything that was needed for anyone. UT had to fundraise for everything. Hart did an exemplary job of replenishing funds while also paying cash for items, such as the Ray and Lucy Hand Digital Studio. It's the nicest in the SEC and there was no fresh debt."

"I will always defend Dave," says a former UT athletic department representative. "Should he have taken the job? Absolutely not. That job was going to eat up anyone doing something different. While everyone is trashing him, enjoy the $10 million surplus that wouldn't have happened without Hart."

After the Music City Bowl, Jones and his coaching staff had to finish up recruiting the Class of 2017. The big get was Trey Smith. The 5-star offensive lineman from University School of Jackson was expected to play right away. He was also an early enrollee, so there was no sweating out National Signing Day. 4-star running back Ty Chandler from Nashville's Montgomery Bell Academy would be needed to help pick up the slack for the now departed Jalen Hurd and Alvin Kamara.

Overall, it was a down recruiting year. 247Sports ranked Tennessee's Class of 2017 seventh in the SEC and seventeenth in the nation, lower than his 2014, 2015 and 2016 classes. Jones tried to put on a good face about that recruiting haul. It did not go well. "We've spoken about the competitive nature, and I think that's really, really big in today's world," Jones told reporters at a recruiting celebration event in Nashville the day after NSD. "Everyone gets into the whole two-star, three-star, four-star, five-star thing. The only five-star that we even concern ourselves with is a five-star heart. We want five-star hearts and five-star competitors."

Doctors in Knoxville warned patients about excessive eye rolling. "I hated that we never got a candid answer," says former WATE-TV Sports Anchor/Reporter Jillian Mahen. "But I understood what he was trying to do. He was trying to maintain the facade. I can't really fault him for that. It felt to me like he was trying to be like Bill Belichick or Nick Saban and hide behind a wall of anonymity, but instead of using short, terse answers he used clichés that sometimes didn't even make sense."

Ideally during a transition year, you'd rather not have big changes on the coaching staff. But Tennessee would see a major shakeup. After two years as offensive coordinator, Mike DeBord was leaving to take the same job at Indiana. There was speculation that DeBord was being forced out, but that wasn't the case. This was not a firing: it was a family decision.

"When you are a coach, you miss so much," DeBord told me. "Our kids are getting older. I was going to sit here and watch their lives go by and I didn't want that. I'm from Indiana. My brother played here, my wife's family is here. Our kids are within four to five hours. We had a grandchild born (recently). If I was at Tennessee, I wouldn't have been there. This was a time in our lives that we decided it was the best thing for us."

So far, the hiring of Bob Shoop as DC had not worked out as Tennessee had expected. Making the wrong decision for the OC job could prove to be devastating in terms of the future of Butch Jones in Knoxville. Jones chose to hire from within. Wide receivers coach/passing game coordinator Zach Azzanni wanted the job. As did tight ends coach/special teams coordinator Larry Scott.

Jones picked Scott. "Coach made the decision that he thought was best with what was needed and all the reasons that went into it," says Azzanni. "But I was not looking to leave. I was full speed ahead. I believed we could still be good... I thought we'd be good at wide receiver and running back. The offensive line was deep, plus we had Trey Smith. Yes, we lost some good players. I still thought we could win."

However, an unexpected opportunity arose a month later, and Azzanni couldn't pass it up. On February 22, Azzanni was named wide receivers' coach for the Chicago Bears. "I got a phone call out of blue and this is absolutely, 100% the truth," Azzanni says. "I wasn't looking to go to the NFL. I had always wanted to coach college football. My goal was to be a college head coach. But that door opened for a reason. There was a reason why I didn't become the OC at Tennessee. I had been there for four years, and then the NFL came knocking. There are only thirty-two of those jobs. It was like arrows were pointing from space telling me that I needed to take this job."

Azzanni, who spent a season in Chicago and today is the wide receivers' coach for the Denver Broncos, has as normal a schedule as possible in the coaching profession. This move to the pros has allowed him to see his wife and four daughters a great deal more often than when he was in the college ranks. Still, leaving Tennessee wasn't easy. "That was a hard decision for me because I didn't like Knoxville. I LOVED Knoxville," Azzanni told me. "My family loved Knoxville. I loved coaching there. Ask other guys that coached there. They'll always tell you Tennessee was one of their favorite places to coach because of the overall experience."

There were more staff changes, including Walt Wells replacing Don Mahoney as offensive line coach, and former Michigan head coach Brady Hoke being brought in to coach the defensive line. Maybe the most important move was with the strength and conditioning program. Jones fired strength and conditioning coach Dave Lawson in early 2016, then added football to associate strength and conditioning coach Michael Szerszen's responsibilities. The results were disastrous, as some players showed up for fall camp out of shape. Tennessee became one of the most injury prone teams in the country.

In 2017, Jones hired long-time NFL and college strength and conditioning coach Rock Gullickson as Tennessee's director of strength and conditioning. Most recently he had been working for the Los Angeles Rams. Jones didn't pick Gullickson on a whim. The two had known each other for decades. Gullickson was even in Jones's wedding. "He is passionate about his work, a tireless worker, detail-orientated and has a tremendous track record of developing and motivating players to reach their maximum potential," said Jones. "He, along with our current staff, will provide our players with the type of training needed to compete at the highest level."

In 2015 and 2016, the Vols didn't have a single player selected in the NFL Draft. But in 2017, the pros took notice of the talent that Butch Jones had collected in Knoxville. Six players were taken that April. In round one, defensive end Derek Barnett went to Philadelphia. In round three, running back Alvin Kamara was picked by New Orleans while defensive back Cam Sutton went to Pittsburgh. In round four, linebacker Jalen Reeves-Maybin was taken by Detroit, wide receiver Josh Malone was selected by Cincinnati and quarterback Josh Dobbs joined Sutton in Pittsburgh. Others, like tight end Jason Croom, went the free agent route.

Barnett would recover a fumble late in the fourth quarter of Super Bowl LII, helping the Eagles beat New England. Kamara became one of the breakout stars of the NFL in 2017, winning the league's offensive rookie of the year award. This success was obviously great news for all those players, but it was clear UT would have a lot of holes to fill in 2017. "In the SEC that happens every year. If you have a good program you are going to lose good players," said Azzanni. "To be a top five program, the guys you recruit have to step up. If you recruit worse, you'll be worse. Ty Chandler has to be as good as Alvin Kamara. That's why recruiting is so vital."

The biggest concern was obviously at quarterback. Josh Dobbs meant everything to those Tennessee teams, and even the most optimistic fan knew that the Vols would be hard pressed to match that kind of productivity with junior Quinten Dormady or redshirt freshman Jarrett Guarantano. Plus, new OC Larry Scott had no experience calling plays at the collegiate level.

The Orange & White Game didn't have the same anticipation as in recent years. Part of that was due to the lowered expectations. Once again Tennessee wasn't playing with a full group, as more than twenty players missed the scrimmage due to injury. The game was shortened by a half due to severe weather.

Jones wasn't prepared to hint at who would be his starting quarterback come September. "There is no timeframe. I want them to compete," said Jones. "Competition is extremely healthy and they've all elevated their games because of it."

Butch Jones spoke on Monday, July 10, the opener for the annual SEC Media Days in Hoover. He was asked by a reporter if he viewed the 2016 season as a disappointment since they were a top ten team that finished ranked twenty-second. "I don't view it as a disappointment," Jones remarked. "The way I view it is we didn't accomplish everything we set ourselves out to. Our goal every year is to win a championship and compete to win a championship."

Jones added, "I don't like to use the term 'disappointment,' because when you still look at it, it's hard to win in this conference. And only three teams have won nine games, and the University of Tennessee is one of those."

He was right, of course. Tennessee, Florida and Alabama were the only SEC teams to win at least nine games in each of the past two seasons. But the Gators and the Crimson Tide won their divisions while the Vols once again missed out on a trip to Atlanta. And there were very few Vols fans that didn't look at the missed opportunity of 2016 as a disappointment.

The next day, Jones arrived at the Big Orange Caravan stop in Kingsport talking about the upcoming season, but he also wanted to discuss what he called "the greatest victory in Tennessee football history that nobody knows about." In the 2015-16 academic year, Tennessee's football team had an APR of 978. The four-year average was now at a program best 972. The national average was 962. That uptick meant UT would not be penalized by the NCAA. "We would never have been able to recover from that," Jones said. For as much criticism as Jones has received, he did help get Tennessee on strong footing academically after the Vols had slipped greatly in that area under Dooley.

Tennessee had a challenging start to the 2017 season. They'd play in the Chick-fil-A Kickoff Game at the new Mercedes-Benz Stadium in Atlanta against Georgia Tech. The Yellow Jackets feature Paul Johnson's triple-option offensive system. They don't throw it very much. Their run game, when operating properly, is a root canal: long, painful, with after effects that keep you awake at night and in misery. It's the type of matchup you would only schedule at the beginning of the year, if at all. In theory, Bob Shoop and the Tennessee defense had eight months to prepare for that unique style. For most of the night, the Yellow Jackets ran wild. Georgia Tech quarterback TaQuon Marshall had five rushing touchdowns. As a team, they took 96 snaps and rushed for 535 yards, gaining 655 yards overall. Time of possession through regulation was 41:27 to 18:33.

ESPN viewers were certainly aware of what the Yellow Jackets offense was doing, but something on the Tennessee sideline got their attention as well. College football teams across the country have props that they use as motivational tools for their players. At Miami, if you come up with a turnover you get to wear the gold chain. At Alabama, there is a WWE style championship belt. Virginia Tech has a lunch pail. Texas A&M has a drum major's baton.

Tennessee had a trash can on the sideline with "Team 121" and "HTB" (Hunt The Ball) labels, along with orange and white checkerboard wrapping. After a turnover, the recovered football would be dunked by the players into the trash can. It's something the Vols did a bit in 2016, to little attention. On this night in Atlanta, the ESPN cameras caught that trash can repeatedly because a Tennessee staff member held it over his head for what seemed like the entire evening.

The players were pumped up to slam the football, which to them was the most important thing. That said, it looked ridiculous. A trash can? Not exactly the best metaphor. This was the kind of thing that Derek Dooley would have come up with. By every measure, this was a game the Vols should have lost by multiple scores. But Tennessee kept fighting. John Kelly was terrific, with 128 rushing yards and four touchdowns. Marquez Callaway looked like an emerging star at wide receiver, with 115 yards and two scores.

Tennessee's ability to rally and their never quit attitude in this game brought back memories of the good times from 2016.

Georgia Tech was up seven with less than five minutes to go when Tennessee defensive back Rashaan Gaulden ran down J.J. Green and forced a fumble that Vols safety Micah Abernathy would recover at the seven-yard line. The way Georgia Tech was bleeding the clock, a score of any kind would have likely put the game out of reach. Abernathy slammed the football into the garbage can. The Vols had new life, and Kelly tied the game on an 11-yard touchdown run with 1:29 to go. A blocked field goal from Tennessee walk-on Paul Bain sent the game to overtime. In the first session, both teams scored touchdowns. In the second OT, the Vols again found the end zone, as did the Yellow Jackets. Johnson elected to go for two and the win.

You can't fault his logic. The Yellow Jackets had mashed the Tennessee defense all night. The Vols were exhausted. On the two-point try, Marshall was taken down by Darrell Taylor (yes, #WGWTFA). A desperate toss to KirVonte Benson was the slightest bit forward and grazed the ground. The game was over. That Tennessee staff member sprinted onto the field, running around the turf, holding the trash can over his head in celebration. It was like the Vols just won the Stanley Cup. Only instead of a silver chalice... it was a trash can.

Tennessee 42, Georgia Tech 41. After the game, Jones was complimentary of his players, yet sounded nervous about the Vols immediate future. "I think this football team showed our grit, but we're continuing to evolve. We talked about three games in thirteen days. We have to turn around now with a short work week. We have to get a lot better and make tremendous progress but I'm just really proud of our players."

There were two main storylines coming out of this game for Tennessee. First, the Vols defense looked Charmin soft. Was this a one-time occurrence against a unique offense? Or was it a sign of things to come the rest of the season? And second, the condition of star wide receiver Jauan Jennings. He suffered a dislocated wrist in the first half and was expected to miss the rest of the season. How would the offense adjust without him?

Five years ago, Derek Dooley was the head coach as the Vols opened the season with a win in Atlanta. But Tennessee ended up suffering through a historically awful 2012, and Dooley was fired. Butch Jones didn't want history to repeat itself. The next Saturday, Tennessee torched Indiana State 42-7. But it was the Florida game a week later that would tell the story of this team. The Vols had finally snapped their 11-game losing streak to the Gators a year before, but their futility in Gainesville was still a problem. Tennessee hadn't won a game down there since 2003. Neither Kiffin nor Dooley nor to this point Jones could figure out a winning formula.

The ghosts of 2015 were still circling. 2017 would prove to cause even more heartbreak.

The Vols were 2-0 and the Gators were 0-1 after a loss in their opener against Michigan. Tennessee was ranked twenty-third and Florida was twenty-fourth. After this game, you would have been hard pressed to find anyone who watched it that believed either team was one of the top 25, much less top 50 in the country. Spencer Miller, a senior at Tennessee majoring in electrical engineering, journeyed to Gainesville. "I actually made the same trip in 2015 and had REALLY expected a win then," he remembers. "Unfortunately, I had to witness fourth and 14. I was on the front row, painted up, in the Florida heat for that one. I was certain of a win in 2015 and was crushed, so this time I was almost expecting us to lose at the end again."

Miller hadn't seen his team play especially well but Tennessee trailed only 6-3 in the third quarter. They had first and goal from the Florida 1. And here is where Butch Jones's critics had a field day. Instead of handing the football to John Kelly (who was having a big day), Dormady apparently audibled. His fade to Callaway was thrown into double coverage and the pass was nearly picked off. But an unsportsmanlike conduct penalty after the play on the Gators gave the Vols a fresh set of downs.

Now, the ball was only 18 inches from the goal line. Dormady had his ankle rolled up and had to go to the sideline for at least one play, which brought Guarantano onto the field. The timing was off. Jack Jones was called for a false start, and now the Vols were 5 ½ yards away. Dormady was put back in the game and Tennessee was still really close to the end zone... yet they wouldn't run the football with Kelly. A pass to Josh Palmer was incomplete, a pass to Kelly lost a yard, and then the capper as Duke Dawson picked off Dormady. Tennessee had four separate snaps inside the six-yard line, including one snap from the one. They lined up in the shotgun each time, and Kelly was never handed the football. "It was awful. We had these two Florida fans behind us and they're laughing at the play calls," says Miller. "We were like, 'Yeah, we don't understand it either.'"

Later in the third, Dormady was picked off again. C.J. Henderson brought it back 16 yards for a score, making it 13-3. Tennessee's defense was playing really well, but the offense was in shambles. Early in the fourth, Gators running back Malik Davis broke free from the Florida 26 and was heading 74 yards to the end zone. But senior defensive back Justin Martin did his best Malik Foreman impersonation, popping the ball free from Davis inside the two-yard line. The football went out the back of the end zone for a touchback and the Vols were back in it.

On their next drive, Kelly busted through the line, 34 yards for a touchdown. He gave three emphatic "Gator chomps" to the Florida student section, which brought forth a 15-yard penalty. It was the kind of celebration that the referees could have let pass, but chose not to. It was also an emotional response to a big play, one that endeared him to Vols fans. Both teams swapped touchdowns, and when Rashaan Gaulden corralled a tipped pass for an interception at the Florida 40, the Vols now, somehow, had a chance to win the game. They were only down three points, and in great field position with 3:57 to go.

Then came another sequence that had Vols fans screaming into their pillows and scaring their household pets. There was 1:06 to play and the Vols had first and goal from the Florida 9. By running the football, they could at worst kill more clock, or force Florida to use up one or both of their remaining timeouts as the Vols kicked a game tying field goal. At best, John Kelly could perhaps run it in himself. On the day, Kelly got 19 carries for 141 yards. Mathematics tells us that he was averaging an impressive 7.4 yards per carry.

But as had happened in the third quarter, Jones and Scott refused to hand the football to Kelly. Instead, they threw the ball three times, with all of those passes incomplete. The first pass looked destined for a touchdown to Kelly, but it fell off his fingertips. Those three plays only took 13 seconds off the clock, and Florida didn't have to use a single timeout. In the second half of this game, the Vols had seven snaps inside the Florida ten-yard line, yet never handed the football to their best offensive player. To many Vols fans, this was coaching malpractice of the highest order.

Aaron Medley and Brent Cimaglia combined to miss three field goals against Florida, but Medley tied the game with a chip shot. There were now 50 seconds remaining. Florida started at their own 25, and the Gators still had those two timeouts. But thanks to a grossly mismanaged clock, the Gators had only moved the ball 12 yards when they called a timeout with nine seconds left. Florida fans booed head coach Jim McElwain for his indifference to the timepiece. However, McElwain had sort of turned into the SEC East's Les Miles. In McElwain's first two years, Florida had its share of good luck and won games they probably should have lost. Of course the bumbling of the clock wouldn't come back to haunt him.

The Gators would need to pick up 25 yards on one play to get into field goal range. Instead, they'd get 63. Tennessee defensive coordinator Bob Shoop didn't repeat Jon Jancek's mistake of 2015. He rushed four defensive linemen instead of Jancek's three linemen and a quarterback spy. Feleipe Franks didn't remind anyone of Danny Wuerrfel, throwing for only 149 yards up to that point. He bought himself some time on this play and looked far downfield. What he saw was inconceivable. Tyrie Cleveland had a step on Tennessee safety Micah Abernathy and was heading to the end zone. Franks heaved it in Cleveland's direction. Abernathy knew he was beat but couldn't catch up to take down the Florida receiver. Cleveland caught the football in the end zone just as the clock struck zero.

Florida 26, Tennessee 20. "When Franks dropped back and launched it deep, I just knew this was how it was going to end," said Miller. "Driving through the night and driving back ten hours over the next day and this is what we came for."

The experience did give Miller a few seconds of those fifteen minutes of fame Andy Warhol talked about. A CBS camera showed a distraught Miller less than a minute after Cleveland made the catch. "Literally as we are walking out of the gate in a crowd of gator chomping Florida fans, I see a text from my fiancée with a picture of my hands over my face on national television," Miller recalls. "Me and my fraternity brothers walked to a local convenience store to get a Coke. While there I got about twenty-five texts and a dozen Instagram and Twitter notifications – all at once. Honestly, it made me laugh, even after such a rough game."

The shot of Miller was a perfect representation of what all Tennessee fans were feeling at that moment. For the second time in less than a year, the Vols had given up a 63 yard touchdown pass in the final moments of the fourth quarter. But unlike Georgia in 2016, on this occasion there weren't any ticks left for UT to pull off a miracle of their own.

Remember the hot seat that Fulmer got put back on the moment Daniel Lincoln's kick at the Rose Bowl stayed to the left in 2008? Butch Jones had a similar experience the instant Tyrie Cleveland secured the catch in the end zone. Fans were angry. Really angry. Immediately after the game, they headed to the airwaves to express their rage on Fox Sports Knoxville. "We started doing 'The Voluntary Reaction' after UT football games in 2017," says host Russell Smith. "We go without commercial breaks and don't screen the calls so there's a sort of 'anything can happen' vibe to the show. The 2017 season went off the rails in a hurry for Butch Jones and the Vols and 'The Voluntary Reaction' ended up being wild, alcohol fueled profane group therapy sessions."

Long-time Tennessee sports talk radio host, Tony Basilio, had a similar option for Vols fans. His "5th Quarter Fan Reaction" was also a must listen in 2017. The biggest fear for an athletic program isn't when fans get mad. Those fans still show up for games and buy the popcorn and hold the "We're #1" foam fingers. The problems come when the fans are apathetic. Tennessee supporters weren't there... yet.

"Fans were pissed," remembers Smith. "The Voluntary Reaction" ended up going over seven hours that night. The following week, while Tennessee was preparing for UMass, Butch Jones spoke about his junior running back, who led the Vols in rushing (141 yards) and receiving (96 yards) against Florida. "What can you even say about the effort of John Kelly and his yards after contact," Jones told reporters. "He is becoming the face of leadership of our football program."

Again, Vols fans were steamed. If Jones indeed felt this way about Kelly, why wouldn't he hand him the football near paydirt?

The UMass game would get a Noon kickoff, so I thought it was a perfect opportunity to bring my younger daughter Emily to her first Vols football game. Emily had just turned eight, and couldn't care less about football, but I convinced her to tag along. She loved it. Emily saw Smokey lead the Vols through the T. She got a big pretzel and a pack of Twizzlers. The game itself was the least of her priorities, which likely made her the happiest spectator in Neyland Stadium.

Emily asked me, "Where's the trash can?" Sadly, it was not on the sidelines, by now retired from game action. Unless this was the mid-90s and Marcus Camby was suiting up for the Minutemen and the sport was basketball, there was no reason in the world for the Tennessee/UMass game to have been close. The Minutemen were 0-4. Two weeks prior, UMass lost 17-7 to Old Dominion. At home.

It was a hot day in Knoxville. Fans who weren't lucky enough to be sitting in the shade felt like they were watching a game taking place on the surface of the sun. Knowing that thirty minutes of football was probably about all I could get out of Emily, we left at halftime, and I listened to some of the game in the car on the way to a late lunch at Chick-fil-A. We didn't miss much. UMass played most of the second half without their starting quarterback. On Tennessee's side, Quinten Dormady struggled and was pulled for Jarrett Guarantano, who was dreadful. The Vols didn't score in the final 22 minutes. Their only points of the half came on an Aaron Medley field goal that certainly looked wide right but was ruled to be within the uprights.

Tennessee barely hung on for a 17-13 win. Even Butch Jones couldn't sugarcoat this result. "At the end of the day, it's all about getting the victory, but the performance was just flat out unacceptable," said Jones. "We'll get back to work tonight, and we'll work to correct our deficiencies. We talked about playing with details. We did not play with details."

The 2017 Vols season was not one to remember, especially the UMass game, which set football back about 25 years. But taking Emily to Neyland Stadium for the first time was a delight.

The Vols were now 3-1, but easily could have been 1-3. With the heart of their schedule about to get underway, the future of Butch Jones at Tennessee was now in serious doubt. And on Monday, Jones had to address reports that defensive tackle Shy Tuttle and safety Nigel Warrior got in a fight at practice the previous week. WNML's Jimmy Hyams reported that Warrior punched Tuttle. GoVols247 reported that Tuttle suffered an orbital bone injury.

Jones denied that a fight even took place. "The injury was not caused by a teammate. He [Tuttle] landed on a helmet. And that's the truth." Jones then went off on reporters with a strange two minute rant. Here are some of the oddest parts:

- "I think we have to understand, what do we want out of our media."
- "Are we focused on Tennessee football from a recruiting standpoint, from all the positive things

we've done, from all the positive things this football program brings to the community, this great fan base? Are we in the reality world of TV?"

- "I'm going to protect our players and I'm going to protect our program. And sometimes the negativity is overwhelming. And if everyone is Vol fans, how do we let our opponents use this in the recruiting process with fake news?"

- "You guys have a job to do, and I'm respectful of that. And I'm friends with a lot of you guys in the room and I appreciate it, but there comes a certain time where enough is enough."

First things first. According to multiple sources, Jones was not telling the truth with regards to the Tuttle/Warrior scuffle. So if Tuttle fell on a helmet, it's because the helmet was attached to Warrior's fist. Secondly, the Knoxville media is not there to serve as a recruiting tool. And I haven't heard many stories about 17, 18-year-old kids choosing not to go to a school because of the media presence in said town. Butch Jones was upset with how things were going with his football team, and he chose that moment to take it out his frustration on the media. This wasn't Bobby Knight yelling at reporters or Bill Belichick mumbling his way through a press conference, but it was an embarrassing moment for Jones.

Making matters worse, an emerging power was heading to Knoxville. Seventh-ranked Georgia was 4-0, with a quality win at Notre Dame on their resume. Sophomore quarterback Jacob Eason was hurt in their first game, but the offense didn't miss a beat with true freshman Jake Fromm taking his place. The run game (Nick Chubb, Sony Michel, D'Andre Swift) was stout, and the defense was aggressive. No, Mark Richt did not leave second-year head coach Kirby Smart a bare cupboard. "The Florida game was where the Butch Jones era died," asserts Smith. "He had a shot at getting things back on track if he beat Georgia, but anyone who watched the Florida game knew that wasn't going to happen."

It was another "Checker Neyland" on a beautiful southern fall afternoon. Tennessee fans packed the old barn, wishing that this would be the weekend that everything turned around. Instead, they saw a butchering. A complete and absolute butchering. On the first play from scrimmage, Dormady took a three step drop from the left hashmark and threw to the right sideline, where fifth-year senior Josh Smith was waiting. But so was Georgia's Tyrique McGhee. He intercepted the pass. The game wasn't even five seconds old, and bad things were already happening to the Vols.

I was on the sidelines for this game. On two separate occasions, I had photographers tell me they wished the SEC would go to a running clock, like high school football games do when a team has a commanding lead. Georgia scored 41 points, but they let up at the finish. The Bulldogs easily could have gone double nickel. By the end of the third quarter, Tennessee fans began to file out. Neyland Stadium looked like a mini-Sanford Stadium in the fourth. Tennessee lost 41-0. It was the first time they had been shut out since 1994 and the Vols worst loss at home since 1905.

During the off-season, Jones talked about how close the quarterback competition was, and how each quarterback was making progress. But what Vols fans were learning was that the decision to start Dormady wasn't one Jones necessarily wanted to make, but he had to pick somebody. The options on his roster were not SEC caliber. Dormady was five of 16 for 64 yards against Georgia, with 44 of them coming on one play. He also threw two interceptions and had a fumble. Guarantano came into the game late in the third quarter, completing six of seven passes for only 16 yards. That's an average of less than three yards a reception.
"It was as bad of an offensive performance as I've ever been a part of, and it's inexcusable," Jones admitted. "This one stings." Tennessee only had 142 yards of offense with four turnovers. They now had gone over six quarters without a touchdown. On defense, they were manhandled at the line of scrimmage for the fourth time in five games.

All was not well on Rocky Top. Tennessee was heading to the bye week as a team in turmoil. With losses to Florida and Georgia, and games against Alabama and LSU still on the schedule, winning the East was no longer a realistic goal. Tennessee now had two weeks to prepare for South Carolina. It was a game Butch Jones and the Vols had to win.

The ship be sinking.

14

A DELAYED ENDING

IN 2016 THE VOLS HAD A BYE WEEK heading into the South Carolina game. But instead of looking like a rested and confident team, they came out sluggish and underwhelming in a 24-21 loss. Tennessee didn't plan on a repeat in 2017. "I think the bye week may have been the most successful since I have been here," said Tennessee offensive lineman Brett Kendrick. "We had three very good practices. They were all full-pad practices, so we had some physicality... I think it was really productive, and I definitely think we got better."

That very well may have been true, but this was still a desperate Tennessee team, and desperate teams make changes. Tennessee did just that with redshirt freshman Jarrett Guarantano now installed as the starting quarterback. "We just felt that Jarrett has earned the opportunity," said Jones. "We need to score points in this conference. It's going to take points to win... it's no reflection on Quinten, he's done some good things, but you're always looking for what you feel gives you the best opportunity to win the football game."

Butch Jones didn't go to Guarantano because he had been impressive in 2017. He was 12 of 24 for only 54 yards and a score. Jones needed to spark his team and maybe the move to

Guarantano would do just that. At the end of his Monday press conference, Jones was asked by WNML's Vince Ferrara about how he would divide the first team reps between Guarantano and Dormady going forward.

"Like I told our quarterbacks, you don't have to get a physical rep to get a rep," Jones said. "You can get a leadership rep by having all the wideouts stand around you and going over your progression and going over what you're thinking. You can get a mental rep... there are a lot of repetitions that can be incurred throughout the course of practice. It may not be a physical rep, but it can be a mental rep and a leadership rep, and as we all know, you need every kind of rep to be able to perform at a high level."

By now Vols fans were delving into every syllable of the press conference transcripts like they were the Warren Commission Report. Needless to say, the "leadership rep" response was not received well in Big Orange Country.

This was VFL reunion weekend, with hundreds of former Vols back in Knoxville. None of those alums ever played on a team that had as many struggles as the 2017 Tennessee Volunteers. South Carolina was 4-2, but not exactly setting the world on fire offensively. Despite being shutout in their previous game, the Vols were installed as a slight favorite by the folks in the tall, shiny buildings in Las Vegas.

College Football Hall of Famer Peyton Manning remains one of the most popular figures in UT history.

The Gamecocks had only beaten Butch Jones once in four tries, but that didn't stop South Carolina fans from piling on. Four Gamecocks fans walked into Neyland Stadium wearing garnet colored t-shirts with white, bold lettering on the front. The words? KEEP BUTCH JONES.

Defensively, the Vols had a bounce back performance, especially in the opening half. They limited the Gamecocks to only three points. Rashaan Gaulden and Nigel Warrior had big games in the depleted secondary with a combined nineteen tackles on the day. But the Tennessee offense approached the end zone like a shy kid at a middle school dance. The Vols made four trips inside the South Carolina 20, yet scored only scored nine points.

There was a delay of game penalty. They had a false start penalty. Two of South Carolina's seven sacks of Guarantano came in the red zone. It's hard to win conference games while making mistakes and settling for field goals. Against Florida, Tennessee's decision making in the red zone cost them a victory. Their inability to finish drives against the Gamecocks produced the same result.

Yet again, intermission adjustments seemed to be non-existent for Tennessee. In the second half, the Gamecocks defense forced three separate 3 and outs. The Gamecocks offense, stagnant in the first half, had a 12-play touchdown drive that took nearly six and a half minutes off the clock. They followed that up with a 16-play drive that burned over nine minutes and led to a field goal. The Vols defense, already undermanned, was now spent. They could have used defensive tackle Shy Tuttle, but he was still recovering from "falling on a helmet." They could have used Darrell Taylor (#WGWTFA), but he had been suspended after kicking Trey Smith in the face during a fight at practice. Tennessee's coaches could not change the direction of the game on the fly.

With 1:13 to go, Tennessee got the ball back on its own 25, trailing 15-9. They had no timeouts. Guarantano had only thrown for 61 yards all afternoon, so chances of a 75-yard drive were slim. But something finally clicked. He found Marquez Callaway on a 16-yard pass, then Brandon Johnson got open on a 39-yard hookup. Incredibly, Tennessee had first and goal from the South Carolina 2 with nine seconds to go. Guarantano was about to be sacked but smartly threw the ball out of the end zone. Now there were four seconds left. There was probably enough time for one more play.

Was it John Kelly time? He had been held to 58 yards on 16 carries, but still was the Vols best offensive option. Instead, Butch Jones and Larry Scott chose to throw. Guarantano's pass was batted down and for a moment, some South Carolina players thought they had won the game. But the home clock still showed that there was one second remaining. The last play of the game was here. Win or lose, this was it. Kelly lined up to the right of Guarantano... and would serve as a blocker. Guarantano rolled to his right and zipped it to Brandon Johnson a step inside the end zone and a stride from the sideline. The pass went through his hands.

South Carolina 15, Tennessee 9.

"We play in the red zone a lot, and you've gotta play well down there," remembers South Carolina head coach Will Muschamp, who was now 6-0 all-time against the Vols. "We understood that they were going to pass and our defense did a great job defending a pick route. We pressured the quarterback and batted the football down. We did the things we had to do to win. I've got to credit our players for that."

After the game, a reporter asked Jones why his team's preparation didn't translate onto the field. "Well, did we not play a good football team?" snapped Jones. "That's a good football team. We got better and unfortunately we came up short... did we think about handing the ball to John Kelly? Yes, we did. But with the four seconds, that's when we thought about it. If you run the ball and don't get it, then that's the final play. Then you're sitting in here and asking me why we handed the ball off."

The pressure was taking its toll on Jones, and it showed. Rumors about Butch Jones's job security were as fast and furious as Vin Diesel in an American muscle car. People in Knoxville that normally started conversations with "How are you?" or "Is it going to rain?" now asked their barber, "Who's going to replace Butch?"

"I don't worry about that," Jones told reporters about the rumors the following Monday. "All my focus is on our players and our football program and getting them ready for the Alabama game. That's all I focus on."

Yeah, the timing for a trip to Tuscaloosa wasn't the greatest. Back when Derek Dooley was the Vols head coach, Tennessee lost to Alabama by "only" 31 points in three consecutive years. Some Vols fans surmised that Nick Saban was going easy on his old assistant coach. Saban, of course, also allegedly stepped over a player that was having convulsions during his time with the Miami Dolphins, so I don't know exactly how much mercy he has in his soul.

Top-ranked Alabama was favored by 34 points, the largest margin ever between these two rivals. It was the CBS Game of the Week, giving the largest possible audience the opportunity to watch two programs going in completely opposite directions. Jarrett Guarantano would get his second career start, and took every snap. Guarantano was sacked four times and knocked down repeatedly. He took a beating at the hands of the Crimson Tide. Guarantano completed nine of 16 passes for 44 yards, an average of 2.8 yards per attempt. He was also intercepted once. ESPN listed Guarantano's QBR at 6.5. (I can't tell you how they come up with that quarterback rating, but I know that 6.5 is not good.) Alabama outgained Tennessee 604-108 in yardage, even though the Crimson Tide played backups at quarterback and running back for most of the second half. The Vols were undisciplined, with nine penalties for 81 yards. Defensive lineman Jonathan Kongbo got called for two personal fouls that helped Alabama score two touchdowns.

Then came Rashaan Gaulden's Twitter-worthy moment. In the third quarter, with Alabama up 28-0 and driving for another score, backup quarterback Tua Tagovailoa was picked off by Tennessee linebacker Daniel Bituli at the Tennessee three-yard line. Bituli raced down the sideline, eventually reaching the end zone. Tennessee finally was on the scoreboard. Rashaan Gaulden had helped keep an Alabama player from getting to Bituli, and while Bituli was catching his breath, Gaulden was giving the Alabama student section a salute. The two middle finger kind.

A national television audience saw it all, and to much of the country, Gaulden came across as being clueless. That's how you react down 28-6? That's what you do? The day's most memorable moment was addressed after the game. "Well that's unacceptable," said Jones. "That's something that will be dealt with internally in our football program, but that's not who we are, that's not what we're about."

"That's not how my parents raised me," an embarrassed Gaulden told the media. "That's not how a leader of the team should show their emotions on the field. I really, sincerely apologize to the student section at Alabama for disrespecting them." Thousands of Tennessee fans immediately shared the video/screen grab on social media. In the weeks to come, a few fans even had the picture blown up and put on their wall.

In the fourth quarter, it looked like the Vols had finally scored an offensive touchdown. Tennessee's special teams made a play, falling on a fumbled punt at the Alabama 20. The recovery, of course, was made by Rashaan Gaulden. A few plays later, John Kelly was credited with a short touchdown run (Kelly running the football in the red zone. What a concept). A streak of more than 13 quarters without an offensive touchdown was over. Not since Dormady threw a touchdown pass to Tyler Byrd at the end of the first half of the UMass game had the Vols offense found the end zone.

But the pesky CBS cameras said otherwise. Kelly was down inside the one-yard line before the ball crossed the goal line. Every Tennessee fan could tell you what was going to happen next. There was a false start penalty, backing them up five yards. Then Kelly was stopped for no gain, and on fourth down, Guarantano was intercepted. The touchdown-less streak continued.

Tennessee would lose on this day 45-7. It was now painfully obvious that it was not going to work with Butch Jones as the head coach of the Tennessee Volunteers. He had gotten the Vols back to respectability, and nearly won the division in 2015 and 2016. But he wasn't going to be the one to get them over the top. Surely this was clear to Athletics Director John Currie. Right? *(Cricket sounds)*

Looking back, it's difficult to remember that John Currie was very popular in his first few months on the job. Shortly after he officially began working on April 1, Tennessee started an online portal called "Hey John!" which gave Vols fans the opportunity to email Currie directly. He also penned open letters to Vols fans, talking about a wide range of topics related to Tennessee athletics. Currie's predecessor never connected with Tennessee fans, nor made much of an effort.   Currie also acted decisively in firing the men's tennis and baseball coaches. While those aren't revenue sports, it was seemingly a sign that when a move had to be made in a more high profile sport, Currie wouldn't be afraid to make it.

The biggest PR win came on September 14, when he and UT Chancellor Beverly Davenport announced that the Lady Vols nickname and logo would return for all women's sports. "By committing to restore the visibility of the Lady Vol brand and showing it the reverence it deserves, our Tennessee family can move forward more united," said Currie.

"I'm just thankful that the University made the decision to reverse the change," said former Lady Vol volleyball player Leslie Cikra. "The Lady Volunteer name and moniker are truly, truly special, not only to the women who have worn it and the fans who have supported it, but to the history of the University. I'm grateful that our leadership understands that enough to say, okay, maybe we made a mistake and choose to make things right."

For John Currie, everything up to that point in his tenure was puppy dogs and ice cream, warm cookies and sunshine, summer breezes and ocean views. Two days later, Tennessee lost at Florida, and everything changed. In the weeks after that defeat, Vols fans were waiting for Currie to make a move. And they let him know that they were losing patience.

The same portal that was at first used by fans to ask about the price of popcorn at Neyland Stadium was now filled with comments about the direction of the football program. Currie's Twitter account mentions were not for the faint of heart. Currie would tweet something that had nothing to do with football and immediately be barraged with comments about Butch Jones.

Case in point: On Sunday night, October 22, the day after the Alabama loss, Currie tweeted: "If your schedule permits, come cheer Timo tomorrow in the ITA Regional Championship!" Timo Stodder was a Tennessee tennis player. Fans had expected a morning announcement that Jones was fired. Instead, they got a tennis promo.

@DuckettStevie replied: "Thanks for sitting back and watching our program fall further and further.. DO SOMETHING!!

@hassell_robert wrote: "Did Mike Hamilton take over this Twitter? Whew that is tone deaf right there. 102,000 are not coming to the tennis match son."

@LoydGravitt said: "Hey @john_currie, it is 8:59pm. Why is Butch Jones still our football coach?"

And there were many, many more of those comments to go around. So this was the backdrop as the Vols headed to Lexington to face Kentucky. Tennessee had only lost to UK once since 1984 and had won five in a row since the legendary 10-7 blunder in 2011. The Vols would be playing without running back John Kelly and linebacker Will Ignont, both suspended after being cited for marijuana possession earlier in the week.

With 8:37 to go in the second quarter, Tennessee quarterback Jarrett Guarantano lined up under center, and handed the football to freshman Ty Chandler, who scored on a one-yard touchdown run, giving Tennessee a 14-13 lead. Church bells rang from Johnson City to Jackson. Fathers hugged sons. Mothers embraced daughters. A street on the UT campus was named after Ty Chandler. Students stormed the Neyland Stadium gates and tore down the goalposts. (Editor's note: This is sarcasm. But it was Tennessee's first offensive touchdown in more than 15 quarters.)

With under a minute to go, Kentucky was only down five points, and they were driving. Stephen Johnson threw into the end zone. C.J. Conrad got a hand on the pass, but that was all. It was tipped right to Tennessee safety Nigel Warrior, but he couldn't make the interception. If Warrior secures the football, the game is over and the Vols win. They were excruciatingly close to a victory, only to see it slip from their grasp. Instead, on the next play,

Johnson ran it in from 11 yards out, giving Kentucky the lead with 33 seconds to go.

The Vols would get one more chance. With two seconds left they lined up at their own 49. Jarrett Guarantano threw a Hail Mary. As in 2016 at Georgia, a receiver made the catch. Unfortunately for the Vols, it was Jeff George with the grab at the six-yard line, not Jauan Jennings in the end zone. George was brought down three yards from victory.

Tennessee was the better team on this night. They dominated the time of possession by nearly seventeen minutes. They forced four turnovers yet didn't cough up the football once. The Vols had more first downs (27 to 17) and yards (445 to 371). But those numbers meant nothing.

Kentucky 29, Tennessee 26.

The Vols were in disarray. They were now 3-5, and winless in SEC action. After the game, Butch Jones said that he believed he still had the support of John Currie and the UT administration. He believed a few other things as well. "I believe in our kids. I believe in our program," Jones said. "I believe in what we're recruiting and it's one of those years and the only way I know is to keep working and driving. I will tell you this, there's nobody who takes more ownership in this football program than Butch Jones. I can assure you that because I take it personal."

The conventional wisdom amongst media and fans was that this has to be the last straw for Jones. Losing to Kentucky for only the second time in thirty-three years was the ultimate sign that the program was in a freefall. "Everybody assumed the announcement would surely come quickly," said Fox Sports Knoxville's Russell Smith. "I remember waiting around the house all day completely convinced we'd hear official news from UT at any moment."

But it didn't happen. "The Butch Jones Show" aired that Sunday morning as usual. And while fans refreshed Twitter with great ferocity, there was no news to report. Butch Jones had survived another week, and was now preparing for Southern Miss. In the days that followed the Kentucky loss, something that had occurred in Lexington cast a shadow over the Tennessee football program.

Beth and Bryan Kendrick had made the trip to Commonwealth Stadium to watch their son Brett play against UK, as they had done for every game in which he dressed over the past five years. This was Brett's final season playing college football, so there weren't many of his games left for the Kendrick family to experience. As always, Beth brought her small binoculars, which fit easily in her clear bag. She's learned a lot about the offensive line in more than a decade watching Brett play... and didn't like what she was seeing.

"In the third quarter we noticed he wasn't himself. He wasn't playing the way he normally played. We wondered, 'What's wrong with Brett?'" Originally, the Kendricks thought that Brett had been poked in the eye since he kept grabbing at his facemask. "You know how the offense huddles on sideline and position coaches talk to them? Brett goes down to his knees on the sideline," remembers Beth Kendrick. "We saw Jashon Robertson, who was playing guard, take some snaps. I thought they were going to move Coleman Thomas to tackle and take Brett out. But Brett goes back in, and it kept getting worse and worse. Only in the last 22 seconds did they take him out, and they only took him out because he threw up."

After the game, the Kendricks were waiting outside the locker room for Brett. Before he came out, UT's trainers told them they believed Brett had suffered a concussion. "[Offensive line coach] Walt Wells comes out," remembers Beth Kendrick. "He never spoke to us after a game. So, this wasn't like Wells. He spent 10-15 minutes telling us what a great kid and what a tough kid Brett was. Wells said, 'Brett played well, we think he has a concussion, but I thought he had a stomachache and thought he wanted to play.' I'm not angry. I'm thinking he is taking care of my son."

Beth says that she wasn't prepared for what happened a few minutes later. "One of his roommates came out and said, 'Mrs. Kendrick, I need to warn you that Brett is messed up. Don't ask him any questions. He doesn't remember anything. He kept asking me while walking off the field who won the game and what was the score. The trainer took his cleats off. Brett thought a Kentucky guy stole his cleats.'"

"Brett comes out with the trainer guiding him. I tell Brett that I love him. My son was out of it. Brett tries to walk other the way. The trainer leads him over and puts him on the bus with the doctor. We drove back to the hotel and I cried for three hours."

Beth Kendrick maintains that Walt Wells did not have her son's well-being at the top of his priorities. "One player told me that Walt said to stay ready because 'BK' could go down at any moment," she says. "And that was in the third quarter. Another player said Walt told him not to let Brett check himself out because he had to have him in the game, and to make sure Brett knew who to block."

Brett Kendrick was a fifth-year senior, and a leader on that offense so the blocking scheme should not have been a concern. "When Brett came off the field, he would go to the end of the bench and gag, then would sit with a towel over his head," says Beth Kendrick. "I don't know how Wells claimed he didn't know [that Brett was concussed]. It's laughable. There is no doubt in my mind they risked his life. I'm angry about Walt Wells. I'm still dealing with anger issues about Wells."

Beth Kendrick is not a fan of Butch Jones, but she doesn't place blame on him for this incident. "I have no reason to believe he knew. I have no knowledge that he was aware. There are a lot of things I don't like about Butch, but not that. I do believe that Butch told people we were accusing him."

In a statement released by the University of Tennessee a few days after the Kentucky game, athletics director John Currie said the following: "The health and safety of our student-athletes is our number one responsibility. Our sports medicine staff and team medical personnel have full autonomy and unquestioned authority during all team activities, including the ability to remove a player from competition and 'return to play' decisions. At all football games, the Southeastern Conference has a trained independent medical observer present who also has full authority to stop play and remove a student-athlete from competition for assessment and/or treatment."

"We have a constant and consistently communicated expectation that all coaches, staff and student-athletes remain attentive to ensure that any potential injuries are appropriately addressed-with full intentions that student-athlete safety is never compromised."

Butch Jones was asked about the Kendrick situation during the weekly SEC teleconference. "John Currie issued a statement earlier today," Jones said. "I'll tell you this. We would never, ever knowingly put a student-athlete in harm's way. Our medical staff has full authority in removing players from competition, but also in the 'return to play' decisions. I have absolutely no say in these decisions. On top of that, the SEC has done a great job placing an independent medical observer in the press box at all games."

In the days that followed, Bryan Kendrick met with UT's trainers (who the Kendricks say took very good care of Brett), Jones and Currie. "Butch told Bryan that he would never have knowingly played Brett if he had a concussion," says Beth. "Now this next part is laughable. Butch said that Brett was one of his twenty most favorite players he ever coached. I would love to see who he didn't like. He was blowing smoke."

An internal investigation took place and the Kendricks say that they hired lawyers to see the results, and also signed a non-disclosure agreement. Everything Beth has talked about for this book, she says was either first-hand knowledge or was told to her by Brett's teammates.

Concussions are a frightening reality in a fast and physical sport like football and changes were made by the time the Vols played their next game against Southern Miss. "Every time the offense came off the field, the trainers had to look each of the linemen in the eye and ask, 'Are you ok?'" said Beth Kendrick. "Coach Wells was not allowed to approach the linemen until this had been done."

I reached out to Walt Wells in an effort to ask for a response to Beth Kendrick's comments. He declined to be interviewed for this book.

The season felt like it had gone on for a year, even though Tennessee still had four games left to play. If adversity builds character, the 2017 Tennessee Volunteers were going to be the most mature football team in the nation. That same week, Antone

Davis resigned as Vol For Life Coordinator. The well-liked Davis cited "constant intimidation, bullying and mental abuse" by Butch Jones. An actual football game couldn't come fast enough for Tennessee. SEC Network's Tom Hart would be on the mic for the Southern Miss game on November 4. "Our television crew had meetings with the coaching staff as usual Friday morning," says Hart. "Butch has always been forthcoming and accommodating. I cannot stress enough how much that is appreciated. Jordan Rodgers, Cole Cubelic and I were invited back for practice that afternoon."

What the SEC Network crew would see first-hand was a coach that knew his fate. This was the end of days. "If there was a typical Butch Jones practice, it was high energy," Hart says. "Jones could be heard on every practice field, as he was often wearing a microphone. If he wasn't barking at players and rushing between position groups, he was instructing coaches to work one-on-one with specific players off to the side. This day was different. The mood was melancholy. It began to rain. The energy level was low."

An announced crowd of 95,551 watched the Vols beat Southern Miss 24-10 as John Kelly returned from suspension and scored two touchdowns. This game is perhaps best remembered for the burning of the redshirts of quarterback Will McBride and offensive lineman Riley Locklear because of injuries. On the offensive line alone, the Vols started their sixth different combination with Kendrick, Drew Richmond and Marcus Tatum all sidelined. Tennessee played that game with only six scholarship offensive linemen available. Redshirt freshmen Devonte Brooks and Ryan Johnson got their first career starts. The off-season changes to the strength and conditioning program did little to stop the rash of injuries suffered by the Tennessee Volunteers.

If Butch Jones wasn't fired after losses to Georgia or South Carolina or Alabama or Kentucky, he wasn't going to be canned after a win over Southern Miss. He and his coaching staff began preparations for a suddenly rejuvenated Missouri team. With all the uncertainty surrounding Jones, the recruiting Class of 2018 was falling part. 4-star running back Brendon Harris reopened his commitment, as did 4-star all-purpose back Lyn-J Dixon. Those were just a couple of the guys that were going to make up what was potentially a top ten class nationally.

The biggest shockwave came on November 7, when Cade Mays announced that he was decommitting. Mays was a 5-star offensive lineman from nearby Knoxville Catholic High School. His father and uncle both played at Tennessee. Mays had been committed to Butch Jones and the Vols since the summer of 2015. With each day that Jones remained the head coach, Tennessee's recruiting efforts were taking a hit.

As for the Mizzou game, Will McBride's redshirt wasn't pulled for no good reason. Guarantano dressed but never played against Missouri, giving McBride his first career start. For the third time in the Butch Jones era, the Vols would start three different quarterbacks in a single season. Josh Dobbs's ability to stay upright for 31 consecutive starts looked more and more impressive.

McBride wasn't half bad against the Tigers, throwing for 139 yards and a touchdown, and completing 16 of 32 passes. He also led the team in rushing with 63 yards. But the patchwork offensive line did him few favors. McBride was sacked five times and hit many more. Brady Hoke's defensive line never got better in 2017. Against Mizzou they allowed 433 yards on the ground. Drew Lock threw four touchdown passes as Missouri beat Tennessee 50-17.

After the game, Jones wouldn't talk about his job status. "It's about these seniors, it's about these players," Jones said. "It ain't about the coach, it ain't about nothing else." Tennessee had two games left, both at Neyland Stadium. They'd need to beat LSU and Vanderbilt to make it to a bowl game for the fourth straight season.

Butch Jones wouldn't be around to lead the Vols in those contests. On Sunday, November 12, Tennessee athletics director John Currie announced that Butch Jones had been relieved of his coaching duties. "We will begin an exhaustive search to identify a coach of the highest integrity and vision to propel Tennessee to championships," said Currie during a press conference that evening. "This is an extraordinary and special place with unique opportunities and a tradition of excellence. This coaching search will be my sole focus, and I will be in regular contact with

Chancellor Davenport. I want to emphasize my commitment to hiring the best coach for the University of Tennessee."

Jones was fired without cause, and will be paid a total of $8.25 million through the year 2021 (that buyout life, y'all). In March 2018, Butch Jones was hired by Alabama's Nick Saban (yes, truth truly is stranger than fiction). In five head-to-head meetings, Saban's Crimson Tide outscored Jones's Volunteers 192-61, all Alabama wins. Butch Jones receives a yearly salary of $35,000. "He's an intern, an analyst, I guess we could have several names for it," Saban said. "He can't coach on the field. He can work with us off the field." Saban allows assistants to speak to the media about as often as a lunar eclipse, so it was not a surprise when I didn't get a

Butch's Coke display was still prominent at the Farragut Kroger in late 2017.

response from Alabama's Sports Information Department to my request to speak with Jones for this book.

Butch Jones went 34-27 at Tennessee, with a couple of nine-win seasons and three straight bowl game victories. Up to that point, nine of his players were drafted into the NFL. But Jones was never able to get his teams to take that next important step. "I'm a trusting person and I bought in. I was a sheep," says Beth Kendrick. "I thought Butch would be great for the program. I'll give him credit. He is a good salesman. That is his skill. He should not be coaching young men. He should be a salesman."

Considering the recruiting, the facilities, and the fact that the SEC East was as down as it had ever been since divisional play began in 1992, why didn't it work out for Butch Jones at

Tennessee? That's a question that has a lot of different answers. "I'm not sure, but I felt like it was time to move on," says former Tennessee defensive back Malik Foreman. "He's a great recruiter and motivator but when it comes to coaching football and winning at a high level, I feel like it was too big for him sometimes. And to win those close games is what it takes to stay a head football coach at the University of Tennessee and other major universities."

"There was a lot of ego and a power structure that didn't work," says former Tennessee defensive back Derrick Furlow Jr. "From a player's perspective, you can tell from the buy in. Knowing what I know, knowing the talent we had, and with NFL guys like Alvin Kamara... overall that locker room didn't buy in. Who was making the guys work? Who was leading those guys? Some years results showed but we plateaued... you had all the great sayings, but no actions."

"I thought 2016 was their best shot and they got decimated by injury," says Mark Elder, an assistant under Jones for nine years. "Butch needed that year for Atlanta because I could have told you 2017 was gonna be a problem. You lost a bunch of players at the same time. He needed to get to Atlanta to have a forgiveness card. It just was not the year that quite gave him the pass. Everyone thought that the writing was on the wall."

"One thing I heard from guys around him before he got to Knoxville was that he coached different. I also think some of the hires on his staff didn't prove to be great fits," says The Athletic.com's Bruce Feldman. "To me the analogy fits... it was like quicksand. The more he struggled the deeper the hole got. For a variety of reasons, that was a tight program. They played tight. I think it became a toxic situation after a while."

No matter the reasons, Butch Jones was out.

It was officially coaching search time in Tennessee.

15

THE GREG SCHIANO FIASCO

DEFENSIVE LINE COACH BRADY HOKE TOOK OVER for Butch Jones on an interim basis and goes down in the history books as the twenty-fifth head coach at Tennessee. While he had a lot of previous head coaching experience, he was not a realistic candidate to replace Jones. The Vols still had flickering bowl game hopes and were looking for their first conference win of the year. That said, the attention of Tennessee fans was not on the final two games of the regular season, but on the coaching search. Tennessee's football alums were interested as well. Late in the evening of Wednesday, November 15, former Vols quarterback Josh Dobbs exchanged texts with Tennessee athletics director John Currie.

Dobbs: "Good evening Mr. Currie. Sooo are the rumors true?
Currie: "Which rumors?
Dobbs: "A lot of buzz around Coach Gruden. Wasnt sure if it was legit or heresay (sic)."
Currie: "Geez even you?
Dobbs: "Hahaha whats that supposed to mean?!"
Currie never responded.

(An open records request was made by multiple media outlets to the University of Tennessee in the weeks after the firing of Butch Jones. The text messages/direct messages/emails with Tennessee representatives cited in this book come from those documents, which were placed in a publicly accessible Dropbox link.)

On Thursday, November 16, Gridiron Now's John Brice and GoVols247's Grant Ramey reported that John Currie and Tennessee powerbrokers were in Tampa the night before, meeting with Jon Gruden. "Multiple attorneys, financial experts, doctors, healthcare leaders and various boosters told some other reporters and me about UT talking with Gruden," said Brice. WNML's Jimmy Hyams reported that those meetings with Gruden did not take place.

Fans took sides on the reporters they believed. Others did their own investigating. The FlightAware website is very popular with college football fans during a coaching search as they can (possibly) track planes connected to their respective schools. Vols fans have memorized the tail numbers for university and prominent booster planes. One such plane was supposedly heading to Knoxville that same day, which allowed Tennessee fans to make the Gruden leap. Was John Currie bringing Jon Gruden home?

"My boss at FanRun Radio, Nate Hodges, jokingly said that one of us should stake it out, and I am always down to try to take nothing and turn it into something," said Fox Sports Radio's Jon Reed. "I figured, at the very least, it'll be funny to say that I did it. People will find it funny that we are out there. And IF something actually happened, it would be really good for business."

A live periscope video of Reed's stakeout in the TAC Air parking lot received over 50,000 views. "I expected to get a couple of thousand views," Reed says. "I thought people would check in for a little bit and then decide to come back when the plane was supposed to land. Look, I think I'm entertaining, but I NEVER thought that people would sit there with me for two hours as absolutely nothing was happening."

Flight plans can be blocked from the public. Fake flight plans can be submitted as well. If the people in charge of a plane don't want you to know where a plane is coming from/going to, you won't know. There would be no moment when John Currie walked off a plane with Jon Gruden. But the fact that tens of thousands broke up their afternoon to watch a live feed from a parked car in a small lot proved that the "Jon Gruden thing" wasn't the desire of an isolated group of Vols fans. A lot of people cared about this story, as unrealistic as it might have been.

"More people kept coming. It was a wildfire," said Reed. "News outlets in Dallas picked it up. Radio stations in Nashville were talking about it. The comments kept pouring in of people talking about how awesome it was and for me to stay there until we had our answer. I knew then that what we were doing was working. I knew people were hungry for any type of 'Grumor.' I didn't know they were starving for 'Grumors' to the point that they would sit with me doing nothing as we waited for a plane that would 99.9% likely not have Jon Gruden on it."

"The 0.1% is a hell of a drug."

The coaching search was now at a fever pitch. The Vols would host LSU on November 18 and that meant the return of former Tennessee assistant coach Ed Orgeron. Last time Orgeron was in Knoxville, he was calling early enrollees and telling them not to go to class. Now, nearly eight years later, he was back as the head coach at LSU. "I have a lot of respect for Ed Orgeron as a coach and how he has done things," Hoke said. "He has a very good football team. He has a very athletic team... He has done a good job bringing that team together."

Before the game there were new "Grumors." And these seemed to have some legs. The 1997 SEC championship team was being honored on its twentieth anniversary. Peyton Manning was back in town, as were many others from that squad. That afternoon, there was a rumor that Manning and Gruden were eating at Calhoun's on the River, the popular establishment that sits an easy walk from Neyland Stadium. Calhoun's is a sponsor of Tennessee athletics. They host the weekly "Vol Calls" show. This is a business with a direct connection to UT. This isn't your cousin Dave saying he saw Gruden driving down I-40 near Dandridge in an orange colored Corvette.

When Calhoun's posted that yes, Gruden was eating there, Tennessee fans went ballistic on Facebook, Twitter, reddit... pick a social media channel and you'd find a Tennessee fan speculating about who Gruden was going to hire as his defensive coordinator for the Vols in 2018. Well, about that. Jon Gruden was 2,500 miles away at the time, preparing for the Falcons/Seahawks Monday Night Football game in Seattle.

"We'd like to take a moment to clear things up and apologize," started a tweet from the Calhoun's account. "Tonight we received word from our management team that Jon Gruden was dining at our restaurant with Peyton Manning. We got excited. We posted something about it. Afterwards, a staff member notified us that they weren't so sure it was him. This is all we know at this moment. We apologize for the misunderstanding."

"Grumors," man. "Grumors..."

LSU fans who made the trip taunted Tennessee players during warmups with chants of "oh and six" and "champs of life." Perhaps that angered the football gods. The weather was dreadful in Knoxville. High winds caused the goalposts in the south end zone to lean to the side before the game (they were uprighted prior to kickoff). Throughout the night orange and white pompon remnants littered the Neyland Stadium turf and circled the air above the playing field. A halftime concert by Knoxville's Chris Blue, winner of NBC's "The Voice" competition, took place in what felt like a monsoon. A bank of lights went out right before the third quarter began, and for some reason there was no delay.

Anyone who wanted Hoke to replace Jones surely changed their minds after watching this game. Marquez Callaway fumbled two punts in the red zone, leading to ten LSU points. He should have been instructed to call for a fair catch in those terrible conditions. In the second quarter, Hoke called timeout a second before a 45-yard field goal attempt on fourth and 3. Incredibly, Aaron Medley made the kick after a whistle blew the play dead. You'd figure that since Hoke called time out, they had decided to go for it. Or not. They kicked the field goal anyway, and this time Medley missed by a mile. Late in the third quarter Hoke went for it on fourth and 1 from his own 21-yard line. Guarantano was stuffed at the line, and LSU scored a touchdown two plays later to put the game out of reach. Being aggressive is one thing, being reckless is another.

LSU 30, Tennessee 10.

Tennessee's injury bug reached yet another low point. They had less than 60 scholarship players suit up. There was a wide receiver named Richard Mize Jr. who saw playing time. Someone named Malik Elion caught a pass while wearing an orange jersey. Where have you gone, Carl Pickens... Vol Nation turns its lonely eyes to you...

The Vols were now 4-7. A bowl game was off the table. A winning season was no longer a possibility. The only thing for Tennessee left to play for was to avoid an eighth loss. In the history of college football, Ohio State and Tennessee were the only programs never to lose eight games in a single season. Vanderbilt wanted nothing more than to do the honors. In the leadup to the game, Tennessee receiver Jauan Jennings, who hadn't played since the first half of the season opener due to a dislocated wrist, tried to convince the lame duck Vols coaching staff to let him play against Vanderbilt. Hoke said no, and Jennings didn't like that decision.

Jennings proceeded to post a video on social media in which he ripped the guys who wouldn't give him the ok to suit up. The post would eventually be deleted, but in the short time it was merely available?

"... You got some lyin-ass coaches, some lyin' ass, fake ass, snake ass coaches... that's what the fuck is wrong with Tennessee..."

"... Fuck the coaching staff right now. I don't give a fuck."

There was a lot more to that expletive laden rant but yeah, he wasn't happy. Neither was Hoke. In a statement released by the University of Tennessee, Hoke said the following: "In consultation with vice chancellor/director of athletics John Currie, I have made the decision to dismiss Jauan from our program. Representing the University of Tennessee football program is a privilege."

The majority of Vols fans sided with Jennings. They were frustrated with how the season had gone as well and believed that a decision on Jennings should have been left to the next coach, not someone that would only be on the sidelines for a few more days. But Currie would be there and didn't want Jennings around after those Instagram comments.

I walked into Neyland Stadium on Saturday, November 25, knowing that the Vanderbilt/Tennessee matchup wasn't going to be a game that would take up much room in the memory bank. The coaching search was my main football interest. Two weeks earlier, when John Currie announced that Butch Jones had been fired, he told reporters that he would not comment on the coaching search until he made a hire. Currie was staying true to his word. He followed the men's basketball team to The Bahamas for the "Battle 4 Atlantis" tournament, but otherwise kept out of sight.

Currie said that he was not using a search firm. After all the money spent over the years on search firms, which assisted in the hiring of guys like Donnie Tyndall, this was seen by some as a fiscally responsible move. This also led to speculation that Currie already had a pretty good idea about who he was going to hire. John Currie was not in attendance at Neyland Stadium for the final game of the 2017 season.

He didn't miss much. An announced crowd of 83,117 walked through the turnstiles, but that was generous. This was two days after Thanksgiving. The students were home on break and there were sales still going on at Belk's. I've maintained that the Tennessee fan base is among the best in the nation. Heck, over 85,000 showed up the week before to watch the Vols get their feet stomped during a hurricane! But for the Vandy game, 60,000 is probably a better estimate in terms of backsides in the seats. For the second straight year Kyle Shurmur looked like the second coming of Joe Montana against Tennessee, throwing for 283 yards and four touchdowns in a 42-24 romp. Vanderbilt, a team with one win in 29 meetings from 1983-2011 versus the Vols, had now won four out of six since 2012, including two in a row. "We own the state for another 364 days," said Vanderbilt linebacker Oren Burks.

At 4-8, "Team 121" will go down as the worst in Tennessee history. "We're not going to allow this to happen again," said Tennessee offensive lineman Trey Smith. He had a tremendous freshman season and was one of the few bright spots for the Vols. "We're going to be great leaders in the locker room, we're going to have a lot of control and we're going to come back better. I promise that."

But who would be his coach in 2018? Tennessee should have moved on from Jones much earlier than November 12, but there were plenty of very good coaches that they could call. Former Oregon coach Chip Kelly, Mississippi State coach Dan Mullen, and Central Florida's Scott Frost were perhaps the biggest names out there that seemed ready for a new opportunity.

Story time? Story time. A few weeks earlier I went on Fox Sports Knoxville's "Voluntary Reaction." I can't remember after which loss, but Vols fans were once again venting for hours. Anyway, co-hosts Russell Smith and Jon Reed were talking about the possibility of Chip Kelly coming to Tennessee. Kelly had some NCAA issues and wasn't the most personable guy to the media or fans. But he was a football genius, with an exciting style of offense that was ahead of its time. Russell asked me if Tennessee was going to hire Chip Kelly and I said no, that wasn't going to happen. Anyone who had been around the program knew that Kelly and Tennessee weren't a realistic possibility. The next caller desperately wanted Chip Kelly to go to Tennessee.

Russell: "Mark Nagi says we aren't getting Chip Kelly."

Caller: "Fuck that guy."

I laughed.

Florida had an opening. They fired Jim McElwain two weeks before the Vols moved on from Butch Jones. McElwain was booted after making allegations that his family received death threats, allegations that were never proven. If he had been fired without cause, UF could have owed him $13 million. Instead, the two sides quickly negotiated a reduced cost at $7.5 million. (That buyout life, y'all.) Kelly was offered the Florida job, but he didn't want to go to the SEC. His recruiting base was out west. UCLA wanted Kelly, so they fired Jim Mora and a few days later hired Kelly. It was a decisive move. There was no wavering. UCLA knew who they wanted to hire, and they got him.

About an hour before Tennessee and Vanderbilt kicked off, I ran into a long-time friend on the sideline. I knew my buddy was close with some people around the Vols program and asked what he was hearing. While neither one of us believed Jon Gruden was ever taking the Tennessee job, neither Gruden nor Tennessee ever spoke out and said that this wouldn't happen.

And that was the biggest problem. Much like Dave Hart let the Grumors drag on in 2012, John Currie was repeating the same mistake to an even greater extent in 2017. Vols fans kept that hope alive for months, because they were never told by their leaders to stop dreaming. I asked my friend what other names he was hearing. My friend looked at me and said one word.

"Schiano."

Greg Schiano was born on June 1, 1966. He grew up in Wyckoff, New Jersey, the northeastern corner of the Garden State. This is about an hour's drive from New York City. Schiano was a standout linebacker at Bucknell University. When he finished playing football, Schiano worked his way up the coaching ranks. Starting as an assistant coach at his alma mater (Ramapo High School), he worked as a grad assistant or defensive coach at Rutgers, Penn State, the NFL's Chicago Bears, and back to college at Miami.

On December 1, 2000, he got his first head coaching job, at the wasteland known as Rutgers football. There was little to no fan base and facilities were a joke by major college football standards. But he was given the time he needed to build the Scarlet Knights into a respectable Big East program. In 2006, Rutgers upset third-ranked Louisville on a nationally televised Thursday night game on ESPN. They'd finish the season ranked twelfth in the nation.

In 11 seasons at Rutgers, Schiano went 68-67, including a 56-33 mark in his final seven years. They finished tied for second in the Big East in 2006 and 2008 and won five bowl games. Schiano did have the good fortune of competing in a Big East without Miami and Virginia Tech during most of his tenure. Those were the best football teams in the conference, and they departed for the ACC after the 2003 season. Schiano flirted with other schools during his time, including Michigan and Miami. In 2010, he reportedly turned down the chance to talk with Tennessee when their job was open after Lane Kiffin's resignation. But it took an NFL opening to woo him away from his home state. On January 26, 2012, the same day his former boss and mentor Joe Paterno was buried, and six days before National Signing Day, Schiano left Rutgers for the NFL's Tampa Bay Buccaneers. "I can tell you when all those other opportunities came up, it didn't feel right," Schiano told reporters the next day. "You know I'm a man of prayer. I prayed about it. I thought about it. I did everything I could within myself and this felt right."

Schiano was back in the NFL, working with some of the same people he didn't have much use for when he was at Rutgers. Paterno was well known for treating NFL scouts with disdain when they'd visit Penn State. Schiano reportedly acted in a similar fashion. "At Rutgers, it was a really unpleasant day," an NFL team executive told Yahoo! Sports Mike Silver in 2012. "You were made to feel like an outsider, like you weren't welcome. And everyone was scared to talk to you." Multiple NFL reps told Silver that Schiano would make them stay far away from the practice field.

When college players make it to the NFL that should be a positive reflection on their college coaches. At least one Rutgers player gives Schiano little credit for his achievements. Former San Francisco 49ers offensive lineman Anthony Davis played for Schiano from 2007-2009 at Rutgers. Davis played part of six seasons in the pros. In 2013, he tweeted, "I'll never let a muhfucka break me. Ask Schiano."

When asked to compare the difference between playing for Kyle Flood (his OL coach at Rutgers) and Greg Schiano, Davis said, "[Flood] wouldn't enable me. But at the same time he wasn't an [expletive]."

Schiano's two seasons as the Bucs head coach were a disaster. Schiano lost big, going a combined 11-21. He had his players diving at quarterbacks who were trying to take a knee in the victory formation. None other than Peyton Manning reportedly swore at

Schiano for this move. The Bucs did this multiple times, including to Peyton's younger brother Eli. New York Giants coach Tom Coughlin, a legendary NFL coach with two Super Bowl titles on his resume, cussed out the NFL rookie coach after the game.

As if all that weren't bad enough, at least three Buccaneers players got MRSA, a serious bacterial infection while Schiano was coach. He didn't seem to be overly concerned. On one occasion he said, "Medicine, as much as we'd like it to be an exact science, is not." Another time he simply cut an interview short when asked about the topic. Some players compared life under Schiano like "being in Cuba" due to his authoritarian ways.

"I felt like Schiano was one of the worst coaches I ever covered. He was absolutely awful," says Bleacher Report NFL National Lead Writer Mike Freeman. "One of the keys to a great coach is adapting. I have never seen a locker room turn so quickly against a coach. The players hated him."

This was never more evident than with the Josh Freeman situation. The relationship between Schiano and his quarterback was already beyond repair at the beginning of Schiano's second and final season in Tampa. Before the opening game, some players accused Schiano of rigging the captaincy vote, allowing him to rip the "C" from Josh Freeman's jersey. On October 1, ESPN reported that Freeman was a stage one participant in the league's substance abuse program. Freeman responded, saying that the medicine was for his ADHD, and that he was being tested voluntarily after making a mistake and taking Ritalin instead of Adderall. In a statement, Josh Freeman said, "Let me be very clear. I have NEVER tested positive for any illegal drugs or related substances. Further, I have agreed to take, and have PASSED 46 NFL-regulated drug tests over the last year and a half... Unfortunately, it appears that some people who may have noticed the testing at my workplace have made hurtful and incorrect assumptions and chosen to disseminate inaccurate and very disturbing information."

"What he's alleged to have done to Josh Freeman was a fucking disgrace," Mike Freeman told me (Josh and Mike are not related). "The NFLPA believed Schiano was the leak and anyone with half a brain believes it as well despite his denials."

On October 2, Schiano was asked if he was the source of the leak. "Absolutely not," he said. "I know what I've done, and I'm 100% comfortable with my behavior. 100%."

On October 3, Josh Freeman was cut by the Bucs.

Schiano was a disciplinarian known to have a scorching temper. The modern-day NFL is not a good fit for most coaches with that description. Nick Saban is arguably the greatest college football coach of all time. Heading into the 2018 season, Saban had six national championships on his resume, and an overall head coaching record of 218-62-1. In his two seasons as the head coach of the Miami Dolphins, he was only 15-17. But in college, head coaches are the stars. They make the big money while student-athletes must make sure they do what they are told to keep their scholarships. In the pros, coaches make less money than some of the adults they are leading. The motivational tools used in the college game most often don't work in the pros. Maybe that why only three coaches (Jimmy Johnson, Barry Switzer, Pete Carroll) have ever won both a national championship and a Super Bowl.

A new term joined football's lexicon. "Schiano Man." There is an entire "Schiano Man" listing on reddit, and it is not meant to be complimentary. There is no real definition for the "Schiano Man," but as U.S. Supreme Court Justice Potter Stewart said in a 1964 case about obscenity, "I know it when I see it."

In the days to come, Schiano would be portrayed by many in the media in a very positive light, while lessening the impact of his flaws. They point out how he has treated Eric LeGrand, his former player at Rutgers who was paralyzed during a game in 2010, as proof of the positive person Schiano is. After he was fired by the Bucs, Schiano worked as a volunteer coach at Berkeley Preparatory School in Tampa, where his three sons played. During those two years he also spent time visiting college and pro teams, trying to learn how to do his job better when the next opportunity presented itself. Schiano understood that his name wasn't held in the highest esteem in many circles. "You know the saying you get the reputation for being an early riser, you can sleep till noon?" Schiano told *Sports Illustrated* in 2014. "Well, it goes the other way too. If you get a reputation for being a jerk, no matter how well you treat the players..."

On December 11, 2015, Schiano was hired by his old friend Urban Meyer to become the defensive coordinator at Ohio State. He was also named associate head coach and safeties coach. "Greg Schiano is an excellent coach," Meyer said. "He is someone I have known for quite some time now and someone who is going to align with our staff extremely well. I think he will be outstanding as a coach and mentor in our program and I am pleased to have him on our staff."

"Of all the guys Urban hired, and we covered all of them, I don't remember Urban being as excited about any coach as he was about Greg Schiano," says Big Ten Network anchor Rick Pizzo.

Seven months after his hiring at Ohio State, and a few weeks before the 2016 season began, Schiano's name was mentioned in connection with one of the most disturbing scandals in American sports history. Schiano was a graduate assistant coach at Penn State in 1990 and served as their defensive backs coach from 1991-1995. The Nittany Lions defensive coordinator at the time was Jerry Sandusky. In 2011, Sandusky was indicted on 52 counts of child molestation which took place over a period of fifteen years. He was convicted on 45 of those counts in 2012, and is serving thirty to sixty years in prison.

In July of 2016, court documents were unsealed in which former Penn State assistant coach Mike McQueary testified that he had been told by another assistant coach (Tom Bradley) that Greg Schiano knew about Sandusky's crimes. According to the testimony, McQueary said that Bradley told him that "Greg [Schiano] had come into his [Bradley's] office white as a ghost and said he just saw Jerry doing something to a boy in the shower."

To those who covered the events at Penn State closely back in 2011-2012, hearing Schiano's name mentioned years later was a surprise. "I spent a combined month of time at State College," Pizzo says. "I was there after the Freeh report came out, there for the NCAA ruling, there when the Joe Paterno statue came down, for the first game with Tom Bradley as the interim coach. I was there for all that. You heard so many names during that time... It doesn't mean there's nothing there, but in every interview and every document, never once did I hear or read anything about Greg Schiano. Not one time."

Schiano has rarely spoken publicly about these allegations. On July 12, 2016, day the story broke, Schiano was firm in his denial. He tweeted, "In response to media reports from earlier today: I never saw any abuse, nor had any reason to suspect any abuse, during my time at Penn State." He was never charged in any crime, and the story didn't stay in the news cycle very long. Conference media days were about to take place and Fall camps would open soon across the country. There were other things to talk about besides a scandal that broke four and a half years ago that everyone wanted to forget.

Schiano had success as the Buckeyes DC right away, helping Ohio State advance to the College Football Playoff in 2016. The following season Ohio State had a major hiccup at Iowa when they gave up 55 points to the Hawkeyes (48 of those points by Schiano's defense), but they rallied and won their division. On the same day that Tennessee lost to Vanderbilt, Ohio State beat rival Michigan. The Buckeyes would begin preparations for Wisconsin in the Big Ten Championship Game. If Ohio State won, they still had a chance to make the College Football Playoff.

As it turned out, that discussion I had with my friend on the Neyland Stadium sideline was spot on. Greg Schiano was absolutely in play for the Tennessee head coaching job. Nationally, his name started to leak a bit. "Earlier in the week, on that Wednesday, I did a story for *Sports Illustrated* saying, 'Here are some intriguing people in this cycle,'" remembers Bruce Feldman. "I reported hearing that Schiano had a shot. Then I heard he was in the mix..."

Gruden, Kelly, Mullen, Frost, Iowa State's Matt Campbell, Purdue's Jeff Brohm, SMU's Chad Morris... those were the guys getting talked about the most locally. Maybe Tennessee alums Tee Martin (Southern Cal offensive coordinator) or Jim Bob Cooter (Detroit Lions offensive coordinator). There were even calls for Lane Kiffin to ride back into town after a successful first season at Florida Atlantic.

No, Greg Schiano was not burning up the Knoxville airwaves. "We mentioned Schiano off and on but it was often when we were running through the list of names and how deep it could go," said WNML's Josh Ward. "We spent very little time talking about Schiano as a serious candidate."

"When Schiano's name got brought up, we pretty much scoffed at it and moved on because we figured there was no way he would actually be involved," says Charlie Burris, co-host of "The Swain Event."

"His name didn't come up once on our show. Nobody wanted him," remembers Brian Rice, co-host of "The Erik Ainge Show" on WNML. "Nobody thought he was a candidate."

On the morning of Sunday, November 26, a posting from CBS Sports Insider Jason La Canfora was getting a lot of attention. La Canfora reported that Tennessee was talking with Jon Gruden, and that they were discussing financials. A deal would be in the $10 million range per year, with another $8 million for assistants. (The Grumors never die... but they should have.) Also that morning, rumors about Tennessee's interest in Schiano started to get more steam from credible news sources. The reaction from Vols fans was one of skepticism. There was no way this was going to occur.

USA Today's Dan Wolken was trying to confirm what he had been hearing about the Tennessee coaching search. Wolken decided to go right to the man making the hire. At 12:23pm, he texted John Currie. "John, are you announcing a coach today? I'm being told pretty strongly that you are"

At 12:33pm, Wolken hadn't heard back from Currie, but tweeted, "Sources: As the last 24 hours have evolved, Greg Schiano has emerged as the focus of Tennessee's search. Vols have also been engaged with Mullen, who has been trying to wait out Florida."

At 12:55pm, Wolken tweeted again. "If Currie can convince Schiano to take the job, it's a home run. Tennessee fans will hate it. I think he is a very good college coach."

Forty minutes after that tweet, and more than an hour since Wolken had originally texted Currie, the Tennessee AD finally responded to Wolken's inquiry about a coach hire at 1:35pm.

"Anonymous yes," Currie texted. Wolken immediately texted back, "Congrats," following up with "And I assume it's Schiano." At 1:39pm, Currie replied, "Hopeso." Wolken texted back a few seconds later. "Great hire, man. Seriously." Currie texted back: "Gonna need some help on the Pr. Our people are wacko"

That afternoon, Big Orange Country was shaken to its core with a single tweet from Wolken. It was posted at 1:40am Eastern time, one minute after Currie told Wolken that it was likely happening. "Tennessee is finalizing the deal with Schiano. Hopes to name him later today, per person with direct knowledge."

After Currie's communications from 2017 were released by the University of Tennessee, many Vols fans took Wolken's follow-up text as a message that Wolken was simply doing Currie's bidding with regards to Schiano. At 1:47pm, Wolken had replied, "I'll help. Not sure they'll listen. LOL. I know he's a very good coach and is about the right stuff."

But when you go through the timeline, you'll see that Wolken wasn't giving Currie cover by saying that Schiano would be a quality hire. He had tweeted similar messages that same day before Currie ever responded to him. In fact, I've gone through Wolken's Twitter postings. Since 2013 he's been consistent on this topic. Wolken likes what Schiano brings to the table as a college football coach. In fact, on October 1, 2017, the day after the Vols got blitzed by Georgia, Wolken tweeted that Schiano might be a good fit at Tennessee.

Vols fans and Dan Wolken have been oil and water since he was working at *The Commercial Appeal* in Memphis. This is back when the Bruce Pearl/John Calipari basketball wars were at their height. Wolken was very critical of Pearl's off the court shenanigans, and Tennessee supporters in turn started to bash Wolken. He remains a Pearl critic to this day. Wolken certainly isn't the only national media member that Vols fans have done battle with on social media, and he won't be the last. But when you examine the Wolken/Schiano/Currie timeline in depth, it's hard to make the leap that Wolken was acting as a Currie patsy.

The conventional wisdom among many Knoxville media members and Tennessee fans was that any talk of Greg Schiano had simply been a smoke screen from John Currie to deflect attention from whatever direction he was truly heading. Schiano had failed miserably in the NFL. He had no SEC experience. He was known in the college football world as a good coach, but also as a hot head who did not handle criticism well. More than a few referred to him as "Butch Jones 2.0" for those reasons.

Schiano also had a link, as loose as it was, to the Sandusky scandal. Considering that only 16 months earlier Tennessee had settled an ugly Title IX lawsuit, hiring someone with even the slightest connection to that sorted time at Penn State should have given Tennessee reason for pause. But none of that was apparently a concern to UT. Greg Schiano was going to be the twenty-sixth head football coach of the Vols.

"[My initial reaction was] Tennessee is making the worst possible decision," says GoVols247's Grant Ramey. "Inexplicable. Surreal. There's no way this is really happening."

"I knew it'd be a PR problem," former Lady Vols sports information department assistant Brian Davis told me. "After having seen these PR nightmares for a decade at Tennessee, you'd willingly attach yourself to someone who brings a potential PR nightmare with him? That goes against all that I've been taught. I'm still stunned they did it."

"Rutgers played in the first college football game in 1869 and between then and 2004 they went to one bowl game," says ESPN's Ryan McGee. "Then Schiano led them to six bowls in seven seasons and laid the groundwork that got them invited into the Big Ten. So, this argument of him not knowing football was always ridiculous. But football wasn't my initial reaction. My first thought was, man, I hope they've prepared a defense for the Penn State thing, because you know someone is going to bring it up."

It had been a decade of mediocrity and emotional pain for Tennessee fans. A decade of beat downs, late game collapses, and empty slogans. It had been a decade of orange dogs, orange pants and Rommel. A decade of mattress burning, five-star hearts and champions of life. A decade of bricks being built on a shoddy foundation. A decade of shower discipline and leadership reps. A decade of a trash can and tearful press conferences. A decade of butt-chugging, field goals from the 1, and open weekends in early December.

Through all of that, Tennessee fans stayed true. They bought the Smokey dogs at the game and shook the pompons. They wore the orange and white and played "Rocky Top" at "11." They believed that their loyalty would eventually be rewarded.

And on Sunday night, November 26, Tennessee was going to give them Greg Schiano. Tennessee fans had had enough.

And this time, they weren't going down without a fight.

16

THE UPRISING

TENNESSEE ATHLETICS DIRECTOR JOHN CURRIE had flown to Columbus. On the morning of Sunday, November 26, he was working out the details on a contract with Greg Schiano to become the next head football coach of the Tennessee Volunteers. In fact, shortly after midnight, Currie sent a text to UT Chancellor Dr. Beverly Davenport. "Have a tentative deal in place awaiting word from you/Prez. Will be up early. Call whenever. Thank you."

Currie wanted the final approval he needed from Davenport and UT President Joe DiPietro. Later that morning, she texted an update.

Davenport: "Joe has gone to Mass and will be back in an hour."

Currie: "Good. Schiano is a devout catholic."

Davenport: "Good to hear."

John Currie and Greg Schiano had signed a memorandum of understanding. Schiano was getting a six-year deal worth an average of $4.5 million per season, a significant raise from the $700,000 he made in 2017 as Ohio State's defensive coordinator. This was also more than the $4.11 million that Butch Jones made in his final season in Knoxville. Schiano would have access to a private aircraft for 40 hours per year. He had a $35,000 moving allowance. There would be twenty season tickets in the lower bowl at Neyland Stadium, as well as use of a suite. There would be four parking passes, which are as good as gold on any SEC campus. In all, this was a deal worth $27 million.

Preparations were underway for a Sunday evening press conference in the Peyton Manning Locker Room at Neyland Stadium. Graphics were being developed by UT's athletics department for promotional purposes. With the Big Ten title game taking place the following week, and a berth in the College Football Playoff still a possibility, there's no way Schiano was immediately leaving Ohio State to take on the responsibilities as Tennessee's head coach. (Urban Meyer's esophagus would never be able to take that kind of stress.) Schiano would return to Columbus after the press conference. If the Buckeyes beat Wisconsin and made the playoff, he'd probably be a part-time Tennessee head coach and part-time Ohio State DC for as long as the Buckeyes were playing. Certainly not an ideal situation, but one both UT and OSU would agree upon. It was business as usual. 'Tis the season for coaching hires and Tennessee was about to add their name to the list. Vols players would meet their new coach shortly, and then he'd speak to prominent boosters and the media.

Greg Schiano would wear an orange tie, introduce his wife and four children, and thank John Currie for the trust he put in him to lead the Tennessee Volunteers. Schiano would talk about the time in 2002 when he brought his Rutgers team to Neyland Stadium, and how he dreamed of the day that he could be the coach at a place like Tennessee. Even with a 35-14 loss, he might say that it was one of the most memorable games of his coaching career. He would take some pictures, shake some hands, and meet hundreds of people of whom he'd remember about five names. And then he'd make the short flight back to Columbus.

This is what was going to happen. There was no reason for John Currie to believe otherwise. But while Currie, Schiano and a few representatives were dotting the i's and crossing the t's in Columbus, Big Orange Country was burning to the ground. The disconnect between Tennessee athletics and the UT administration, and the fans who buy the tickets and make the donations and watch the games had built up for years and was now at its peak.

And this wasn't only limited to Knoxville and the surrounding area. The Schiano news was statewide, regionwide and nationwide, and Vols fans were nearly unanimous in their disgust with this potential hire. What transpired over the next few hours was something never seen in college athletics. A fanbase was in open revolt before a hire was official. "I was driving from Columbus (GA) to Auburn the day after Iron Bowl," CBS Sports writer Dennis Dodd remembers. "I wasn't checking my phone. This was playing out in real time." From the moment Dan Wolken tweeted that the Vols were closing in on Schiano, Vols fans began to mobilize in an effort to stop the hire dead in its tracks, even if they didn't realize that's what they were doing. At that moment, all they felt was helplessness and desperation.

Chris Hayes was at Disney World's Animal Kingdom. "I had been on Twitter off and on all day while in lines. I read about Schiano being hired and immediately decided I would not renew my tickets. I'm from Nashville and I grew up going to every home game. It's a part of my family's life. I looked down and saw my son standing there, thinking about him not getting to have those same experiences as me and I lost it. There I was... crying like a baby."

"It was pure anger. I'd stood by this university, crawling through *The Shawshank Redemption* river of crap they'd let run freely for a decade," says Tennessee grad Will Warren. "The day before, I publicly stated on my Twitter account I'd divest myself entirely of Tennessee football if they were to hire Schiano. I knew that he was involved to some extent with the Penn State/Sandusky scandal, but it was more than that for me. His former players hated him. Half the dang team got staph infections. He dove at Peyton's knees! How was a thinner-skinned Butch Jones supposed to be our 'big, expensive, explosive' hire?"

"I remember the time I looked at my phone," says Tennessee fan Joe Fowler. "I was out playing golf. It was a beautiful day. I remember when I saw the news I didn't say anything but my friends immediately asked what was wrong by my facial expression."

"I was at Disney World, the happiest place on Earth," recalls Tennessee fan Brandon Orrick. "When the reports started coming out, I was sick. I couldn't fathom Schiano becoming the head coach. I was physically sick. I was ready to give up Tennessee football until he was gone."

"I am on the praise team at my church and I got the alert on my phone just before services started that Tennessee may be pursuing Schiano," says Tennessee fan Cory White. "After services ended I jumped to #VolTwitter to see what the latest was and it hit me. 'Oh my goodness they are trying to hire this guy.' It was a firestorm."

"The news broke while my 17-year-old and I were eating at Arby's in Jonesborough," UT fan Jason Hensley told me. "I saw the first tweet, then spent the next 2 ½ hours tweeting about wanting no more carpetbaggers at UT."

"I was feeling sick to my stomach on the way home thinking we might hire Schiano," remembers Tennessee grad Jackie Clowers. "I told my wife that I would never root for UT football until he was fired. For me it was both the presence at Penn State as well as the allegations against him when he was with Tampa Bay. I could care less about his win-loss record as I have suffered through Kiffin, Dooley and Butch."

"I actually called my die-hard Tennessee football fan Mom, my football buddy because my husband isn't a football fan, almost in tears," says Tennessee fan Nickie Rhoads. "I told her it looked like UT was actually going to hire Schiano. We discussed [rooting for] Clemson or Miami if we hired Schiano because we are fans of Dabo and Richt."

"After getting out of church that Sunday, my wife thought I was sick," Tennessee fan Paul Orgain says. "We went to the Chinese buffet to eat with my extended family. 'Are you ok?' asked my Mom, Dad, and sister. My wife says, 'It's the Tennessee coach.' My Dad says, 'I understand.'"

"I live in Nashville and my best friend, also a Vols fan, was in town from Brooklyn," says Shea Antunes. "When news broke we went for a walk in the woods to escape phone coverage. We broke multiple sticks and were brainstorming future fall activities to replace Tennessee football."

"I'm a server and when I caught wind of the hire, apparently I was physically distraught to my tables," said Amber Selvage, a Tennessee fan from Athens. "I'm a great, cheery server typically. I had one specific table of eight, mixed with four Alabama fans and four Auburn fans. They noticed something was up and joked that I couldn't be a Tennessee fan. So, there I stood, with Alabama and Auburn fans, agreeing that there was no way we could hire 'that guy.'"

#VolTwitter's @volblood took that a step further. "When the Schiano news started bubbling to the surface, I set all my Dooley/Adidas era UT apparel on fire."

Tennessee football alums were taking notice of this development as well. "I was actually trying to emotionally disconnect," said former Tennessee wide receiver Jayson Swain. "I was raking leaves and was following everything on my phone. Then I just put my phone down and processed it. I had a buddy I played with who was gonna come with Schiano. I heard good things from him, but I also heard a lot of other stuff about Schiano from his time at Tampa Bay. He just didn't fit the profile as a UT coach, especially after previous coach. We need more of a people person. I didn't think he was a good coach anyway. I was trying to wrestle with it all."

The potential hiring of Greg Schiano had a profound effect on some of the people who cover the Vols. "I pulled up the report about Schiano's connection to the Penn State case, read it carefully, and then I talked to my parents," remembers Charlie Burris, co-host of "The Swain Event." "They are long-time UT fans and just happened to be eating lunch at my wife and I's house that day. I told my parents that Tennessee was about to hire Greg Schiano and that I think I'm going to have to quit my job because I cannot in good conscience cover someone who may have ignored the sexual assault of a child. I was pretty distraught. I tweeted, 'Shame on you, John Currie' because I couldn't really think of what else to do."

Back on November 3, Tennessee announced plans for a two-phase, $340 million renovation to Neyland Stadium. "We're excited about the long-term impact of this undertaking on future generations of Tennessee fans," said Currie in a statement. Now, only four weeks after that ambitious financial goal was announced, Tennessee was going to have Greg Schiano be the face of their program. "Folks who flat out love UT pondered their future, said that you can't sell, market or raise funds for this guy," says Gridiron Now's John Brice. "There are so many great people who go above and beyond to give UT athletics a chance to be premier... folks were devastated and angry. No other terms fit."

"Within an hour I had talked on the phone to three people that have given the University seven figures over the last five years," said WNML's Brian Rice. "They were all ready to walk away from donations if Schiano was hired. Each of those people had already contacted the Tennessee Fund to pass that along."

Mike Evans is a 1985 graduate of the University of Tennessee. He has lived in Dallas since graduation. Still, he's been a season ticket holder for twenty years. "In addition to calling Beverly Davenport and texting John Currie, I texted someone in the UT College of Engineering's Development Office. I had been working with them to endow a scholarship and said I'd be reconsidering if the hire went through."

"I just spent hundreds at Alumni Hall," said Chad Loposser, a Tennessee fan who lives in Ohio. "My dogs are named Smokee, Neyland and Knox. I wear UT gear in the heart of Buckeye country. I got engaged the night before Eric Berry played his final home game. I looked at my wife and said as long as Schiano is the coach we won't spend a dime."

Zach Hill is a two-time graduate of the University of Tennessee. He is the co-owner of Remedy Coffee, a business located in downtown Knoxville. "We had been following the coaching search since the middle of season," said Hill. "Schiano was never on our radar, then I realized when it got serious that this is really bad. The thing is, you don't even need to get into the Penn State stuff and the hire makes you even madder."

That afternoon, Hill went onto his business Twitter account, and put out an eight word tweet that got a lot of attention. "Greg Schiano is not allowed in our establishment."

"Honestly that whole tweet was entirely a joke," says Hill. "He is never gonna go to our coffee shop and I'm not turning down a customer. It's illegal. My Mom even called me and said, 'You can't do that.' I think most people realized that the tweet was symbolic.. We were taking a stand against the hire from a morality point of view, from a coaching view, and every way possible. There had been so many disastrous decisions at Tennessee. That's why we sent the tweet."

People with Tennessee ties were transfixed on their phones, their tablets, their laptops... anything with a lifeline to the latest Vols coaching search information. This led to its own set of problems. #VolTwitter's @GTA-Redhead attended UT, is a season ticket holder and the proud Mom of a recent Tennessee grad. "I actually broke my nose because I was reading Twitter," she told me. "I tripped and hit the footboard of my bed. I grabbed some ice and tissues and got right back to #VolTwitter."

"I was driving from Miami to Atlanta with my girlfriend that day," says Tennessee fan Jim Scroggs. "We had been in the car and on the road since 3am. Around Noon or so my brother calls and tells me that a deal is being finalized with Schiano. I-75 isn't a place to be scrolling Twitter on coaching news but that's what I was doing for about fifteen seconds. We stopped at a Chili's to grab lunch in Tifton (GA), which didn't have a strong cell signal, and I'm trying to get on their Wi-Fi to find out more. This whole time, my girlfriend is trying to calm me down and keep things positive."

"I was driving home from Nashville to Dallas, right before the rumors started trickling out," said Tennessee fan Kyle Illgen. "I checked my Twitter feed when we stopped for gas. Obviously, I freaked out and wanted to keep up, but because my girlfriend won't let me check my phone while I drive, I had to figure out reasons to stop. So, I faked having to pee twice and convinced her that a restaurant we stopped at was too dirty to eat at so that we could stop again in the next town. I ate in the car for forty-five minutes because 'I didn't want to eat and drive' and I was

THRILLED to be stuck in traffic at one point just so I could check in on the situation. A scheduled 9 1/2 hour trip took us 11 1/2 hours, mostly because I was trying to keep up with the whole fiasco."

"I was traveling back from my in-laws in Huntsville to Louisville," says Clowers. "My wife drove, and I sat in the backseat with our 20-month-old to feed her lunch on the way home. I just kept refreshing Twitter."

"The Schiano news broke as my wife and I left our house to go to our friend's one-year-old's birthday party," said Tennessee season ticket holder Derek Woolbright. "Before the kid had ever gotten to finish opening his presents, the entire party had turned into all the adults sitting around on their devices. We were all questioning, mourning, and trying to do our part to stop the hire. Luckily, the kid got to eat his cake while being the center of attention prior to the total meltdown of partygoers."

Allie Lynn is a law student at the University of Memphis. She's a Vols fan who had her most difficult final exam in two days. Understandably, she was distracted from studying by the news coming out of Knoxville. "I had the right top corner of my laptop dedicated to Twitter," she says. "Seemed like I was refreshing every 30 seconds. An hour after the news broke I couldn't take it anymore and started calling the athletic director's office. No one answered so I finally talked to the sweetest lady from alumni affairs. We talked for about seven minutes and she told me the phones had been ringing non-stop since the news broke."

"It was the first time I've ever texted an athletics director or member of the athletic staff," said Tennessee fan Cory Varner. "That was the breaking point. I didn't think I would have continued my fandom if that hire happened."

Lynn and Varner weren't alone. The University of Tennessee's athletic department and main switchboard received a barrage of calls throughout the afternoon and evening from angry fans to protest the decision to hire Greg Schiano. In addition, John Currie's cell phone number had been posted to social media. When credible sources like Dan Wolken and Bruce Feldman began posting first about the possibility, and then about the probability of the hiring of Greg Schiano, fans started calling and sending texts to Currie, warning him how they would respond to this move.

"If you hire Schiano I'm out. We're all out. You're killing this program if you do that."

"You can not hire Schiano. This fan base will revolt."

"you do this to this university and community, just resign and never come back."

"Long time season ticket holder. I will not be renewing if you hire Greg Schiano. Listen to your fans."

"I have been a season ticket holder for 20 years. If Greg Schiano is our next coach, I along with THOUSANDS will not spend another dime supporting this program."

There were more than a few fans who believed the Tennessee athletic department was more interested in making money and upgrading facilities than they were about winning. Those communications were a desperate attempt to make someone— anyone—finally listen to them.

Many of the text messages also treated the allegations about Schiano as fact. Again, nothing like this was ever proven in a court of law about Schiano, nor was he ever even questioned by investigators. But those who weren't completely educated on the Sandusky case were expressing their anger in this manner. Many other texts were simply sent to attack John Currie. Some were vicious in nature. Text messages of varying degrees of disapproval continued for hours. They came in by the thousands, and they didn't stop. The emails to Currie had the same themes as well.

"I have set up 2 scholarships at UT (in my will), donate each year to the Tennessee Fund, buy season football tickets and make other donations. I can easily stop it all. ALL."

"You and the Administration just proved to every Vol fan that you do not give a damn about our beloved football program."

Yes, there was a sliver of support mixed in for the hire, but Tennessee fans were telling the leader of Tennessee's athletic department directly that in no uncertain terms, they didn't want Greg Schiano. Many of the messages in approval of Schiano were actually from opposing fan bases. Not long after Wolken's tweets started making the rounds, two local radio shows powered up their bat signals. Tony Basilio's "5th Quarter Fan Reaction" and Fox Sports Knoxville's "Voluntary Reaction" were broadcasting and would do so throughout the afternoon and evening.

"As soon as I saw the level of outrage on Twitter, I knew we had to get on the air ASAP," remembers Fox Sports Knoxville's Russell Smith.

"I was a horrible father that day," admits Dave Denning, who was keeping up with the events in Knoxville from his home in New Orleans. "Spent the whole day saying, 'Yeah, I'll be there in a minute' while refreshing Twitter and listening to Russell Smith and the crew via the app."

Fox Sports Knoxville is located at 1340 WKGN-AM on your radio dial in East Tennessee. That was an NFL Sunday, and the station is contractually obligated to air NFL games that day. The station would broadcast exclusively from their website and app. "It was some of the most raw, visceral radio I've ever done," says Smith. "People were absolutely shocked, appalled and devastated."

Janna Abraham is a small business owner who graduated from Tennessee in 2001. Abraham lives in Los Angeles, so she had the unique experience of seeing Lane Kiffin leave her beloved school in the lurch, and then come to her town to coach. As it did with Vols fans across the country, the Schiano news struck a chord with Abraham. She emailed Tennessee's athletics director, then posted the email that afternoon as an article on 247Sports.com.

"An Open Letter to Currie" was read over 2400 times. "I have been an unrelenting ambassador out here on the west coast for my alma mater and for its athletic program, but today, I have to end it," Abraham wrote. "I have to stop supporting you and this program because the forthcoming hiring of Greg Schiano is a toxic, incomprehensible and unforgivable action. Instead of giving back to the community and the state, you are outright damaging it – tainting a beautiful, historical program that many people rely on to make an honest living. From Memphis to Bristol, small businesses and brands have been holding out hope that you would right the ship... Please do not bring Schiano to The Hill. All of us deserve better."

Abraham explained to me what she was feeling at that moment. "The first thing I did was send a text to a national media friend that said, 'It can't be. They will lose this fanbase,'" she says. "What an accurate take, huh? And then as the news grew stronger, I went straight into crisis PR mode. 'Take action' was all that I could think. 'Stop this. We have to stop this,' was the only thing running through my mind. Looking back at those couple of hours, I can honestly say that something in me was saying we could make them take it all back. I knew it was farfetched, but I also know #VolTwitter. I believed if we could harness that power that something amazing could happen and we could force them to change course. *We have to stop this.*"

For a long time, Tennessee fans felt ignored when it came to the direction of their football program. They were split on the Fulmer firing, lost the coach they liked [Kiffin], got a coach they didn't want [Dooley] and had another coach fail to meet expectations [Jones]. There would be no rally of support for Schiano. In fact, if he was indeed coming to Knoxville for a Sunday evening press conference, he was going to be greeted by a campus in turmoil.

At 1:30pm, Davenport texted Currie. "Social media is beyond brutal."

Currie texted back, "I'm working on it."

At 1:57pm, shortly before Russell Smith began broadcasting on the Fox Sports Knoxville website and app, he tweeted the following: "If there's anything inside you that still gives a damn about this University, get your ass down to Neyland and protest Schiano if he's hired tonight. This is bigger than football. We can't allow them to do this to our community."

Smith doesn't back away from what he posted that afternoon. "I took some heat for that, but I'm glad I did it. I stand by it and I'd do it again."

Will Warren, who had graduated from Tennessee in 2015, saw Smith's tweet and felt inclined to act. "I respond and basically say I'm headed to Neyland Stadium and going to drop off any article of Tennessee clothing I can find, because if this hire is real, I don't plan on wearing it again," said Warren. "At some point after this, I call my grandfather, who doesn't use Twitter, to tell him the news. We both get choked up because we know if this goes through, we can't support the program any longer."

If Currie didn't have an understanding of how Tennessee fans were going to react that morning, he definitely understood by that afternoon. The texts, voicemails and emails were piling up, but damage control was underway. At 3:05pm, Currie emailed Executive Associate AD Reid Sigmon a draft addressing the Penn State situation. In part it read, "We thoroughly vetted Greg Schiano's character with former colleagues, players, and university personnel at multiple institutions including The Ohio State University."

At 3:39pm, Currie proofread an email from Sigmon. It was a draft that was going to go out to VFL's. "Listening to many of you, I focused on finding a coach with proven experience identifying, recruiting and developing toughness and accountability. We knew that in our next leader we needed head coaching experience, a national recruiter, and a program builder. We believe we have found that."

Another email was being worked on that would be sent to UTAD staff. In both drafts, Currie said that the press conference time should be changed to "later this evening." A minute after emailing Sigmon about the drafts, Currie sent a direct message to Schiano to see if he could make a 7:15pm flight, presumably to Knoxville.

"Be close but I believe yes," Schiano responded at 4:06pm. A direct flight from Knoxville to Columbus takes about an hour. They were probably looking at a 9pm press conference. Currie and Schiano were hoping that the inferno of public opinion would die down by that time. That wasn't going to be the case.

"I woke up to our apartment door slamming open," says Skip Garner, who would graduate from Tennessee a few weeks later. "This was followed by two angry voices that proceeded to walk into my living room. Both of my roommates stood in the doorway holding poster boards and permanent markers. You can imagine my confusion. Before I could say a word, I was told to 'Get up, get dressed, and make a poster. Tennessee is attempting to hire Schiano.' That is likely the fastest shower I have ever taken. We had a coaching hire to stop."

At first, Warren, Garner and their buddies were among only a handful of people who gathered outside Gate 21 at Neyland Stadium. As time went on, the group swelled. Remember, Tennessee students had been home for the Thanksgiving holiday weekend and were getting back to campus throughout the day. Smith's fellow Fox Sports Knoxville host, Jon Reed, who broadcast live via Periscope from TAC Air a couple of weeks earlier was at it again, beaming the campus unrest to the world.

"I knew that fans would be upset. I didn't know HOW upset they would be," Reed says. "I was shocked at how many grown adults of all ages drove by honking and rolling the window down to thank us for what we were doing. My mother took to the streets to join in, and she's a Facebook Vol for Lifer who is always positive!"

Protestors would eventually make their way to the UT football complex. They brought signs that said "#FireCurrie," "Dear God No" and "SchiaNO!" They chanted, "Hell No Schiano" and (you guessed it) "Fire Currie." The protest, which started in daylight with a few people, was at least a couple of hundred strong after sunset. "I had to call family who were visiting from out of town to tell them why I'm 35 minutes late to dinner," Warren said. "They don't watch football. It was a long conversation of telling them I accidentally created a campus protest and I don't even go here anymore."

"The experience was thrilling," Garner remembers. "Every member of the crowd was working for one common goal."

At 6pm, Reed got on a bullhorn, fired up the crowd, and tore up Tennessee t-shirts on the steps in front of the UT football complex. "I was done with Tennessee," Reed says. "Football, basketball, tennis, soccer... whatever you want to say. I no longer needed Tennessee apparel. Shout out to Hulk Hogan and wrestling and whoever brought the pocket knife to the rally for preparing me for the shirt ripping moment. I cut a little piece at the top of each shirt to make sure that I was able to rip them."

The uprising was taking place in four forms simultaneously: direct communication (via text, phone call or email), social media, broadcast and boots on the ground. It was definitely having an impact. Dyron Birdwell is the boys' basketball coach at Siegel High School in Murfreesboro. "We had practice on that Sunday. When I went into practice we were hiring Schiano. My parents, who were season ticket holders for twenty-five years, were dropping them. When I left practice two hours later I had 20 texts, seven missed calls, and [still] no head coach in Knoxville."

The Rock on the UT campus became the symbol of the uprising. This statement, which is not known to be factual, helped put Vols fans in the crosshairs of most of the national media (Courtesy: Louis Fernandez Jr./WBIR-TV)

Multiple media sources, including Saturday Down South's Dan Harralson and Gridiron Now's John Brice tweeted throughout the afternoon that Tennessee representatives and Greg Schiano were growing more and more concerned about the reaction from Tennessee fans. General Neyland had seven "Maxims," which have been recited by the Vols in the locker room before games for decades. Number three was coming to life for the fans.

"If at first the game – or the breaks – go against you, don't let up... put on more steam."

Tennessee politicians were not ignoring the events of the day either. Jeremy Faison is a state representative in East Tennessee. He was the first state politician to comment publicly on the potential hiring of Greg Schiano. "I had constituents calling me all day Sunday afternoon saying, 'Jeremy, you have to get involved,'" Faison told me. "I never took it seriously until I saw that a tweet that it wasn't a rumor and that we were fixing to hire this guy. I thought surely, we are not this stupid. So, when I realized that it was for real, after seven, eight of my constituents called me in a panic, I tweeted..."

His messages to @UTKnoxville were simple, yet strong.

At 3:18pm, Faison tweeted: "if you hire him, the backlash will be insurmountable and devastating to the University and the state."

At 3:27pm, he tweeted: "your money comes in large part from the citizens of TN. They will demand a refund and I will help lead the charge. Don't hire him!"

Faison explained his thinking on this matter. "The economic boom and potential with a viable football program is huge," he says. "When the UT system is working well, it brings unbelievable revenue into Tennessee. We as legislators... we appropriate $2 billion a year that goes to UT, and I vote on that. I chair the operations committee. The Board of Trustees will be in front of me. I carry a bill for UT. The people in my district want to have an influence. It's their money. Between economic impact and the fact that all the power lies in the legislature, I have to have a say."

Many other state legislators joined Faison in making their feelings known on the matter in the hours to come. "We have seventy-three members in our GOP caucus," Faison said. "We have a group text that we use if something has to get out immediately. I said, 'Guys, if there was any time that we stood together, now is the time. I need y'all to get on board with me and fight this.'"

If there is one lasting image from "Schiano Sunday," it was The Rock on the UT campus. A man named Trip Underwood painted the words, "Schiano Covered Up Child Rape At Penn State."

Underwood told WBIR-TV, "I want to put something so provocative on here that if Schiano sees this, he'll realize we don't want him here."

Sports Reporter Louis Fernandez Jr. did that interview with Underwood. "Harsh words, no doubt, but I felt he spoke for a big chunk of the Tennessee fan base," says Fernandez. "They didn't want Greg Schiano, and they wanted him to know that. The words on The Rock made allegations and hearsay toward Greg Schiano seem like the undeniable truth. That isn't the case."

As time went on, some prominent Tennessee boosters came forward to express their displeasure with the situation, as did many former Vols players. There also seemed to be confusion and outrage amongst some members of the Tennessee Board of Trustees as well. At 6:15pm, George Cates, a member of the BOT, traded emails with Raja J. Jubran, the BOT Vice Chair. Cates was asking if the agreement with Schiano had been finalized.

Cates: "Done deal? bad odor. Have gotten outrage call from booster of over 25 years and top 900 donor who says no more. What's the story here? Jubran emailed back at 6:36pm: "No contract signed yet. Regarding the bad odor, it is so disappointing that our fan base and our media are willing to condemn a man of being a criminal even though he might be innocent... I just hate that we are ruining someone reputation unfairly."

After an entire day filled with unrest from fans, media, and politicians on the interwebs, airwaves and the UT campus, Tennessee pulled the job offer. At approximately 6:40pm, the news broke on Twitter. It was over.

Tennessee Fans 1, University of Tennessee 0.

"Fanbases have more power than ever before," says Big Ten Network anchor Rick Pizzo. "They say that they pay for so much, plus donations to keep season tickets. They want a say. With social media, the Tennessee uprising is a perfect example of what happens when they didn't do what fans wanted and the fans made the AD powerless. Whether you agree or disagree, it shows the amazing power that fans have to effect change. Huge change."

So, was the revolt because of Greg Schiano's loose connection to the Sandusky scandal? Was it because Tennessee fans didn't want the guy from Rutgers? Because he failed in the NFL? Was it the inevitable byproduct from the decade of on and off field problems? There is no one answer, but the majority of the comments that fans sent to UT were about the Penn State connection. Every fan had their reasons for speaking out, but they all seemed to share an overall level of exasperation that finally boiled over.

"There had been ten years of frustration [for Vols fans]," said TheAthletic.com's Bruce Feldman. "They saw other schools getting Chip Kelly, and others don't want us, and now we are getting this. So many factors went into it... it was ripe for an implosion."

"My reaction was a mixture of relief that he wasn't going to be my coach, shock that someone actually pulled the plug, and proud of how UT fans came together to finally say 'no, Tennessee is better than this,'" Lynn says. "All in all, it probably took fourteen years off my life."

"I was proud of those connected fans and boosters for taking a stand and stopping it from happening," said Hayes, who had been keeping up with the Schiano news from Disney World. "I think my wife was more relieved than I was that it wouldn't ruin our entire vacation!"

"I watched fans talk themselves into Dooley and Butch and just assumed the same was going to happen with Schiano," said WNML's Will West. "Then I started getting emails, texts, and social media messages. By the end of the night I had probably a hundred people tell me they were cancelling their donations and season tickets if the hire goes through."

"At first, we didn't believe it was possible," said Antunes. "Good things don't happen to the Vols anymore, so it was hard to believe. We went out and had a nice dinner to celebrate. Then we spent the rest of the night looking at the coaching big board and refreshing Twitter every thirty seconds. Such a wild, emotional roller coaster of a day."

"I do think that the 200 of us that actually stood outside of the athletic department doing a variety of chants and voicing our displeasure delayed everything," Reed says. "We stalled. We gave the legislators and the powerful boosters enough time to keep making phone calls and sending tweets and voicing their displeasure. It was important."

"That night a number of my co-workers were at Barley's in downtown Maryville and Coach Fulmer was there having dinner," Charles West remembers. He's a Tennessee alum, and the President of West Chevrolet in nearby Alcoa. "One of them walked over to his table and asked Fulmer what he thought of the days events. He looked up and said, 'I have no comment at this time,' and continued his dinner... I felt bad they were annoying him while he was just trying to eat. But Phil wouldn't give them anything on the subject when they pressed. He knew better."

Phillip Fulmer would eventually play a major role in a story that was not soon ending.

In the weeks that followed, the memorandum of understanding was a hot topic. From Fulmer to Pearl to Hamilton to Dooley to Hart to Jones (not to mention all the assistant coaches following different staff turnovers), financial separation agreements over the past decade had cost UT tens of millions of dollars.

Forget "Wide Receiver U." Tennessee had become *"Buyout U."* Did they now owe Greg Schiano $27 million? Currie signed the MOU on November 26, as did Schiano. But the document was not signed by UT Chancellor Dr. Beverly Davenport. It was also lacking the signature of Chief Financial Officer David Miller. According to UT's contract policy, without a John Hancock from the CFO, the MOU was not legally binding.

Tennessee fans hadn't seen very much in terms of winning over the past decade. "Schiano Sunday" served as their biggest victory in a decade, and nary a football was kicked, thrown or caught.

Sunday, November 26, 2017, will go down as the wildest date in the history of Tennessee athletics. Vols fans had stopped the hiring of Greg Schiano.

But the backlash was just beginning.

17

KNOXVILLE VERSUS EVERYBODY

ON NOVEMBER 27, TENNESSEE ATHLETICS DIRECTOR John Currie was scheduled to speak at the Knoxville Quarterback Club luncheon at Calhoun's on the River. In a perfect world, this would have been a victory lap of sorts for Currie. He'd talk about the new football coach and how excited he was about the future of Tennessee's football program. But after the wild events of the day before, Currie was in no man's land. John Currie was an AD without an HC.

Understandably, he canceled his appearance. Currie had vowed not to speak until a head coach had been hired. However, Sunday was such a complete dumpster fire that he had to say something. That morning he released a statement. Currie was making an effort to... well... let's just go to the statement.

"As we began our search for our next head football coach earlier this month, I promised that I would pour all my energy and effort into this process.

I have followed Coach Schiano's accomplishments throughout his career and have been fortunate to get to know him and his family over the last several years. As reported by the media, he was a leading candidate for our position. Among the most respected professional and college football coaches, he is widely regarded as an outstanding leader who develops tough, competitive teams and cares deeply about his student-athletes.

We carefully interviewed and vetted him, as we do candidates for all positions. He received the highest recommendations for character, family values and commitment to academic achievement and student-athlete welfare from his current and former athletics directors, players, coaching colleagues and experienced media figures.

Coach Schiano worked at Penn State from 1990-1995. Consequently, we, of course, carefully reviewed the 2012 investigation report by Louis Freeh. Coach Schiano is not mentioned in the Freeh report and was not one of the more than 400 people interviewed in the investigation. We also confirmed that Coach Schiano was never deposed and never asked to testify in any criminal or civil matter. And, we conferred with our colleagues at The Ohio State University, who had conducted a similar inquiry after the 2016 release of testimony. I know that Coach Schiano will continue to have great success in his coaching career and wish him and his family well.

I am grateful for your patience as our search for the next leader for the Tennessee football program continues, and I look forward to making that introduction soon."

Currie had an extremely difficult job to do in regaining the trust of Tennessee fans. He read the emails, saw the texts, and heard the voicemails. It got so bad that he had to abandon his cell phone and start using a new one that Monday because of contact he was getting from displeased members of Big Orange Country. Currie knew that his approval level was minimal. But his statement did nothing to make Tennessee fans feel any better. There was no apology, no understanding of the angry response that took place the day before. Instead, it was Currie giving a glowing description of Greg Schiano while stating that the vetting was good.

"I have no doubts that John Currie talked to powerful boosters and Greg Schiano," Fox Sports Knoxville Jon Reed's says. "But he failed to vet his own fanbase. So, no. HELL NO."

"What's the proper vetting?" WNML's Will West said. "Calling the guy that currently employs him or a trustee at Penn State that has a vested interest in saying Schiano didn't know?"

"What Currie failed to realize was being the defensive coordinator for a powerful, national championship winning authoritarian like Urban Meyer is far different from being the most visible employee in the state like you are as the head coach of Tennessee," said Chad Withrow, host of "Midday 180" on 104.5 The Zone in Nashville. "He also failed to gauge the level of hope of his fanbase which would lead to the level of disappointment when word leaked that Schiano was the choice. The decision was just... strange."

UT Chancellor Dr. Beverly Davenport, who had hired Currie, was feeling the pressure from Tennessee fans herself. She released a statement shortly after Currie's was made public. "I deeply regret the events of yesterday for everyone involved," Davenport's statement read. "The university remains steadfast in its commitment to excellence, and I look forward to John Currie continuing the search to bring the next head football coach to the University of Tennessee, Knoxville."

She was publicly reaffirming her support for Currie. They needed to present a united front at a time when the UT administration/athletic department and Tennessee fans were more divided than they have even been. Currie also had support in other crucial areas. Tennessee Board of Trustees Vice Chair Raja J. Jubran emailed some members of the BOT about an hour after the offer to Schiano was pulled.

"I need to also let you know how impressed I was with John Currie this past 3 weeks. He is doing a great job with all the vetting and due diligence."

In the days to come, athletic department influencers came under scrutiny from Tennessee fans. Some placed blame on Jimmy Haslam, the owner of the Cleveland Browns. The Haslam family has been a major part of the University of Tennessee for decades, donating over $100 million to UT academics and athletics. The family patriarch, Jim Haslam, played on the 1951 national championship team under Robert Neyland.

Jim Haslam has credited the University of Tennessee for much of what he has achieved in the business world. Jim is the founder and chairman of Pilot Flying J, a multi-billion dollar company. He is adamant in his assertion that the reports stating that they were pushing for Schiano are false.

"Anyone saying that the Haslams screwed all this up, that's completely wrong," Jim Haslam told TheAthletic.com in December 2017. "All we want to do is what's in the best interest of the University of Tennessee. If you asked the people over there they will tell you we have never gone in there and said, 'You do this and you do that.'"

Here's how you know that things were bonkers during this coaching search. Some Vols fans were mad at Peyton Manning after reports were published that he was on board with the Schiano hire. Manning had contacted some fellow alums in what was considered to be an effort rally support for Schiano.

ESPN's Kirk Herbstreit went on ESPNU radio and spoke about a conversation he and Manning had that weekend. "Manning said, 'We're really excited about this. We vetted him. Everything's clean. It's good.' I said, 'Awesome, man, Congrats. He's going to do a great job and put a good staff together.' And that was it. That was before everything went down, and then everything went down."

Peyton Manning is so popular in Tennessee that hundreds have named their children after him, and even he was fair game for criticism from Vols fans.

Bob Yarbrough is a morning anchor at WVLT-TV in Knoxville. He is also the host of a daily news talk show on 98.7 WOKI-FM. On the Monday after the attempted hire of Greg Schiano, there was no doubt about the topic of the day. "Here's the thing. We rarely get into sports," Yarbrough says. "We are typically local news and pop culture... but Schiano was 100% of the show. Rarely do we have a topic that is 100% of the show, but this was a no brainer."

Yarbrough's program is based in Knoxville, but the Schiano story reached far beyond East Tennessee. This was dominating the national sports scene. It was such a unique situation that everyone seemed to have an opinion. Nationally, the prevailing judgement was that Tennessee fans went crazy for no good reason.

The takes… oh the takes that week were hot my friends…

"You people are ridiculous," wrote Yahoo! Sports Pat Forde about Tennessee fans. "Not all of you, but the delusional loudmouths who somehow think a program with a 62-63 record over the last decade is too good for Schiano. The internet vigilantes who want to bully their way into running the school's coaching search. The piling-on politicians. The protestors. The rock painters. The rubes who still are waiting for Jon Gruden to slide down the chimney. But the worst among the Tennessee lunatic fringe are the disingenuous liars who say this Schiano backlash is about Mike McQueary's testimony regarding Jerry Sandusky and things that happened at Penn State, when in reality it's because they don't think Schiano is going to win a Southeastern Conference title. Don't go getting righteously indignant when this has nothing to do with being righteous and everything to do with trying to beat Georgia."

Forde finished with a bang. "Who would want to deal with this fan base right now?"

Dan Wetzel, also from Yahoo! Sports, had spent as much as any reporter covering the Sandusky scandal. "Did it happen? Maybe. Maybe Greg Schiano is every bit as terrible as you can imagine. Anything is possible," said Wetzel. "No Tennessee fan knows for sure, though. It's just one loose accusation, based on what a guy said a guy said that no one with the authority or interest in pursuing criminally or civilly proved, or even pursued because no one really believed it. That isn't a lot of reason to go paint rocks – and use them to crush a man's career and reputation."

Joel Klatt from Fox Sports tweeted: "The Tennessee fanbase and the media members that led them off this cliff via group think and the mob mentality should be EMBARRASSED…You trashed a good man and a high-quality coach today based on ZERO evidence"

Long-time NFL writer Peter King wrote about the Knoxville controversy in his weekly MMQB column. "Whether Schiano saw something or didn't, whether he shielded Sandusky or didn't, only Schiano knows. He denies it. The legal system in Pennsylvania found no reason to charge him with a crime. NO matter. On Sunday, he was convicted in the court of public opinion, and the

University of Tennessee dropped a man charged with nothing. Innuendo won. The witch-hunters won. It's a sad time in America."

CBS Sports Senior Writer Dennis Dodd has covered Schiano since his days at Rutgers. Dodd looked at the problems in Knoxville and wrote that Lane Kiffin should be hired to give Tennessee the stability it needed. "My article was a knee jerk, tongue in cheek reaction... but not really," Dodd says. "Considering everything that went on, Kiffin was a better option. Lane looked like the voice of reason."

Dodd told me that article was one of his most read on the website. "The more time goes on, a case had to be made for sticking to your guns if you are Currie," Dodd says. "Don't let the minions tell us what to do. Tennessee fans, not unlike other fans... they feel an investment in process. But this was way over the top. This empowered fans and a lot of people that didn't know better. It empowered everyone that was angry. The results were shameful. What do you tell Schiano? This had been made public for years and it was now a false narrative. There was no proof. If I was the Tennessee administration I would have sat at the podium and stood by it. I know that was the plan, but they just couldn't get to the presser. Tennessee fans damaged the brand and they ruined the reputation of a good man."

"I think this is a travesty," said professional screamer Stephen A. Smith on ESPN's "First Take" program. "And I want to be on the record saying that I think Greg Schiano is being royally screwed over in all of this. This is a travesty of justice and it needs to be pointed out adamantly so."

"Now all of a sudden Tennessee is too holy that they don't want Greg Schiano? Who the hell does Tennessee think they are right now," SEC Network's Booger McFarland said. "I think they are disillusional (sic) and I think they ultimately gonna pay the price for it."

"When mobs gather, there is little time for reasonable," Mike Vaccaro wrote in the *New York Post*. "And make no mistake: What happened in and around Knoxville on Sunday was mob rule... It was also an abject disgrace."

The Schiano situation was tricky for the Guarantano family. Tennessee quarterback Jarrett Guarantano is from New Jersey and played his high school football at Bergen Catholic. Jarrett's father James was a wide receiver at Rutgers and is a member of the University's Hall of Fame. The day after the Schiano hire was squashed, James Guarantano tweeted about it. And he wasn't happy.

"I have a fair question for all the Vol fans that protested the Schiano hire. When our AD hires our next HC, and if all of you "like" the hire, are the players allowed to protest and say that's not who they wanted? Get ready cause Pandora's box just got opened!"

Many who have worked with Schiano and/or known him for years went public in their support, including his old boss in Tampa Bay. The night Tennessee backed away from the MOU, former Buccaneers general manager Mark Dominik tweeted the following: "We spent hours & hours interviewing & background checks on Greg Schiano. Yes we didn't win. Fact-he's honest, awesome father/husband, & an excellent coach. This shouldn't be whether YOU think you like him or not, you don't even know him. #Meyer #Belichick ask them."

Penn State trustee Anthony Lubrano said the decision to pull the offer to Schiano was influenced by a "grossly uninformed social media mob."

Ohio State's Urban Meyer and the New England Patriots Bill Belichick, two of this generation's most successful coaches, vouched for Schiano in the days that followed. "I'm not angry. He's an elite, elite husband, elite father and an elite coach," said Meyer. "I stand by my coach."

"I have great respect [for him] and think he's a great football coach," Belichick said. "Speaking about him as a coach and as a person, [I have] the utmost respect and zero reservations. None."

Across the country, Tennessee fans were seen as a collection of country bumpkins who were mad the Vols weren't hiring Jon Gruden, so they pitched a hissy fit. Locally, the perception of the events of "Schiano Sunday" could not have been more different. "I am disappointed at the national narrative on this subject because I think it is lazy and unfair," said Gridiron Now's John Brice. "UT is special for lots of reasons, but its fans' passion pokes near the top of that chart. And fans were sick of being charged the same or higher prices for tickets as Alabama, Georgia, LSU, etc., and seeing it deliver inferior results and tone-deaf decision-making."

"I'm troubled by the national media's reaction to this story," Fox Sports Knoxville's Russell Smith says. "I can tell you as someone who was at the heart of this story, that this characterization of the fan base is categorically false... The bottom line is that if he had been hired here, anytime Vol fans saw Schiano lead the team onto the field there would be a little voice in the back of their head wondering if it were really true. That's a hell of an ugly thing to have to think about every time you watch your favorite team play."

Today, Tom Hart is a play-by-play announcer on the SEC Network. A few years before getting that gig, he was on the mic for the AA baseball Tennessee Smokies in Kodak, only a twenty-five minute drive from the UT campus. In addition, Hart's time at ESPN/SEC Network has coincided with the Butch Jones era, and he has called more of Jones's games at Tennessee than anyone not associated with the Vol Network. Hart knows the Tennessee fanbase better than most.

"I was surprised how out of touch some of my colleagues in the national media were on this subject," Hart told me. "Tennessee doesn't deserve someone better or more accomplished because the program has a losing record over the last decade? They were a top ten program as recently as October of 2016. They were a win away from the Sugar Bowl. Butch won nine games in consecutive years. Vol Nation should not be forced to apologize for having high standards."

Greg Schiano was the number one trending topic on twitter that Sunday night. This wasn't just a sports story. Jeremy Faison is a Tennessee state representative, and his comments embodied what many Tennesseans were thinking after hearing almost universal criticism of Vols fans from national media. "I'm not challenged at all about what some Yankee says about my state. Number one, I don't care what they do in their state so why should they care what we do in our state? Number two, if you are going to call us ignorant hillbilly rednecks, maybe you should take a chill and look at which state in America is doing better than any other state and then load your blank shots. We are the fastest growing state for jobs, lowest unemployment, our education is doing great. We have more work covered up, lowest debt... We are about the best state financially in America. So, when some Yankee pundit for *Sports Illustrated* or some liberal outlet or ESPN has something to say about my state, I say that you don't know what you are talking about. You are completely ignorant about this state to say anything."

The deification of coaches has been going on as long as games have been played. In college athletics, it has proven to be even more worrisome. Fans backed Oklahoma's Bob Stoops when he kept running back Joe Mixon on the team, even after Stoops watched the video of Mixon punching a woman in the face. They gave Nebraska's Tom Osborne a pass for allowing Lawrence Phillips to play for the Cornhuskers. Phillips had dragged a woman down a flight of stairs by her hair. They ignored the arrests of more than thirty Florida players during Urban Meyer's six years in Gainesville. In those cases, and countless others, victories trumps all.

Schiano's case is different. He wasn't in the category of those national championship winning coaches I just mentioned. So why were so many who cover the sport of football willing to stick their necks out for Schiano while ripping Tennessee fans for challenging the hire? "One of the reasons many in the national media liked Schiano was because he was a good leaker of info to writers," says Bleacher Report's NFL National Lead Writer Mike Freeman. "Not all writers, but a lot. They liked him for that. Not because of his coaching skills."

"You had a variety of national personalities that are represented by the same agency that Jimmy Sexton works for start being critical," says WNML's Brian Rice. "That's the whole problem now in most of the national media in sports, politics and everything else. I had several people that I've met in the media reach out to encourage me to walk back my criticism of Schiano on Twitter. That was a real eye opener."

Greg Schiano had interviewed for other Power 5 head coaching jobs between the time he was fired by Tampa Bay and before McQueary's testimony leaked. But it wasn't like Schiano was a hot commodity during this coaching cycle. Looking back to how the coaching search went, this is what I could put together. John Currie really was giving Butch Jones every chance to keep his job. If Tennessee had gone 7-5, Jones wouldn't have been fired. It would have meant losses to almost all of their biggest conference rivals, but Tennessee would have stressed a fourth straight bowl appearance and what was potentially a top ten recruiting class.

That said, Currie had a short list of potential coaches ready before Butch Jones was fired. At the top of that list were Dan Mullen and Greg Schiano. What about Jon Gruden, you ask? There were overtures made on both sides and Gruden loved the attention, but that was never going to happen. Gruden wanted to return to the NFL, and would do so after being re-hired by the Oakland Raiders in January 2018. Still, Currie was more than happy to play along, using "Grumors" as a distraction during the search.

What about Matt Campbell? Well, the bloom from Iowa State's upsets of top five opponents Oklahoma and TCU lessened a bit after the Cyclones lost to West Virginia, Oklahoma State and Kansas State. He didn't turn 38 until after the regular season had ended, so you'd be taking a risk by hiring such a young coach. The Vols did that in November 2008 and it didn't turn out well. The buyout was a major factor as well. Tennessee would have had to pay $9.4 million to get Campbell. Factor in the buyout for Jones and his staff and you are easily in the $20 million range, and Tennessee was never going to pay that kind of money for Campbell.

It doesn't appear there was any contact between Campbell and UT. But the Dan Mullen talk? That had legs. He spoke with Tennessee about the opening. Mullen, Clint Dowdle (assistant to Mullen's agent Jimmy Sexton) and Currie swapped direct messages the week of Thanksgiving 2017. Peyton Manning called Mullen in an effort to presumably convince him to take the Tennessee job.

Mullen and Currie were scheduled to be in touch in some form at 11am on Sunday, November 26. This was likely to be an in-person meeting in Starkville. But Mullen was also biding his time for the Florida job. That was the one what he wanted. And after Chip Kelly and Scott Frost turned down the Gators, Florida finally called Mullen. Once that happened, the Vols were not going to be a consideration.

On Saturday, November 25 at 7:11pm, Currie sent a direct message to Mullen. "So tomorrow work?" Mullen never responded. He accepted the Florida job the next day. In a way, this was karma coming back to bite Tennessee. Five years earlier, Butch Jones was waiting on Tennessee to call while mulling an offer from Colorado. Once the Vols made contact, the Buffaloes were an afterthought. So, Currie went to Schiano. According to Currie's statement that Monday, he already had gotten to know Schiano over the previous few years. This was someone who he was familiar with personally and absolutely wanted to work with. The Currie/Schiano combo was going to be in place in Knoxville for years to come.

Or not. In November 2008, Phillip Fulmer famously said, "I love Tennessee too much to let her stay divided." Nine years later, the attempted hiring of Greg Schiano unified Big Orange County even more than an SEC title would have.

John Currie was moving on with the job search. Over the next week and a half there would be hirings, firings, rumors and plane trips as the search took strange turn after strange turn. This coaching search wasn't even close to being over.

I made multiple requests with Ohio State's Sports Information Department to speak with Greg Schiano about the Tennessee coaching search.

The response: "He says the time to talk about that time isn't now."

18

CURRIE GOES ROGUE

THE GREAT AXL ROSE ONCE SANG, "WHERE DO WE GO NOW?"
Tennessee fans were wondering the same thing after "Schiano
Sunday," as the coaching search resumed on Monday, November
27. ESPN reported that Tennessee got in touch with David
Cutcliffe to see if he was interested in the job. "Coach Cut," now
sixty-three years old and finishing his tenth season at Duke,
politely declined.

On Outkick the Coverage, Clay Travis reported that if offered,
former Tennessee Volunteers tight end Jason Witten would leave
the Dallas Cowboys to take the Tennessee job. "Coaching is
something I can see myself [doing] down the road... but right now
I'm all in with this team and my feet are planted firmly here,"
Witten told ESPN. It wasn't likely that John Currie would have
considered Witten for the job, but the reality that this was even
being talked about showed how desperate things were getting in
Knoxville. Currie was under the microscope and everyone knew it.

That night, a national television audience tuned in for
"Monday Night RAW" on USA Network. The weekly WWE event
just happened to be at Thompson-Boling Arena on the UT campus
that evening. Fans cheered for their favorite son, Kane. Outside the
professional wrestling world, "The Big Red Machine" is Glenn

Jacobs, 2018 GOP nominee for Knox County Mayor. (On a side note, if you've never been to Knoxville, you really should visit. It's never boring here.)

Throughout the night, fans had a variety of chants, but one in particular stood out and could be heard loud and clear by those watching at home.

"Fi-re Cur-rie."

Clap. Clap. Clap Clap Clap.

"Fi-re Cur-rie."

A single video of such chants got over 122,000 views from the *Sports Illustrated* Twitter account. Lane Kiffin, who by now has established himself as college football's top troll, retweeted the same video. At Alabama, Nick Saban's media policies kept Lane in the witness protection program for about three years. But in 2017, with those shackles now removed, Kiffin tweeted at will.

I asked Lane if he was ever contacted by Tennessee with regards to their coaching opening. "I was not," he says. "What normally happens in those things is when jobs come open there is usually communication with the agent and the athletics director. The agent says something like, 'Hey I got these eight to ten guys... what do you think about this guy here or there?' Then the AD says, 'I want to interview those two guys, those sound good.' In that conversation with [agent] Jimmy Sexton, who has a million guys obviously so it's not just about me... John Currie says, 'Lane will never be the head coach as long as I'm the athletics director here.' So, once he said that I didn't think about it. So that kinda answered that."

Currie's refusal to consider Kiffin isn't a surprise. Back in 2008, when Tennessee was looking for Phillip Fulmer's replacement, John Currie was one of athletics director Mike Hamilton's top associates. Hamilton was at the top of a small committee of about four or five people deciding on the next coach. Currie has said in private conversations that he was the only one in the group who voted against hiring Lane Kiffin. Instead, he wanted Air Force's Troy Calhoun.

The top of Currie's short list had both names crossed off, so he had to look elsewhere for a coach. His first stop was to visit the ghost of Tennessee searches past. Back in 2012, Oklahoma State head coach Mike Gundy was Tennessee athletics director Dave Hart's first call. The five years that followed have only strengthened Gundy's resume. From 2013-2017, his Cowboys were regulars in the national rankings. They won 47 games and finished 10-3 four times. In twelve seasons at the school, he had won 68% of his games. While Gundy was looked at as a guy who probably would never leave his alma mater willingly, his relationship with Oklahoma State athletics director Mike Holder was a bit strained. Currie felt that there was an opportunity. Even while working the Mullen angle on Saturday, November 25, Currie scheduled an interview with Gundy in Oklahoma City for Monday, November 27. Like any good AD doing a coaching search, Currie wanted multiple options.

Currie and Gundy swapped direct messages on that Monday. Gundy said that he cleared his schedule after the events of Sunday. But instead of meeting that day, they'd get together on Tuesday, November 28 in Dallas. Currie messaged Gundy, "This is the plane I'm flying you back to rocky top on."

Former ESPN reporter Brett McMurphy tweeted that Peyton Manning had called Gundy in an effort to get him to Knoxville. Before the Vols AD and the Oklahoma State coach met face to face on that Tuesday morning, Currie messaged Gundy that it was a beautiful day in Dallas. "Looks like Tenn orange," Gundy replied. That afternoon, Currie sent Gundy a Memorandum of Understanding. He told Gundy he'd be standing by in the area, waiting for an answer. Currie even offered to fly him back to Stillwater, regardless of his decision. Tennessee backed up the Brinks truck. It was a six-year deal reportedly worth $7 million per season.

In 2017 you are never more than a cell phone away from being discovered. That night, a Tennessee fan contacted Fox Sports Radio's Russell Smith. He had pictures of Gundy at the Renaissance Dallas Hotel restaurant/bar. Gundy was sitting at a table, alone. The "source" said he overhead Gundy on the phone saying that he was waiting for someone. Was the new dynamic duo about to head to the airport and fly to Knoxville? Were mullets (Gundy's hairstyle of choice) going to be back in fashion in Big Orange Country?

At 8:28pm CT, Gundy made his decision known on Twitter. "Cowboy For Life! #GoPokes #okstate"

"There was no way Gundy was taking that job," says TheAthletic.com's Bruce Feldman. "That's the third best job in the Big 12 at his alma matter and his roster is stocked. Tennessee has a great history, but at best that's the fifth or sixth best job in the SEC. He lives on a dude ranch! It just didn't make sense."

A few days later, Mike Gundy got a $675,000 raise, and will make $5 million for the 2018 season. Gundy should send a healthy check to a Knoxville area charity, because that's now twice in five years that merely speaking with UT got him a large salary bump. "I think he [Currie] looked desperate," says Bleacher Report National College Football Columnist Brad Shepard. "Did he really think he could pluck Gundy away from his alma mater or was that just a tire kick to show the fans, 'Look! I'm going after a big name here!'"

On Wednesday, November 29, the next person on Tennessee's magical mystery tour seemingly was Purdue's Jeff Brohm, considered to be one of the up and coming coaches in college football. He played quarterback at Louisville. In 1991 he fractured his right ankle playing in a Thursday night loss to... you guessed it... Tennessee. Jeff Brohm's professional career wasn't much to speak of, and he bounced around six different NFL teams, throwing a total of 58 passes. But there was a memorable moment in 2001, when Brohm suited up for the Orlando Rage of the soon to be defunct XFL.

Brohm loved the XFL. He wanted to put "J Bro" on the back of his jersey, as nicknames were allowed on jerseys in this league, like Rod "He Hate Me" Smart. Sadly for Brohm and "bros" everywhere, Rage players voted against using nicknames. Midway through the season, Brohm got knocked out of a game, wheeled off on a stretcher and taken to the hospital. He returned later that night in a neck brace and suited up to play in the next game. XFL sideline reporter Chris Wragge asked one of the most important questions of our age before kickoff.

"Jeff Brohm, how in the world are you starting this game tonight after taking that hit six days ago?"

"Well, let me answer that question by asking two questions," Brohm replied. "One, is this or is this not the XFL? Yes, it is. Two, do I or do I not currently have a pulse? Yes, I do. Let's play football." Vols fans shared that video on social media throughout the day. Personally, I was imagining what VFL Films could do with the clip. Play that on the Jumbotron before the Florida game and you'll win 50-0.

Brohm had worked his way up the coaching ranks, eventually becoming the head coach at Western Kentucky. Brohm's teams could certainly score points. The Hilltoppers led the nation with an average of 45.5 points per game in 2016. Brohm had just finished his first regular season at Purdue. The Boilermakers improved from 3-9 to 6-6 (7-6 after a Foster Farms Bowl win over Arizona in December).

Vols fans felt like a deal with Jeff Brohm was going to happen. This was Tennessee. Of course they'd get the guy from Purdue if they wanted him. That afternoon, the Brohm talk hit a new level when WNML's Jimmy Hyams tweeted: "Tennessee will soon announce the hiring of Purdue coach Jeff Brohm after going 6-6 this year. Brohm was 30-10 at Western Kentucky. Buyout is $5 million, drops to $4 million Dec 5. Still owes Purdue about $750K for leaving WKY."

Hyams then went on ESPN's Outside The Lines program and said basically the same thing, that Tennessee offered Brohm the job and that he thought Brohm accepted it. According to Feldman, Jeff Brohm's son Brady, who is in the seventh grade, was heading to the bathroom at school when he got stopped by a teacher who told him his Dad was taking the Tennessee job. But the reports that he was Knoxville bound were not accurate. It didn't take long for many other media members to say that there were discussions between Brohm and Tennessee, but that nothing was imminent. A Purdue recruit named Elijah Ball texted Brohm that afternoon, asking him if he was leaving. Brohm texted back that those reports were false.

Sadly, there would be no XFL highlights playing on the Neyland Stadium Jumbotron. Jeff Brohm was staying in West Lafayette. In May 2018, Brohm was asked by *The Courier Journal* if there had been any contact with Tennessee. "Where there's smoke, there's fire," he admitted. This was the Space Mountain of coaching searches. So many twists and turns and highs and lows. But that ride times out eventually, whereas this search showed no signs of stopping.

Brohm was known to be a no go by the time Tennessee's men's basketball team tipped off that night against Mercer. Throughout the game, Vols fans chanted "Fire Currie," "We Want Kiffin," and "Hire Tee." When these chants started up during timeouts, the band would often begin playing or music would be pumped into the arena through the PA system. Fans felt this was a deliberate attempt to drown out their voices, and it's hard to argue otherwise.

Unless the students at UT are studying to be doctors or are still spending their parent's retirement fund on the eight-year plan (stay in school, kids), they weren't on campus during Kiffin's short tenure. Certainly, Lane Kiffin still has his share of critics in Knoxville, but time has healed at least some of the wounds from January 2010. "What you do lately... that's what people look at so much," Kiffin says. "I think the success we had on the field at Alabama and this last year [at Florida Atlantic] as one of the hottest teams in America for a team that really hadn't won anything here for ten years. Just to see the difference now, from burning things to years later [fans] doing polls for Tennessee to hire me... just to see that change is kinda crazy. I don't think anyone would have thought that the week I left there."

Kiffin says that the support he's gotten from some Vols fans speaks to the work he has put in since his firing at Southern Cal. "To see that pay off and see Tennessee's fans react like that... it's natural to say, yeah this is worth it."

As tabulated by TheAthletic.com, John Currie received 160 emails that week from fans wanting Lane Kiffin to return, by far the most of any coach. But Kiffin was a non-starter for the UT job. Would Tennessee approach Southern Cal offensive coordinator

Tee Martin, a Vols legend still waiting for his first head coaching job? Would it be too much of a reach to offer SMU's Chad Morris? Would they go back to Gruden with Nick Saban level cash? Is Bill Belichick looking for a new challenge? Was the ghost of Vince Lombardi available?

Despite the madness, the Tennessee job did get its share of interest. On Tuesday, November 28, Tennessee Associate AD Tyler Johnson texted Currie, telling him that Dallas Cowboys assistant head coach/special teams coordinator Rich Bisaccia wanted to talk to him about the Vols opening. Bisaccia had SEC football ties from previous stints at South Carolina and Ole Miss, plus decades of coaching experience in college and the NFL. Currie replied: "Who's he?" Bisaccia made contact multiple times with UT that week, but it doesn't appear that he was ever considered. Bisaccia ended up leaving the Cowboys in January to become the assistant head coach/special teams coordinator for the Oakland Raiders. Yes, Bisaccia is now part of Jon Gruden's coaching staff.

On Wednesday night, reports circulated that Tennessee offered the job to a guy UT fans disliked a great deal, North Carolina State head coach Dave Doeren. Currie began contacting Doeren's agent, Jordan Bazant, back on Monday, November 27. The next night, Currie messaged Bazant that Gundy had turned Tennessee down. Bazant messaged back, "Ok. Let's get this done."

Currie had gone from Columbus to Knoxville to Dallas within forty-eight hours, and now was flying to North Carolina. Shortly after midnight on Wednesday, November 29, he arrived in Raleigh and messaged Bazant again.

Currie: "I gotta go buy clean clothes."

Bazant: "Ok. He won't care if you are wrinkled."

Was the disheveled coaching search going to end here? Currie slept for a few hours, and then texted N.C. State athletics director Debbie Yow. He expressed an interest in speaking with Doeren about the coaching vacancy at Tennessee. What kind of a coach would the Vols be getting with Dave Doeren? In five years, Doeren is 34-30 at N.C. State. 2017 was his best season in the ACC, finishing second in the Atlantic Division. But a 15-25 conference record was hardly anything to put at the top of a resume.

"He's not a glad-handler, politician type," says Joe Giglio, a sportswriter for the *News & Observer* in Raleigh. Giglio has been at the newspaper since 1995 and covered N.C. State football for past eight seasons. "He's more guarded than other coaches. He's not necessarily media savvy, but that's by choice. He was at Northern Illinois for two years and you don't deal with a lot of media there."

After his first game at N.C. State in 2013 against Louisiana Tech, Doeren made an error that initially hurt his relationship with Wolfpack fans. "They have a pass out rule here, so you can leave after halftime and then come back," Giglio says. "It was a foreign concept to him. Fans had gone outside and didn't come back in for the start of the second half. He was pretty vocal about it, and that was a complicated mistake on his part. Ever since then he has tried to go out of his way to compliment fans. He made a mistake and learned from it."

During a 38-31 loss to Clemson in 2017, he chose the postgame press conference to take an odd stand. "I'd like to know why there was a laptop on Clemson's sideline that people were looking at... I'd like that to be investigated," said Doeren. "Maybe they weren't doing anything, but I was told it was illegal to have technology on the sideline." The laptop in question was being used to transmit pictures and videos for Clemson's social media platforms. There was nothing nefarious going on.

Currie and Doeren met on Wednesday, November 29. Tennessee fans were not inspired by the choice. There were too many similarities to Butch Jones for their liking. Records, personalities, thin skin... As they had a few days earlier, fans took to social media to express their displeasure. Staying quiet was no longer as option. While Currie was waiting for an answer from Doeren, he got a text from Brady Hoke. Remember, at this time, Hoke was still technically UT's football coach.

"JOHN I HOPE YOU DO KNOW I WOULD LIKE TO BE YOUR HEAD FOOTBALL COACH I DO KNOW THE ENVIRONMENT WE LIVE IN AND WHAT NEEDS TO BE DONE AT TENNESSEE"

The fact that Brady Hoke sends texts in all caps was the most predictable part of the entire coaching search.

For weeks, Dave Doeren had been working on a contract extension at N.C. State, but talks had slowed considerably. Funny how a call from Tennessee speeds up negotiations for a coach isn't it? Late Thursday morning, November 30, Doeren announced that he was staying at N.C. State. He was getting a raise, and a new contract that would pay him $15 million over five years. The *News & Observer* reported that the Vols had been willing to pay $1 million more per season. That's not Greg Schiano money, but still a sum considerably higher than what Doeren would end up accepting.

"Did he probably take temperature of the Tennessee fan base? I'm sure he did," says Giglio. "That's part of it. You can have confidence in your own ability and it's hard not to get caught up in situation where they were offering more money. But on the comfort and confidence scale, N.C. State checked off more boxes."

Since Sunday, the Vols had gone through Schiano, Gundy, Cutcliffe, Brohm and Doeren. It didn't work out with any of them for a variety of reasons, so Currie continued his nationwide journey. One intriguing name from the past was starting to get bantered around a bit. In 2010, Houston's Kevin Sumlin was the next guy on Mike Hamilton's list when Tennessee settled on Derek Dooley. Sumlin would later go 51-26 in six seasons at Texas A&M.

The timing could be perfect. Tennessee was paying approximately 728 contract buyouts at this time, and if they hired Sumlin, there would be no buyout as he had been fired earlier in the week. Back on November 4, I tweeted a poll question, asking Vols fans if they wanted Sumlin at Tennessee. 87% of the 356 respondents said no. I asked the same question on November 30. This time, 77% of the 517 respondents said yes. Opinions can change quickly. All it takes is a mess of a coaching search.

Over the next few hours the coaching search took yet another odd twist, a twist very few people saw coming. John Currie wasn't approaching Kevin Sumlin. John Currie was now going after Washington State coach Mike Leach.

Wait... Mike Leach? Let's backtrack a bit first. Currie was weary of what social media was doing to his pursuit of Dave Doeren. He had been down this road before. He needed another option should Doeren back out. At 3:52am on Thursday, November 30, he sent a direct message to Leach.

Currie: "Coach – Currie here. You available for a call?"

Leach replied immediately: "I will call in 5"

Mike Leach was up late on the west coast, and the two apparently conversed. Later that morning, Currie was trading direct messages with Doeren's agent, Jordan Bazant. But suddenly, the communications stopped.

Bazant at 7:37am: "Are you on plane"

Bazant at 9:17am: "He Is fired up"

Bazant at 9:51am: "Really need to hear from you"

There would be no response from Currie. Maybe Bazant and Doeren took the hint and knew that UT wasn't going to happen. Or maybe Doeren was deciding to stay at N.C. State regardless. Doesn't matter. Both sides were moving on.

My first thought upon hearing the Mike Leach rumor was that it would be the ultimate buddy cop movie. Currie, the straight-laced administrator and Leach, the wild card coach. They'd make the police captain very upset, but at the end of the day they'd put the bad guys behind bars. Leach is one of the rare big-time college football coaches that never played a down of college football. His innovative offensive systems lit up scoreboards as an assistant at Valdosta State, Kentucky and Oklahoma. The points and yards kept coming when he became a head coach. Leach has a career record of 122-81 in sixteen seasons at Texas Tech and Washington State, with the last six years in Pullman. If you want to see a team that airs it out, Leach is your man.

At a time when college football coaches show as much personality as a paper cup, Mike Leach is a combination of Richard Pryor and Bill Walton. "[Leach] is like no one I've ever dealt with in just about every way," says Dale Grummert, a sportswriter for the *Lewistown Tribune*. Grummert has been at the newspaper since 1985. "He's intensely focused on what he wants to focus on. You may not feel that it is relevant, but in Mike Leach's world, he is tuned in."

His media opportunities are must see TV because you have no idea what's going to come out of Leach's mouth. "He details opponent's tendencies but gives brief answers," Grummert says. "It is not in his interest to talk about his opponent. He would rather talk his team, but even that bores him. He would really rather talk about anything but football, and once you accept that in your interviews, a lot of us go along with it. Why not? A press conference can be superficial, so why not talk Woodstock or Hunter S. Thompson?"

When talking with the media late in the 2017 season, Mike Leach addressed a reporter that was getting married in a couple of weeks. Leach spent more than three minutes giving him wedding advice. Mike Leach loves pirates, so much so that he titled his 2011 autobiography *"Swing Your Sword: Leading the Charge in Football and Life."* The Vol Navy would have had a field day.

Leach's teams have never won a conference championship, but he was still getting a lot of victories with two and three-star athletes in Lubbock and Pullman. What could he do with four-star and five-star kids in Knoxville? John Currie wanted to find out. While Tennessee was offering the job to a few guys this week and that news was being made public, it wasn't like Currie was showing up in the town squares of Stillwater or Raleigh with a bullhorn and a sack of loot. He wanted to stay hidden. After the Doeren deal was dashed (in whatever way you believe), Currie was missing in action the rest of that day. Not just to Bazant, but to anyone.

That Thursday morning, John Currie took a direct flight from Raleigh to Los Angeles to meet with Leach. He didn't tell UT Chancellor Beverly Davenport or UT President Joe DiPietro that he was making the trip. He didn't tell those on the Tennessee Board of Trustees. He didn't tell his associates in the Tennessee athletics department.

John Currie had gone rogue. For six hours in the middle of the day, with the coaching search still ongoing, Currie was not able to be reached. Maybe there was some anger on the part of Tennessee officials due to the confusion on Currie's whereabouts. There was absolutely some concern.

"Have we confirmed that john is safe?" Raja Jubran texted in a group message later that afternoon. Reid Sigmon texted Currie as well. "Lots of people worried about your whereabouts. Please call Ryan Robinson or Peyton."

Currie eventually texted back, "I'm fine." In a separate text, he typed, "I'm still alive."

Jubran texted the group after it was learned that Currie was ok. "Good that he is safe Now we need to know what the hell was going on This is ridiculous"

Currie said in communications shortly after he landed in California that WiFi was not working on his Delta flight, which is why he was missing for all that time. At 4:05pm ET, Leach sent Currie a direct message. "Text whenever you're ready. I'm on the bike path by the water." Currie replied at 4:12pm. "Ok – sounds nice! Give me a few more minutes."

Saturday Down South's Dan Harralson reported that they had a lunch meeting at the Cast & Plow restaurant in Marina Del Ray. At the same time, Currie was in full damage control with Davenport.

At 4:26pm, the two exchanged a terse set of texts.

Davenport: "We need you to come back to Knoxville tonight."

Currie: "What should I tell coach leach"

Davenport: "Tell him you have nothing more you can talk with him about."

In an email sent at 4:55pm to Davenport, DiPietro, and UT General Counsel Matthew Scoggins, Currie explained what happened in further detail. "I had every intention of being able to communicate and that we could still get DD [Dave Doeren] deal done while I was traveling but without an immediate answer, the negative social media assaults against him and the media news of their negotiating with NCSU, I was concerned that I needed to be in position to meet with other candidate including Coach Leach who's was in LA recruiting. This presented an opportunity for a quick meeting, as there are direct flights from RDU. I apologize to all involved."

Currie told Davenport, DiPietro and Scoggins in the email that he had not offered Leach the Tennessee job, nor that they even discussed terms of a deal, but that Leach would take it if offered. Davenport replied to the email, telling Currie that she wanted to meet with him in her office the next day at 9am.

While Currie was heading back to Tennessee late that Thursday night, NBC in Dallas reported that both sides were working on a deal. Feldman reported that the Currie/Leach meeting went "very well." So that night, Tennessee fans went to bed believing that this wild coaching search was nearing its conclusion. This belief was given even more support when a reporter from cougfan.com found Leach in the early morning hours on Friday at the Pullman airport. Leach was asked if he met with Tennessee representatives in Los Angeles. "If I had I wouldn't tell ya and if I hadn't I wouldn't tell ya," Leach said as he walked towards the parking lot. That wasn't a denial.

Currie was back in Knoxville shortly after 1:40am. It has been reported that Currie used a Kansas State booster's plane to return to Tennessee. When Currie landed, he and Leach began trading direct messages again. Leach said that he hoped that Currie would be ok and that they'd be able to work together. If it did in fact happen, Leach was going to be a breath of fresh air for a program that needed the energy after going from nine wins in 2016 to four wins in 2017. Could Leach win an SEC title? In the age of Nick Saban at Alabama, very few coaches have broken through that wall. But considering how the past few weeks had gone, getting someone of Leach's caliber to run the Tennessee football program would be shocking. How exactly the eccentric coach would mesh with UT's administration remained to be seen.

This was going to be the move that saved the job of the much-maligned John Currie. His popularity with fans would be somewhat restored. Buzzards were circling within the athletic department and just outside it, but it might be tough to fire him following a popular hire. "The paperwork was ready to go, and they just needed the Chancellor to sign off on it," Feldman says. "I think that's a hire if Currie makes gets the fans excited. They'd think Currie didn't screw it up and now they are excited about direction of the program."

Mike Leach was John Currie's Hail Mary. That Friday morning, Vols fans learned about the meeting Currie was having with Davenport and shortly after 9am, Currie walked into her office. On Twitter, WBIR-TV's Michael Crowe said that the meeting lasted about twelve minutes. "I can't say anything to you just now," Currie told Crowe after the meeting as he walked into an elevator.

Things were about to get weird. Shortly after 9:30am, WVLT-TV reporter Chynna Greene tweeted that John Currie had been fired. But a couple of minutes later, that tweet was deleted. The heck was going on? Has he been fired or not?

For maybe ten minutes, #VolTwitter was even more wild than normal and rampant speculation was everywhere. At this time, you could have told me that Charlie Sheen was going to coach the Vols and I wouldn't have discounted the possibility. At 9:47am, Greene tweeted again. "#BREAKING: According to sources, UTAD John Currie has been fired after only 8 months on the job"

One minute later, Sports Director Rick Russo tweeted a similar message from the main WVLT account. Soon, local and national media representatives followed with the same news. It was over. A week earlier, John Currie was getting some sun in The Bahamas. Now, he was out as Tennessee's athletics director.

"I think the post-Gundy candidates were more indicative of the waters Currie actually thought he was fishing in," says Shepard. "Unfortunately for him and us, it became a 'Honk if you turned down Tennessee' situation. When he went covert ops? It turned to panic."

"I understand that it can be difficult to feel sympathy for those who have financial wealth," says David Cobb, Tennessee athletics beat writer for the *Chattanooga Times Free Press*. "I also recognize the deep divisions that were caused when Fulmer was fired in 2008 and how that pain resurfaced when Beverly Davenport hired Currie as athletic director. Even with all that, I feel bad for John Currie and his family. They moved across the country, his kids enrolled in new schools and his wife probably devoted a ton of time to getting them settled while John worked around the clock. Now all that has been burned to the ground in a very ugly, public manner at a place that he loved."

Cobb added, "I hope John will one day share an open and honest account of the coaching search from his viewpoint."

Currie received text messages throughout the day from coaches and employees in the department expressing sadness at what had transpired and showing their support for him. Brady Hoke shout-texted as well. "JOHN VERY SORRY TO HEAR WHAT HAS HAPPENED THIS IS THE BULLCRAP THAT COLLEGE FOOTBALL HAS BECOME. IF I CAN BE OF ANY HELP PLEASE LET ME KNOW."

Technically, Currie wasn't even fired at that point. He was placed on leave with pay. On March 22, 2018, both sides agreed to a contract buyout of $2.5 million. John Currie had made over $3.3 million for eight months of work, which included the most inept coaching search in the history of collegiate athletics. I texted Currie to see if he would be willing to be interviewed for this book. I didn't get a response.

Davenport was going to hold a press conference on the afternoon of Friday, December 1, and would briefly touch on the Currie dismissal.

The press conference would also serve as a homecoming.

19
RETURN OF THE BATTLE CAPTAIN

ON NOVEMBER 29, 2008, Phillip Fulmer was carried off the field after coaching his last game. Almost nine years to the day after that emotional scene at Neyland Stadium, Phillip Fulmer was back, newly installed as Tennessee's athletics director.

Shortly after 3:30pm, UT Chancellor Dr. Beverly Davenport sat at the podium with Fulmer in front of a packed house in the Ray and Lucy Hand Digital Studio. "It has indeed been a difficult week," Davenport said. "It's been a difficult road at times to get where we are. This hasn't been an easy process for any of us, and I want you to know that I regret deeply any hurt that has been caused."

She addressed the Currie situation during those opening remarks. "Early yesterday afternoon, I asked John Currie to return to Knoxville before going forward with the search... When there are high expectations about a great place, those expectations come with challenges and challenges require tough decisions. Today required one of those decisions."

Davenport wouldn't answer questions about Mike Leach or why she decided to fire John Currie. But she did emphasize that Currie had been given "full authority" to hire a coach. She thanked him for his efforts but admitted that the coaching search process was "not satisfactory." Davenport's decision to remove Currie from the equation and replace him with Fulmer was widely supported by Tennessee fans.

When Phillip Fulmer began to speak, one of the things that stood out to me was that he looked better in 2017 than he did in 2008. Coaching years aren't normal years. The money at that level is significant, but so is the stress.

Phillip Fulmer Way runs parallel to Neyland Stadium on the UT campus, a perfect spot for one of the legendary figures in the history of the University. Fulmer's hiring as Tennessee's athletics director brought much needed stability to the department during a time of great controversy.

The sixty-seven-year-old Fulmer immediately presented an image of calm as the waters were still raging. "All of our sports at the university are the front door to the university and to our entire state, and we are proud of them all," he said. "Our athletic program's history is a bond that connects students and alumni, fans and the Tennesseans who support our great university. The success of our student-athletes in all sports is a source of inspiration, pride and unity that we must have as an athletic department and that fosters energy, an example of success at the highest level."

Fulmer's message to Vols fans was that this downturn was only temporary. "Our football program has the history, the facilities, the tradition and the resources to play with anyone, anytime, and that is what we're going to do again... our first job is turning around our football program. Our football teams in recent years have struggled for a variety of reasons, but through it all we have been supported by the most passionate fan base in the country. These great fans deserve teams that make them proud."

Fulmer finished his opening remarks with a plea for togetherness. "I have seen and been a part of the University of Tennessee's athletics program when it's been at its best. I have seen what honest communication, trust and hard work achieve. Turning our situation around will require teamwork. There's an old saying that says it is amazing what can be accomplished when no one cares who gets the credit. That cooperative spirit will drive my approach. We need energy, passion and focus from every Vol fan, alumni, coach and athlete. Let's be so unified and enthusiastic we even win over the naysayers. I'm asking all of our fans, our alumni, our student-athletes and coaches: *Let's go have fun winning championships.*"

If indeed there had been too many cooks in the kitchen with regards to Tennessee athletics over the past decade, the hiring of Phillip Fulmer was a huge step towards stability, something that in recent years had been severely lacking at Tennessee. From 1993-1999, Tennessee had Joe Johnson as president, William Snyder as chancellor, Doug Dickey as athletics director and Phillip Fulmer as head coach. Those were some of the most successful years for the football team and the UT athletics department overall. The baseball team made it to the College World Series in 1995. The Lady Vols basketball team won three consecutive national championships from 1996-1998. The men's basketball team finished the decade with two trips to the NCAA tournament.

A couple of hours after the Davenport/Fulmer press conference, UT President Joe DiPietro tweeted the following: "The process of searching for a football coach for the Vols has obviously not gone as expected to this point, and I regret the damage it has caused to the University's reputation. I'm very grateful to Phillip Fulmer for stepping in to act as athletics director at this critical juncture..."

That was a pretty telling admission from DiPietro. Or perhaps it was one he felt he had no choice but to make. The coaching search indeed had damaged UT's reputation.

"I was shocked by the Fulmer hire," David Blackburn told me. "I felt like, why didn't they just hire him in round one?" UT was calling on Fulmer in desperation. This was Wyatt Earp returning to Dodge City to restore law and order. The former players I've talked to believe that Fulmer will turn things around. "I feel that Fulmer being the AD is the best move Tennessee has made in years," former Tennessee linebacker Daryl Vereen says. "Fulmer knows coaches and players and knows the direction the program needs to go. He is the perfect AD for Tennessee."

"I believe that having Coach Fulmer back as AD is a no-brainer," former Tennessee kicker James Wilhoit told me. "As a head coach at Tennessee he was always heavily involved in academics and the student-athlete experience. He is the type that knows what he does best and will hire people around him to do the rest. He is the perfect person to run our athletic program and be the face of Tennessee athletics."

"Exuberating. That might be the best way to describe how I and many other alumni feel about having Coach Fulmer in charge of righting this ship," says former Tennessee defensive lineman Charles Folger. A few days earlier, there were Tennessee fans protesting on the steps of the UT football complex. On this day, they stood on those same steps to show their support for the return of "The Battle Captain."

"[Fulmer] knows what it takes to win championships and truly connects with the players," says recent Tennessee grad Skip Garner. "I think he will make a great AD for the next three to five years and will do all he can do help this program." In the days and weeks that followed the hiring of Phillip Fulmer, I spoke with men and women who have held a variety of roles inside the athletics department. Some of these folks are still at UT, others are working elsewhere. There wasn't one person that felt Fulmer's hiring was a negative.

"It felt like we won," says Brian Davis, a former Lady Vols Sports Information Department assistant. "I didn't win, but at the end of day we went through all that we went through and had gone full circle with one of our guys back in charge. We had to find stability to be a family again and care about each other. The fanbase wants this. Listen to the fans. Listen to your people."

"I'll give you an example of what Tennessee means to Phillip Fulmer," says former Vols assistant coach Trooper Taylor, who coached under Fulmer from 2004-2007. "We are walking to the dining hall next to the football complex. We are walking up the hill and in the middle of a conversation; Fulmer picks up paper that had been blowing in the wind. He was the first person to stop and do that. He makes millions of dollars and stops to pick up trash? That was a valuable lesson. This is home to him. It was just different. Another coach might just say to have a grad assistant get it. But not him. He's not that kind of way. Accountability... I learned that from him."

But there are those who believe that this AD switch was 1992 all over again, that this was another coup d'état with Phillip Fulmer waiting in the wings. The morning Currie was dismissed, former ESPN reporter Brett McMurphy tweeted the following: "Sources: John Currie was prepared to hire Mike Leach but university officials wouldn't allow him to do so. Phillip Fulmer has been sabotaging search process in hopes to become Tennessee's AD"

"The viewpoint I got and heard from numerous people was that Fulmer wanted the AD job and they blew it up from that point, and then Fulmer took over," Feldman says. On December 2, ESPN's Rece Davis spoke about the reports that Fulmer undermined the coaching search on College GameDay. "I talked to Phillip Fulmer this morning and those are allegations he flatly denies. He said he made two calls at the request of John Currie and visited a coach at the request, or with, Currie."

Up until Schiano Sunday, Currie hardly seemed to involve anyone else in the process. Had there been a few dissenting voices allowed in the conversation, perhaps someone could have explained to Currie why Greg Schiano was such a risky choice. But after that debacle, Fulmer was now included in communications with Currie, Davenport and others. Records show that Fulmer did indeed make phone calls on Currie's behalf and traveled to Raleigh to meet with Dave Doeren.

I made a request with the University of Tennessee to speak with Fulmer for this book. That request was denied.

Fulmer said that he would not serve as Tennessee's head coach or interim head coach. "I've done my duty that way and enjoyed it very, very much." That doesn't mean he hadn't thought about it. In a text message from long-time UT booster John "Thunder" Thornton and UT President Joe DiPietro on November 29, Thornton said that he asked Fulmer if he would consider coaching the Vols. "All they would have to do is ask," Fulmer responded.

But that wasn't going to be the case now. Currie was out, and Fulmer was in. Was Mike Leach still a possibility for the coaching job? No. Both sides moved on, and a couple of weeks later, Leach agreed on a five-year, $20 million contract extension to stay at Washington State. Fulmer began the search with a clean slate. Be it a sitting head coach, a coordinator, an assistant... all options were on the table.

In the days that followed there were a few names bantered about, and a couple of rumors got some attention. Of course, being Tennessee, there were times of panic for Vols fans. It had been reported that Fulmer spoke with former Texas coach Mack Brown, who was sixty-six-years-old and had been out of coaching since 2013. But that communication was most likely to obtain recommendations or background information on prospective candidates.

It finally felt like a traditional coaching search. The week after his hiring, Phillip Fulmer attended the College Football Hall of Fame induction ceremonies. His former quarterback, Peyton Manning, was a member of the Class of 2017. In New York City, Fulmer did interviews with three defensive coordinators. Auburn's Kevin Steele, Georgia's Mel Tucker, and Alabama's Jeremy Pruitt. It was the second time he had interviewed each candidate.

One coach conspicuous by his absence was another coordinator, and one with major Tennessee ties, Southern Cal's Tee Martin. Back in 1998, Martin had the seemingly impossible task of replacing Peyton Manning as the Vols quarterback. All Martin did was lead Tennessee to a 13-0 record, with SEC and BCS national championships. In his two years as the starter, the Vols went 22-3. Martin played six seasons of professional football, with stops in the NFL, NFL Europe, and the CFL. He has bounced around the high school and college ranks as an offensive assistant coach since 2006 but has yet to get a shot as a head coach.

In 2012, he joined Lane Kiffin's staff as wide receivers coach at Southern Cal and in 2016 moved his way up to the offensive coordinator position. Martin had been offered jobs on Tennessee's coaching staff in the past, but turned them down. However, he was very interested in talking to Tennessee about the head coaching opening. On December 2, Martin's Trojans beat Stanford 31-28 in the Pac 12 championship game. A couple of UT fans were seen holding up signs on the television broadcast. One read, "Come Home Tee." Another read, "Tee 2 UT #PhilzLike98."

Martin tweeted a screen grab of that scene. "And to the loyal Tennessee fans. Showing some California Love!! That's what up! #Pac12Champs!"

Martin did in fact speak with Tennessee, but was never really in the mix to replace Butch Jones. "That Monday, Tennessee still hadn't reached out to Tee," said TheAthletic.com's Bruce Feldman. "Finally, they called Tee, but not to interview as the head coach. It's just a bad look. You talk about 'VFL' and then you have a guy that is qualified enough to get an interview and you don't even offer him the chance to interview for head coaching job..."

"I don't know if there were some forces against Tee. I don't know if they thought that he wasn't ready. I don't know if they thought we don't have a lot of time to waste on someone we know is not a head coach right now," says former Tennessee wide receiver Jayson Swain. "It stinks because he has been successful and will be a head coach someday, so why not take a hard look at him. I wish he had gotten an interview. It could have helped him, and you never know what kind of ideas he might have had..."

There had been speculation about Martin possibly returning to Knoxville as the offensive coordinator and "head coach in waiting" had a veteran head coach been hired. Former Tennessee women's athletics director Joan Cronan, who held the interim job for both departments after Mike Hamilton resigned in 2011, texted Currie the night before he was fired. She said former LSU coach Les Miles had called her asking about the Tennessee opening. She said she was brainstorming about a Miles as HC, Martin as OC coupling.

But both Martin and Tennessee wanted different things, making a reunion impossible. In late December 2017, Martin spoke with reporters at the Cotton Bowl about the Tennessee coaching search. "It was a situation where if I was going back to Tennessee, it was to be as the head coach, not as coordinator. I made that message very clear."

Considering what a mess the coaching search had been, Fulmer's three options weren't too shabby. Kevin Steele did have Tennessee ties, and many fans were in favor of getting more Tennessee guys in the program. But considering his failures as the head coach at Baylor, Steele would have been a tough sell for Fulmer. It would come down to a choice between the defensive coordinators from the eventual national championship finalists.

Mel Tucker was forty-five years old and had been in coaching for the better part of two decades. He worked under Jim Tressel at Ohio State, Romeo Crennel with the Cleveland Browns and Jack Del Rio with the Jacksonville Jaguars. He had three stints as a Nick Saban assistant. But it was his most recent work at Georgia that was deservedly at the top of his resume. Tucker's Bulldogs were the sixth-ranked defense in the nation at the end of the 2017 season, allowing less than 300 yards of offense per game. Tennessee fans were aware of what a Tucker defense could do. Back on September 30, Georgia shutout the Vols 41-0. The Dawgs forced four turnovers as the Vols only picked up seven first downs all day.

The following month, Georgia head coach Kirby Smart was asked about how Tucker might fare as a head coach in the future. Tucker had no head coaching experience aside from five games as the interim head coach of the Jaguars in 2011. "Mel's a great leader. He commands great respect," Smart said. "Players really follow

Mel's lead... I know he'd do a tremendous job if given the opportunity."

Twenty years earlier, when Tucker's playing days were over, he made ends meet by selling steaks door to door. Now, he was on the cusp of getting the main job at one of the SEC's traditional powers.

As for Jeremy Pruitt, his resume looked a lot like Tucker's. Pruitt was forty-three years old and had two decades of coaching experience as well. He was Florida State's defensive coordinator during their 2013 BCS title winning season and was Georgia's defensive coordinator from 2014-2015. Like Tucker, Pruitt had multiple go-rounds working for with Nick Saban. Pruitt's Crimson Tide were the top-ranked defense in the nation in 2017, allowing just over 260 yards per game. Tennessee fans saw first-hand what a Jeremy Pruitt defense could do. In the past two seasons against Pruitt's Tide, the Vols offense produced a combined 271 yards of offense and ten points.

Sixteen years earlier, Pruitt was teaching elementary school Physical Education so that he could be an assistant coach on his dad's staff at Fort Payne High School in Alabama. Now, he was closing in on getting the head coaching job at a school that had won six national championships.

On Thursday, December 7, Fulmer's decision was made official. Jeremy Pruitt would become the twenty-sixth head football coach in Tennessee history.

Pruitt played his final two seasons of college football at Alabama. He served as a grad assistant at Alabama. He's from Alabama. There is something fun about Fulmer going to the Alabama well for this hire, because there is no fan base that despises Fulmer like that of the Crimson Tide. In the sixteen games in which Fulmer was the head coach against Alabama, he was 10-5-1. Tennessee's success in the Fulmer era (1993-2008) was coupled with Alabama's struggles.

Yes, there was indeed a time in which Alabama wasn't always a national title contender. Their efforts to replace Gene Stallings were failures. From Mike DuBose to Dennis Franchione to Mike

Price ("It's rolling, baby, it's rolling!") to Mike Shula, the Crimson Tide was mostly an SEC afterthought until Nick Saban arrived. Fulmer and the Vols were thriving during the pre-Saban era. But it was an off the field situation that forever cemented Fulmer's legacy as public enemy #1 in the minds of Alabama fans.

In January 2001, *The Commercial Appeal* reported that a Crimson Tide booster paid a high school coach $200,000 to get a recruit named Albert Means to go to Alabama. This was the fourth time in fourteen years in which they were penalized by the NCAA. In theory, as a repeat violator, they could have been facing the "Death Penalty." But that program ending move has only been used once (1987, SMU) and likely will never be used again.

Instead, Alabama got five years' probation and a two-year bowl ban. Three years after the story broke, a lawyer representing former Alabama assistant coaches Ronnie Cottrell and Ivy Williams contended that Fulmer provided information about the Crimson Tide to the NCAA that helped lead to those sanctions. Court records showed that Fulmer had called an NCAA investigator twice in 2000. Eventually, this would lead to the most bizarre moment in SEC Media Days history. In 2004, I was working as a sports reporter at WATE-TV and awaiting UT's appearance in Hoover. Offensive lineman Michael Munoz and linebacker Kevin Burnett were there representing the Vols. But Phillip Fulmer was not. Had Fulmer traveled across the Alabama state line, he would have been served a subpoena in Cottrell's and Williams's lawsuit against the NCAA. Fulmer stayed in Tennessee and was fined $10,000 by the conference for failing to attend SEC Media Days.

This led to Fulmer been criticized by many media outlets and Alabama fans. They were saying that Fulmer had left his players in the lurch by not showing up in Hoover. Even if Fulmer wasn't there physically, he wasn't going to let that condemnation go unanswered. Fulmer addressed the media horde... via speakerphone.

"You can talk about my coaching if we lose," Fulmer said, and you could hear in his voice how mad he was about this entire circus. "You can talk about my play-calling in games. You might talk about my physique if you chose to stoop that low. But 'coward' is way over the line. The same people that used the space to call me a 'coward' have used that same space to talk about cleaning up the SEC from cheating."

"People in Alabama think Phil Fulmer is a hypocrite," wrote Cecil Hurt later that year. Hurt is the long-time sports editor at *The Tuscaloosa News*. "They just don't like him."

"Phillip Fulmer is one of most hated men in Alabama. That's just the easiest way to put it," says Wendy Jardet. She's been an Alabama fan since the day she was born. Her Dad played for Bear Bryant as part of those great Ken Stabler teams in the 1960s. "We know Fulmer as a snitch and a coward. It all boils down to the way he handled everything. When he was fired in 2008 there was a party in Tuscaloosa... it was intense."

Jardet has a unique perspective on the Tide/Vols rivalry, as she's lived most of her adult life in Knoxville. "I love everything about the rivalry. I hate Tennessee more than Auburn and that's saying a lot. It seemed like Fulmer took pleasure in all of that happening. At the time Tennessee was dominant. I think that's what threw us fans off because Alabama wasn't dominant at all back then."

I can tell you from working in Knoxville at the time that this episode wasn't that big a deal in Tennessee. The Vols were still in the SEC championship mix most seasons, and that story didn't get much play after Hoover. But in Alabama, this was huge. There were even some fans who wanted the Alabama/Tennessee series ended. In 2008, Fulmer was finally served a subpoena at SEC Media Days, this time by the law firm representing booster Wendell Smith in his lawsuit against the NCAA.

Now, all these years later, Fulmer believed that it would be addition by subtraction. Of course, he didn't pick a top Nick Saban assistant just to hurt Alabama football. But if that would be one of the end results, I don't think he'd mind either.

On Thursday, December 7, five years to the day after Butch Jones was hired by Dave Hart, Phillip Fulmer and Jeremy Pruitt stood at the front of the Peyton Manning Locker Room, holding a number 26 orange Tennessee jersey with "Pruitt" on the back.

Nearly a month after Jones's firing, the Vols had a new head coach.

The craziest coaching search in the history of college football was finally over.

20

JUST PRUITT

UT CHANCELLOR DR. BEVERLY DAVENPORT opened the introductory press conference for new Tennessee head coach Jeremy Pruitt. This was certainly a much more pleasant occasion for Davenport, as well as the UT athletic department and administration, when compared to the last media opportunity six days before when she announced the firing of athletics director John Currie.

When Davenport spoke, she was also addressing the country. As UT President Joe DiPietro said the previous week, the entire episode damaged the University of Tennessee's reputation. This was a day to try to get some of it back.

"We're really excited that you're going to be a part of this Volunteer family, and I promise you, you're going to love it," Davenport said to Pruitt. "I think you're going to quickly see how passionate our fans are and how warm and welcoming they are."

Next up was Fulmer, who shed some light on the coaching search. "I've spent five exciting days interviewing outstanding men to be our new football coach. I interviewed head coaches, and coordinators with both offensive and defensive backgrounds." SMU's Chad Morris was a head coach who was reported to have communicated with Tennessee during this time. He was offered and accepted the head coaching job at Arkansas the day before the Vols hired Pruitt. Clemson defensive coordinator Brent Venables was also contacted. Gridiron Now's John Brice reported that discussions had been held with former LSU coach Les Miles. But remember, as always, in college football no one is ever offered the job until they *accept* the job.

"My obligation to our alumni and our great fans, and especially to our former and future players who have or will pour their hearts into this program, was to go find the best coach to get our proud program back to the level of its championship tradition," said Fulmer.

Pruitt was getting a six-year deal for $3.8 million annually, and he made sure to give the proper respect. "Coach Fulmer, it's very rare for a first-time head football coach that you get an opportunity to work with a boss that has not only done what Coach Fulmer has done, he's done it at the place that you're about to do it. Thank you for giving me this opportunity and I'll probably be knocking on your door."

"I know Jeremy Pruitt. I call him a friend," said former Tennessee assistant coach Trooper Taylor. "He is smart enough to know that he has all that knowledge right down the hall. You'd be a bad coach if you weren't a sponge. Fulmer has been there. There is no substitute for experience. One thing I know is if Fulmer doesn't know something, he won't blow smoke. Pruitt and Fulmer will fit like a glove."

"I think having Fulmer there now helps Tennessee," says South Carolina head coach Will Muschamp. "He will have everyone pulling in the right direction. When everyone isn't, that makes things really difficult. I think that's why they had problems before. But hiring Fulmer and hiring Pruitt, who is a really good coach, they'll all be pulling in the right direction."

Pruitt's press conference was filled with a lot of the quotes that Tennessee fans liked to hear. "There was a time and place that this university was feared among the rest of the SEC. My goal as the head football coach at the University of Tennessee is to get us back to that point."

"What kind of football team do we want to have here? My vision for our football team is we want to be a big, fast, dominating, aggressive, relentless football team that nobody in the SEC wants to play."

"Recruiting. It's the lifeblood of any organization. We're going to start right here in this state. We're going to start from Knoxville and work our way out. This is going to be our state."

But what fans will remember the most was Pruitt's penchant for saying "aight" following what felt like every sentence. It was a little bit quirky, but it was endearing. Nick Saban has a habit of saying "all right" during interviews so perhaps he picked it up from his now former boss. In all, the press conference wasn't all that different than what Tennessee fans had seen four times since 2008. The new coach was projecting confidence following what was a rough period for Vols football. Pruitt though wasn't brash like Kiffin, goofy like Dooley or filled with clichés like Jones.

Kiffin, Dooley and Jones each had their chances. Now, it was Pruitt's turn on the throne. "Jeremy has done a tremendous job for our program, and we appreciate everything he has done to contribute to our success," said Alabama head coach Nick Saban in a quote released by the University of Tennessee. "He is hard-working, dedicated and organized with exceptional knowledge of the game."

Tennessee fans remembered the glowing recommendation Saban gave Derek Dooley in 2010 so they can be excused for taking that quote with a grain of salt. Jalen Ramsey had perhaps the best summary of Pruitt. Ramsey played at Brentwood Academy in Nashville. He was a 5-star cornerback and the top high school football player in the state of Tennessee for the Class of 2013. Ramsey was pretty much ignored by Derek Dooley's staff. He was committed to Lane Kiffin and Southern Cal until Jeremy Pruitt came calling. Pruitt had just been hired as the Seminoles' defensive coordinator and got Ramsey to flip to Florida State shortly before National Signing Day.

In 2016, Ramsey was the fifth-overall pick in the NFL Draft by Jacksonville and has become a Pro Bowl player for the Jaguars. "Coach P was one of my favorite coaches because he had a good balance of work and play," Ramsey said in a statement. "I was never a Tennessee Volunteer fan growing up and that's a main reason I didn't go there, but now I hope nothing but the best for their program and Coach Pruitt. Maybe I would have made a different decision back then."

Two days after that press conference, Tennessee was hosting Lipscomb in a men's basketball game. During a timeout, Phillip Fulmer walked onto the court at Thompson-Boling Arena. Fulmer received a loud ovation from Vols fans. The guy he introduced got an enthusiastic cheer as well. It was Jeremy's Pruitt's first opportunity to connect in person with Tennessee fans. "We're gonna have one goal. And that's to win every one of them [games]."

The pep band played "Rocky Top" and the crowd cheered Pruitt as he walked off the court. This was during a TV timeout and in all the entire PR effort probably took about 90 seconds. From there, Pruitt had to get back to work on his two most important duties. Securing a coaching staff, and recruiting the Class of 2018.

In December 2017, t-shirts hit the stores in Knoxville, welcoming the arrival of the newly hired Tennessee Head Coach, Jeremy Pruitt.

Getting both of those things accomplished was going to be tricky, because Pruitt wasn't completely Tennessee's yet. Much like Kirby Smart did two years before; Jeremy Pruitt made the decision to stay with Alabama as defensive coordinator throughout the college football playoff.

"I am in this business for the kids," said Pruitt. "I work for the University of Tennessee, and I am all in for the university. I also have a commitment to the kids whose homes I sat in with their parents and recruited them to go to the University of Alabama. Coach Saban has been wonderful to me. I would not be here today without his help, so I am going to go back as soon as dead period starts and coach those kids."

New NCAA rules allowed recruits to avoid waiting until National Signing Day in February. The Class of 2018 could sign with their schools during the third week in December. The early signing period was a game changer. Instead of having two months to establish relationships with some recruits, Pruitt would have less than two weeks. The first early signing period was December 20-22, 2017.

In the hours after his hiring, Pruitt was in touch with committed recruits like Farragut tight end Jacob Warren and Gibbs offensive lineman Ollie Lane, two local kids who weren't going anywhere. He also reached out to players like Coffee County Central High School quarterback Alontae Taylor, who was projected to play wide receiver in college. Taylor was ranked by 247Sports as the twenty-third best receiver in the country for the Class of 2018. Taylor, one of the best prep players in the state of Tennessee, was originally committed to the Vols, and then de-committed the day Butch Jones was fired. Pruitt called Taylor and got him to Knoxville for an official visit that Saturday, December 9.

"I'm a Tennessee boy," Taylor told me the night before making the trip to the UT campus. "I love the Orange and White. I love the fanbase. I have a lot of family so them being able to come watch me play is important." Taylor, a 4-star prospect, re-committed to Tennessee on December 13.

The news was not as positive regarding the player Tennessee fans wanted more than any other, 5-star Knoxville Catholic offensive lineman Cade Mays. On the first day of the early signing period, Mays chose Georgia over Clemson and Ohio State. "We just signed the greatest class in the history of football," Mays told reporters. "We are gonna do something special with it, I promise you that."

In recent years Clemson went to East Tennessee to swipe highly sought-after recruits Tee Higgins (Oak Ridge High School) and Amari Rodgers (Knoxville Catholic High School) from the Vols. Now, it was Georgia with Mays. The SEC East is improving. Pruitt is going to have his work cut out for him in seasons to come.

"Tennessee high school football is getting better but that won't sustain your program," says former Tennessee assistant coach Mark Elder. "You have to go into someone else's yard and beat them. You don't realize it. You lose your home field advantage at Nashville (two and a half hours from Knoxville). It's not like Ohio State going into Cincinnati. You don't go to Memphis and see everyone wearing UT stuff. It's a melting pot out there. You lose your advantage at Nashville. I know people don't like to hear that but guess what, it's real. They haven't walked in these shoes..."

Elder's point is a valid one. Knoxville is a little under 400 miles from Memphis. You can get to Charlotte or Atlanta or Greenville-Spartanburg or Birmingham much quicker than you can the in-state city that traditionally has the most high school football talent. And in Memphis, you are competing with Arkansas and Ole Miss and Mississippi State, schools that are much closer than Tennessee. Plus, the University of Memphis has proven they are a program to be reckoned with in recent years too.

"Tennessee high schools will always have players, but not the total numbers like Georgia or LSU," says former Tennessee assistant Trooper Taylor. "Just look at the proximity. So they have to go into other states for players. If you get them on campus you have a chance because Knoxville is a great place. They see the tradition and all the great players. That's going to be the key for that staff."

Pruitt is considered to be one of the top recruiters in college football. He and his (in progress) staff brought in fourteen early signees, including five of the top ten players in the state. Two Cordova High School standouts, offensive lineman Jerome Carvin and running back Jeremy Banks, were important gets in this cycle. Nashville Christian defensive lineman Brant Lawless had been committed since May and didn't reopen his commitment even after Butch Jones was fired. Greg Emerson, a defensive end from Jackson, didn't play football in 2017 due to injury, but was picked for the U.S. Army All-America Game.

"We are excited to welcome this group of outstanding young men who signed with us today," said Pruitt in a statement on December 20. "They are terrific football players, who also display exceptional character off the field. We appreciate the commitment they have made to the University of Tennessee."

With the early signing period done, Pruitt was back in Tuscaloosa, working for Tennessee's traditional rival as the Tide were trying to win yet another national championship. This put Vols fans in an odd spot. Rooting for your new coach meant rooting for Alabama. Some fans boast about "conference pride." Chants of "S-E-C!" break out often when an SEC team is beating a team from another conference. Some fans root for other SEC teams when they don't have a dog in the hunt. That said, for Tennessee fans, watching Alabama control the league while going 0-11 against them since 2007, has been torture.

If Alabama lost to Clemson in the semifinals on New Year's Day, the Vols would have their coach all to themselves starting January 2. But of course, if the past decade has proved anything, it's that Tennessee fans couldn't be that lucky. Pruitt's defense only allowed a couple of field goals in a 24-6 Sugar Bowl victory over Clemson, so Pruitt would be Alabama's for another week. Oh, and Georgia beat Oklahoma 54-48 in overtime at the Rose Bowl. That meant two of the Vols three biggest rivals would play for the national title.

Back in 2009, to make way for the new UT Student Health Center, "The Rock" was moved about 275 feet to its current home at the corner of Pat Head Summitt Street and Volunteer Boulevard. Was the 97-ton stone now placed over ancient burial ground? No other way to explain the misfortune. For Tennessee fans, that National Championship Game was like that scene in *The Dark Knight Returns.* If they were to have a rooting interest, they were choosing "Death or Exile," with both choices resulting in their demise. If Alabama won, it's yet another year of Saban ruling the country. If Georgia won, now you have a division rival at the top of the food chain and coming off a massive early signing period recruiting haul too. Either way, it was awful and the 2017 football season couldn't end soon enough. The football gods wouldn't even let the game end in regulation as Alabama beat Georgia 26-23 in overtime. Jeremy Pruitt was now part of a fifth national championship team. The next day, he walked into his new office in Knoxville and finally could begin working full-time on rebuilding the Vols.

In the weeks that followed, Pruitt filled out his coaching staff. Tyson Helton was the offensive coordinator. He came over from Southern Cal, where he was working as quarterbacks coach and passing game coordinator. For defensive coordinator, Pruitt brought in Georgia linebackers coach Kevin Sherrer, someone he's known since they were teammates at Alabama in 1995.

Pruitt got some Tennessee blood on his staff with the hiring of Terry Fair as the Vols' defensive backs coach. Fair was a key member of the 1997 SEC championship team and a first-round draft pick of the Detroit Lions in 1998. Pruitt also brought in former Vols Kevin Simon and Montario Hardesty to join his staff in an off-the-field capacity.

"I think it is vital," says former Tennessee Vols wide receiver Jayson Swain. "I know what they are about. I know how they related to players. A lot of guys need someone that have been in their shoes to communicate with them the way they need to and still have the respect there."

According to 247Sports, Tennessee's Class of 2018 was ranked twentieth in the country. The Class of 2019 needs to fill a role like the Class of 2014 did for the Vols. Young players will not only get the chance to play right away, but Pruitt will need them to make an immediate impact the way Derek Barnett, Jalen Hurd, Josh Malone and others did. The Class of 2018 got a late boost when Stanford grad transfer quarterback Kelly Chryst chose to play at UT for his final season of college football. Everything appeared to show a program moving forward. A new era in Tennessee football was underway. One slight problem. The most visible remnant of the previous era of Tennessee football was still present.

From the moment Butch Jones was fired on Sunday, November 12, Tennessee fans began looking to the Neyland Stadium Jumbotron, and waiting for the image of Butch Jones to be removed. Perhaps that week or after the regular season, but certainly it would happen in due time. There were no changes made to the Jumbotron in December. On January 2, a Tennessee fan tweeted to UT Chancellor Beverly Davenport, wanting the Butch Jones picture taken down. She tweeted a response: "Please hang on. A crane has been ordered." A few weeks later, Fulmer spoke with WBIR-TV about the Jumbotron. "That's not an easy process," he said. "There's mechanical things involved to get that done. It's not just, 'Let's take down a picture off the wall or a graphic.' We're working through that."

But January came and went, as did February. The one hundred day mark was eventually reached and passed. Tennessee told Butch Jones they didn't want him to be their football coach, yet his picture still greeted those visiting the UT campus three months after his firing. On one of my stops on "The Hill," I took the picture that you see on the cover of this book. The delays felt like a sign that the dysfunction that had plagued Tennessee athletics wasn't done just yet.

Finally, on the morning of Monday, March 5, a truck from Sycamore Sign Service was spotted at the Gate 10 ramp, which leads up to the South End Zone at Neyland Stadium. Throughout the morning, people showed up to document the historic events from the G10 parking garage. On gamedays, G10 is the site of much revelry. Whether the Vols are winning or losing, the fans will pregame for hours with a beverage of choice and a conversation.

But on this day, a smattering of fans were there to witness something 113 days in the making. There was no crane, but at approximately 11:40am, three workers on a platform you'd see used by window washers brought the Butch Jones picture to the ground. And that was that. As of March 14, the Butch Jones/General Neyland/Reggie White Jumbotron was now the Al Wilson/General Neyland/Jason Witten Jumbotron. Wilson was the heart and soul of the 1997 and 1998 Tennessee teams that won two SEC titles and a national championship. Witten is the pride of Elizabethton, and a future NFL Hall of Famer. Neyland is still there, with a new picture.

To an outsider, the Jumbotron picture situation might seem trivial, but for Tennessee fans the removal was therapeutic. The recent past had not been kind, and this was a final page that needed to be turned. After a decade in which the Vols went 4-26 against their three biggest rivals (Alabama, Florida, and Georgia), the Vols and their fans needed a fresh start. They have that with Jeremy Pruitt.

"I said all along that all Tennessee needed was a good person and a good football coach," says Swain. "You don't need a marketer... you just need to know how this place is. This is warm place. We know our football, and we really respond well to good people. Now we have Fulmer and his past success and Pruitt fits well. He's a good guy and I've heard good things about how he treats people."

Tennessee football has only had a few moments of relevance recently, but Vols fans have very good memories. They'll tell you where they were when Dale Jones made a point-blank interception to secure the 1985 win over Alabama, or when Jeff Powell outraced the Miami defense in the 1986 Sugar Bowl. They tell you how they watched the 1991 Miracle at South Bend and remember how it felt when Collins Cooper's kick went wide left for Florida in 1998. They still get chills when hearing clips of John Ward call a game or seeing Peerless Price grabbing the deep ball from Tee Martin on that cool January night in Tempe in 1999.

They want to have those feelings again. "The power is in the people, not the buildings. And we got away from that for a while," says Swain. "Stadiums don't win games. Miami had awful facilities but in 2001 they won a national title because they had dudes and guys that they recruited, and that team was together. That's what wins games. If money was everything then Oregon would be undefeated every year. It's the people. We got away from that, realized it and now got Fulmer. He understands that."

On November 26, the future of Tennessee athletics was going to be Currie/Schiano. This would be coming on the heels of the

Hamilton/Dooley duo and the Hart/Jones tandem. Instead, it is Fulmer/Pruitt. It's a trade Tennessee fans wanted. The November 2017 revolt made that happen.

What was it Fulmer said on the day he was hired as AD? *"Let's go have fun winning championships."*

It'll happen again… it's only a question of when.

EPILOGUE

SINCE PHILLIP FULMER'S FIRING IN NOVEMBER 2008, the University of Tennessee's revenue sports (football, men's basketball) hadn't won a national championship, a conference championship or even a divisional title. There have been a few close calls, but the Vols simply haven't been a factor in the sports their fans care about the most. Football and men's basketball hold an important place in the financial and emotional standing of an athletic department.

This made the timing and the achievement of the 2017-2018 Tennessee men's basketball team so special. It was the third season at the helm of the Vols program for Rick Barnes. He is a Hall of Fame coach who was fired after 17 seasons at Texas, where he went 402-180 with three conference championships and a trip to the 2003 Final Four.

"We are very, very fortunate today to have hired an elite basketball coach," said Tennessee AD Dave Hart in quite the understatement. Barnes walked into a program in upheaval. Even though UT had been to four of the previous nine Sweet Sixteens, Barnes was now the Vols fourth coach in six seasons. Bruce Pearl left in disgrace. Cuonzo Martin bolted a situation that had become toxic. Donnie Tyndall was fired because Tennessee didn't use Google.

But Rick Barnes was the right man at the right time, and a gift from the gods for Hart. For Barnes, it was a chance to be close to his boyhood home in North Carolina, as well as his alma mater Lenoir-Rhyne in his hometown of Hickory.

"When Dave and I started talking... the one thing he said to me is, `we've got to create stability,'" Barnes said. "I just want you to know that I'm really, truly, really excited about what's happening here on Rocky Top."

During the first two seasons under Barnes, the Vols didn't do very much, finishing a combined 31-35. In 2017-2018, Tennessee was picked by the media to finish a lowly thirteenth in the SEC. Skeptics said Barnes had mailed it in, that this was just one last paycheck before he rode off into the sunset. But to most everyone's surprise, the Vols were actually pretty good, and on March 3, 2018, they were looking to achieve something that hadn't been done in a decade at Tennessee, and that's win an SEC championship. A sold-out crowd of 22,237 at Thompson-Boling Arena watched the Vols rally from a late deficit to beat Georgia 66-61. The game showed off some of Tennessee's best qualities. They were unselfish. They found a way to win despite their best player, SEC player of the year Grant Williams, fouling out with 3:33 to go. They played stifling defense, allowing only 19 points in the second half. Tennessee shared the conference title with Bruce Pearl and the Auburn Tigers.

"The last two years we have had a group of guys that are blue collar guys that worked hard, said Barnes. "I found out early that Tennessee likes that." After the game, SEC championship t-shirts and hats were passed around, and "Rocky Top" was sung at peak volumes. Tennessee athletics director Phillip Fulmer stood on the court named after his good friend Pat Summitt and smiled ear to ear. Fulmer looked like a proud papa while watching the Vols celebrate a title along with Tennessee fans.

The Vols would receive a three seed in the South Region of the NCAA tournament. Tennessee beat Wright State 73-47 in the opener and seemed to get a break when eleven seed Loyola Chicago shocked six seed Miami at the buzzer. If the Vols could beat the Ramblers, they'd advance to the Sweet Sixteen for only the eighth time in program history.

And then it happened. Actually, not it. Her.

Sister Jean Dolores Schmidt is the ninety-eight-year-old team chaplain for Loyola Chicago. After the win over Miami, Sister Jean was interviewed on the truTV broadcast. She was sitting in her wheelchair and looked like everyone's grandma. America instantly fell in love with Sister Jean.

Her Ramblers hadn't lost a game since January, and they showed Tennessee why they were on an 11-game win streak. Loyola Chicago led by four at the half, and with 3:25 to go; they were on top 60-51. Things looked bleak for the Vols. But with 27 seconds left, the Vols had pulled within two. They had the ball, and Barnes drew up a play for Grant Williams, who delivered with a short jumper. He was fouled, made the free throw, and somehow, Tennessee was in the lead 62-61.

The Vols were one defensive stop away from a trip to the Sweet Sixteen in Atlanta. For those who believe in curses, what happened next added fuel to the fire. Loyola Chicago's Clayton Custer took the inbounds pass and drove near the lane. He hoisted a fall-away 15-footer from the right side of the court. The shot hit the side of the rim, then bounced high off the glass, rattled around the iron, and dropped in with 3.6 seconds left. The Vols inbounded to Jordan Bone, who pushed up court quickly and got a good look from the top of the key. His shot hit the back rim and bounced away.

Loyola Chicago 63, Tennessee 62. After celebrating with her players, Sister Jean revealed on the TNT broadcast what she said to the Ramblers during the pre-game prayer. "I told them that we were going to win, that we could do it. God would be on our side and we were just going to do it today." It was hard to argue against her. Loyola Chicago would go all the way to the Final Four.

Everyone loves the Cinderella story until it comes at the expense of your team.

Phillip Fulmer had made the trip to Dallas and tweeted later that night. "I remain proud of their season, their coaches, their leadership, character, fight, and grit. It was a fun team to watch play, and be around."

Throughout that evening I checked out my Twitter timeline and there were two themes that stood out the most. First, Tennessee fans tweeted their appreciation for what the Vols accomplished this season. It had been a long time since a Tennessee team had won a championship, and this group delivered a trophy. 2018-2019 has the potential of being an even more special season for Tennessee basketball.

Second, that this is a communal experience. Vols fans are in this together. Tennessee is consistently in the top ten nationally in attendance for football, men's basketball and women's basketball and Lady Vols softball. The losing feels ten times as bad as the winning feels good. That is the contract you enter as a fan. Even after a decade of struggles in Tennessee athletics, the fans are rarely deterred from showing up.

On April 21, 2018, Jeremy Pruitt led the Vols into Neyland Stadium for the Orange & White Game. Come September he'll be on the sidelines for games that count. Will his coaching career end up like Fulmer's? Kiffin's? Dooley's? It's impossible to predict.

One thing is certain. Tennessee's coaches will come and go. Tennessee's players will come and go. Tennessee's administrators will come and go.

But it's the Tennessee fans who will remain.

This was proven even more so when on Wednesday, May 2, UT President Joe DiPietro fired UT-Knoxville Chancellor Beverly Davenport. In a statement released by the University of Tennessee, DiPietro said, "Dr. Davenport and I have had several conversations during her tenure as chancellor to lay out expectations, and discuss concerns. Unfortunately, issues arose that have progressed and, while I am disappointed to have to make this change, it is necessary and in the best interests of the University."

In the letter of termination that DiPietro wrote to Davenport, he detailed the reasons that she was fired. Not since Tupac's "Hit 'Em Up" has there been a diss track this severe.

Some of DiPietro's most pointed criticisms are as follows:

- "The relationship between us, as well as that between you (and some members of your cabinet) and some on my leadership team continues to be unsatisfactory. More times than I find acceptable, there has been a lack of trust, collaboration, communication and transparency in these relationships and it has been counterproductive to the collective success of the university."
- "You would have benefited from a professional coach, and your unwillingness to routinely engage one, despite my recommendation that you do so, has been frustrating."
- "You have not acclimated yourself to the UT system and still appear unwilling to try to understand or acknowledge the value of the UT system. I continue to detect that you (and some members of your cabinet) have an 'us (UTK) vs. them (UT system and UT Board)' mentality."
- "Your one on one, small group, and business transactional communication skills are very poor. I have had multiple people on multiple occasions complain that you do not listen to the person talking to you or pay attention to the details of written communications you receive. I also have received multiple complaints from multiple people about your ability to communicate orally."

Davenport wasn't being kicked off campus. Instead, she was to be re-assigned. Starting on July 1, Davenport would become a "full-time faculty appointment as Professor, with tenure, in the School of Communication Studies."

She would make 75% of her Chancellor's salary, meaning that for the next four years, she was eligible to earn $438,750 annually. Yes, a big reason why Davenport was fired as Chancellor was for having poor communication skills, and now she could receive over $1.75 million to teach a couple of classes... in the Communications Department.

If you think that's absurd, you're right. But wait, there's more... Just as this book was going to print, the University of Tennessee Board of Trustees Audit and Compliance Committee was going to vote on a recommendation from DiPietro. He was asking them to approve a separation agreement, which would end Davenport's employment immediately.
The settlement? $1.33 million.

That buyout life, y'all...

The day after Davenport's firing, DiPietro named Wayne Davis, dean of UT's College of Engineering, as her replacement on an interim basis. Since 2008, twenty-four people (including interims) have held some of the most important administrative and athletics positions at the University of Tennessee:

- Seven football coaches (Fulmer, Kiffin, Dooley, Chaney, Jones, Hoke, Pruitt)
- Four men's basketball coaches (Pearl, Martin, Tyndall, Barnes)
- Five UT Athletics Directors (Hamilton, Cronan, Hart, Currie, Fulmer)
- Three UT Presidents (Petersen, Simek, DiPietro)
- Five UT-Knoxville Chancellors (Loren Crabtree, Simek, Cheek, Davenport, Davis)

We are counting Fulmer and Simek twice as they worked two separate positions. We are not counting Kippy Brown because he officially isn't in the record books as head coach, since he didn't coach a game.

With that kind of instability at the top, it is not a surprise that the past decade truly has been one of dysfunction at the University of Tennessee. Until that revolving door is slammed shut for at least a reasonable period of time, it will be very difficult for UT's athletics program to return to its glorious past.

On the morning of Monday, March 5, 2018, a picture of Butch Jones was finally removed from the Neyland Stadium Jumbotron, more than 16 weeks after he had been fired. Jones would eventually be replaced on the structure by Al Wilson, one of the most revered players in Tennessee history.

ACKNOWLEDGEMENTS

WRITING A BOOK IS NOT EASY. I knew that going in. For months, whenever I've had free time, I've been on my laptop. I've done my best to tell the complete story of the past ten years at Tennessee, not only with the football program, but all that led to the coaching search of 2017. There are so many people for me to thank, and I know that I am going to leave some folks out. If I forgot you, my sincerest apologies.

First of all, I couldn't have done this without my smart and beautiful wife Jennifer. She designed the book and cover and was on top of the printing and distribution every step of the way. I love you bunches.

Thank you to my daughters Lillian and Emily. Daddy tries his hardest to give you a good childhood and hope I'm succeeding.

Thank you to my Mom and Dad, who taught me the importance of education. I hope that I've been even close to as good a parent as they have been to me.

To my dogs Mattingly and Bailey. Mattingly is named after my favorite baseball player of all-time (Donnie Baseball should be in the Hall of Fame) and Bailey got her name from the Knoxville bar/restaurant where I met my wife. Mattingly and Bailey would hang out with me during most of the writing. Thanks, ladies.

Thank you to former Tennessee assistant coaches Zach Azzanni, Dave Clawson, Mike DeBord, Mark Elder and Trooper Taylor. They gave up some of their valuable minutes to talk for this book. Thank you to former Tennessee football players Ben Bartholomew, Charles Folger, Malik Foreman, Derrick Furlow, Jr., Daniel Hood, Cody Pope, Jayson Swain, LaMarcus Thompson, Daryl Vereen, Fred White, James Wilhoit and Justin Worley. Their insights were critical.

Thank you to former Tennessee athletic department representatives David Blackburn, Brian Davis, Roger Hoover, Brian Rice and Jimmy Stanton.

Thank you to Ty Darlington, Amarlo Montez Herrera, Lane Kiffin, Will Muschamp, Patton Robinette, Kyle Woestmann and others in the world of college football.

Thank you, Beth Kendrick.

Thank you, State Representative Jeremy Faison.

Thanks to all the current and former media members that took time out of their schedules to help me. There's no way I could have written this book without you.

Thanks to my copy editor, Amanda Clark Youngers. SUNY Geneseo Pride.

And finally, thank you Tennessee fans. Your support and your stories made this book happen.

NOTE OF SOURCES

Chapter 1
https://247sports.com/college/tennessee/Article/Playing-the-what-if-game-The-1992-changing-of-the-guard-Tennesse-53306106
http://articles.latimes.com/1992-11-30/sports/sp-1050_1_johnny-majors
http://www.espn.com/college-football/recap?gameId=273002633
http://www.espn.com/college-football/recap?gameId=273142633
http://www.espn.com/college-football/recap?gameId=273280096
http://www.asapsports.com/show_interview.php?id=46795
Chapter 2
http://www.utsports.com/news/2008/1/11/Vols_Name_Clawson_Off_Coor_QB_Coach.aspx?path=football
http://www.utsports.com/news/2008/9/2/UT_UCLA_Postgame_Quotes.aspx?path=football
http://www.utsports.com/news/2008/11/1/Tennessee_South_Carolina_Post_Game_Quotes.aspx?path=football
http://www.utsports.com/news/2008/11/3/Press_Conference_Comments_What_Others_Said_About_Fulmer.aspx?path=football
http://www.utsports.com/news/2008/11/29/Kentucky_Tennessee_Postgame_Quotes.aspx?path=football
Chapter 3
http://www.nfl.com/news/story/0ap2000000296707/article/lane-kiffins-pitch-to-alshon-jeffery-comes-back-to-haunt-him
http://www.utsports.com/news/2009/2/16/Blackburn_Expands_Role_Returns_as_UT_Football_Operations_Director.aspx?path=football
http://www.nytimes.com/2009/09/20/sports/ncaafootball/20gators.html
https://patch.com/california/santamonica/ex-college-football-player-gets-11-year-prison-term-killing-mothers-boyfriend
http://www.utsports.com/news/2009/12/31/Vols_Fall_to_Virginia_Tech_in_Chick_fil_A_Bowl.aspx?path=football
Chapter 4
http://www.espn.com/nfl/news/story?id=4816494
Chapter 6
http://www.sandiegouniontribune.com/sdut-tennessee-ad-mike-hamilton-to-resign-2011jun07-story.html
http://www.espn.com/college-football/recap?gameId=313232633
http://www.utsports.com/news/2011/11/26/Tennessee_Kentucky_Postgame_Quotes.aspx?path=football
https://scout.com/college/michigan-state/Article/Arnett-Releases-Statement-104864490
http://www.utsports.com/news/2012/1/3/Derek_Dooley_s_Media_Session.aspx?path=football
https://www.sbnation.com/2010/5/5/1646874/two-more-examples-that-in-the-end
http://www.al.com/sports/index.ssf/2011/06/aaron_douglas_drugs_autopsy_report.html
http://www.local8now.com/home/headlines/Bray-throw-beer-bottles-as-car-no-charges-filed-163758016.html

http://theknoxvillejournal.com/bad-boy-tyler-bray-at-it-again/
http://www.utsports.com/news/2012/8/27/UT_Athletics_Provides_Financial_Update.asphttp://www.utsports.com/news/2012/9/15/Post_Game_Quotes_No_18_Florida_37_No_23_Tennessee_20.aspx?path=football
http://www.utsports.com/news/2012/9/29/No_5_Georgia_51_Tennessee_44_Post_Game_Quotes.aspx?path=football
http://www.utsports.com/news/2012/10/14/No_19_Mississippi_State_41_Tennessee_31_Post_Game_Quotes.aspx?path=football
http://www.utsports.com/news/2012/10/20/Tennessee_Alabama_Postgame_Quotes.aspx?path=football
http://www.utsports.com/news/2012/11/10/Post_Game_Quotes_Missouri_51_Tennessee_48.aspx?path=football
http://www.utsports.com/news/2012/11/18/Dooley_Will_Not_Return_As_Vols_Head_Coach.aspx?path=football
esaewhttp://www.utsports.com/news/2012/11/18/Dave_Hart_Addresses_Vols_Football_Future.aspx?path=football

Chapter 7
https://www.cbssports.com/college-football/news/how-mike-gundy-nearly-became-a-tennessee-vol/
https://www.youtube.com/watch?v=JKaNm6gZjnM
http://gobearcats.com/news/2009/12/16/Butch_Jones_Press_Conference_Quotes.aspx?path=football
https://www.knoxnews.com/story/sports/college/university-of-tennessee/football/2016/12/15/tennessee-makes-final-buyout-payment-derek-dooley/95217948/
http://www.tennessean.com/story/sports/college/ut/2016/08/18/butch-jones-first-meeting-dave-hart-all-night-conversation/88978914/
http://www.utsports.com/news/2012/12/7/Jones_Press_Conference_Transcript.aspx?path=football
https://www.usatoday.com/story/sports/ncaaf/2012/12/07/butch-jones-leaving-cincinnati-new-football-coach-tennessee/1754835/
http://www.utsports.com/news/2013/2/6/Family_Effort_Produces_Jones_1st_UT_Class.aspx?path=football
https://247sports.com/college/tennessee/Article/Jones-touts-Vols-academic-turnaround-74884923
http://www.al.com/sports/index.ssf/2013/08/phillip_fulmer_says_administra.html
http://www.utsports.com/news/2013/9/14/Postgame_Quotes_Vols_At_Oregon.aspx?path=football
http://www.utsports.com/news/2013/9/21/Postgame_Quotes_19_Florida_31_Tennessee_17.aspx?path=football
http://www.utsports.com/news/2013/10/5/Postgame_Quotes_6_Georgia_34_UT_31_OT.aspx?path=football
http://www.volnation.com/volsblog/2013-10-15/johnny-majors-agrees-that-butch-gets-it/
http://www.vucommodores.com/sports/m-footbl/spec-rel/111813aac.html
http://www.utsports.com/news/2013/10/19/A_Meaningful_Day_for_Vols_Seniors.aspx?path=football
http://www.utsports.com/news/2013/11/23/Postgame_Quotes_Vandy_14_Tennessee_10.aspx?path=football
http://www.espn.com/college-football/recap?gameId=333272633

Chapter 8
http://www.utsports.com/news/2014/2/5/Butch_Jones_VolsNSD14_Press_Conference.aspx?path=football
http://www.utsports.com/news/2014/7/15/Jones_Players_Transcripts_At_SECMD14.aspx?path=football
http://archive.knoxnews.com/sports/vols/other/bud-fords-claim-against-ut-dismissed-ep-631765070-354227451.html
http://newsok.com/lawyer-lady-vols-media-director-forced-to-retire/article/feed/385650
http://www.tennessean.com/story/sports/college/vols/2014/10/02/debby-jennings-tennessee-vols-lawsuit-dave-hart/16611729/
http://www.espn.com/womens-college-basketball/story/_/id/14503557/settlement-reached-lawsuit-ex-lady-vols-officials-tennessee
http://www.utsports.com/news/2014/8/16/_VolReport_40_000_Fans_For_Practice_.aspx?path=football
http://www.timesfreepress.com/news/local/story/2014/sep/30/tennessees-checker-neyland-movement-emerged-humble/268364/
http://utsports.com/news/2014/10/4/Postgame_Quotes_UF_10_UT_9.aspx?path=football
http://utsports.com/news/2014/10/19/Postgame_Quotes_Ole_Miss_34_Vols_3.aspx?path=football
http://utsports.com/news/2014/10/20/Media_Monday_Players_Preview_Alabama.aspx?path=football
http://utsports.com/news/2014/10/20/Media_Monday_Jones_Previews_Bama_Game.aspx?path=football
http://utsports.com/news/2014/10/26/Postgame_Quotes_Bama_34_Vols_20.aspx?path=football

http://www.montgomeryadvertiser.com/story/rankinfile/2014/10/26/lane-kiffin-exit-had-some-drama/17950103/
http://utsports.com/news/2014/11/2/Postgame_Quotes_Vols_45_SC_42_OT_.aspx?path=football
http://utsports.com/news/2014/11/29/Postgame_Quotes_Tennessee_24_Vandy_14.aspx?path=football
http://utsports.com/news/2014/12/7/VOLS_HEADED_TO_TAXSLAYER_BOWL.aspx?path=football
http://www.espn.com/college-football/recap?gameId=400610224
http://utsports.com/news/2015/1/2/Postgame_Quotes_Tennessee_45_Iowa_28.aspx?path=football
Chapter 9
http://utsports.com/news/2015/2/4/_VolsNSD15_Vols_Welcome_Newcomers.aspx?path=football
http://utsports.com/news/2015/2/6/DeBord_Named_Vols_Off_Coordinator_QB_Coach.aspx?path=football
http://bleacherreport.com/articles/2370528-tennessees-butch-jones-opens-up-on-mike-debord-hire-developing-qbs-and-more
http://www.tennessean.com/story/news/crime/2015/02/17/former-vol-aj-johnson-booked-rape-charge/23558461/
http://utsports.com/news/2013/11/22/Pat_Summitt_Plaza_Dedication.aspx
http://www.tennessean.com/story/news/2014/11/17/two-ut-students-accused-rape-sexual-assault/19169563/
http://www.tennessean.com/story/news/local/2015/02/16/dave-hart-helm-florida-state-athletics-mishandled-rape-claim/23458011/?from=global&sessionKey=&autologin=
http://www.utsports.com/news/2015/6/7/Gruden_s_Message_For_Team_119.aspx?path=football
http://www.utsports.com/news/2014/11/10/One_Tennessee_Branding_Restructure.aspx
http://www.utsports.com/news/2015/7/14/Quotes_From_SECMD15.aspx?path=football
http://www.utsports.com/news/2015/9/12/Postgame_Quotes_Oklahoma_31_Vols_24.aspx?path=football
http://www.utsports.com/news/2015/9/21/_MediaMonday_Florida_Week.aspx?path=football
http://www.utsports.com/news/2015/9/26/Postgame_Quotes_Florida_28_Vols_27.aspx?path=football
http://utsports.com/news/2016/1/1/Outback_Bowl_Postgame_Quotes_23_Tennessee_45_13_Northwestern_6.aspx?path=football
Chapter 10
http://utsports.com/news/2016/1/6/Tennessee_Announces_Staff_Change.aspx?path=football
http://utsports.com/news/2016/1/9/Shoop_Agrees_In_Principle_To_Become_Def_Coordinator.aspx?path=football
http://utsports.com/news/2016/2/3/Butch_Jones_TSD16_Press_Conference.aspx?path=football
http://www.tennessean.com/story/news/2016/02/09/sweeping-sexual-assault-suit-filed-against-ut/79966450/
http://www.espn.com/espnw/sports/article/14829201/tennessee-volunteers-head-coaches-address-questions-title-ix-lawsuit-sexual-assault-complaints
http://www.espn.com/espnw/voices/article/14832662/tennessee-coaches-press-conference-leaves-some-sounding-tone-deaf
http://www.utsports.com/news/2016/4/16/Orange_Prevails_for_70_63_Win_in_DISH_Orange_amp_White_Game.aspx
https://247sports.com/college/tennessee/Article/Butch-Jones-Tennessee-Vols-football-enjoying-new-strength-coach-45007685
http://utsports.com/news/2016/7/12/Quotes_From_SECMD16.aspx?path=football
http://utsports.com/news/2016/7/15/UT_Picked_to_Win_SEC_East_9_Vols_Named_All_SEC.aspx?path=football
http://utsports.com/news/2016/8/27/Butch_Jones_Press_Conference_Kicks_Off_App_State_Game_Week.aspx?path=football
http://utsports.com/news/2016/9/1/Postgame_Quotes_Vols_20_App_State_13_OT_.aspx?path=football
http://www.bristolmotorspeedway.com/fans/news-archive/bristol-motor-speedway-transform-into-worlds-largest-college-football-venue-for-battle-bristol.html
Chapter 11
http://utsports.com/news/2016/9/20/Vol_Report_Vols_Talk_Gators.aspx?path=football
http://utsports.com/news/2016/9/24/Postgame_Quotes_Tennessee_38_Florida_28.aspx?path=football
http://www.espn.com/college-football/recap?gameId=400869007
https://www.seccountry.com/florida/teez-talks-star-cb-jalen-tabor-speaks-ahead-of-floridas-showdown-at-tennessee
http://utsports.com/news/2016/9/27/Vol_Report_Vols_Talk_Dawgs.aspx?path=football
http://utsports.com/news/2016/10/1/Postgame_Quotes_Vols_34_Georgia_31.aspx?path=football

Chapter 12

http://www.utsports.com/news/2016/10/3/FOOTBALL_CENTRAL_9_Tennessee_at_8_Texas_A_amp_M.aspx?path=football

http://www.utsports.com/news/2016/10/3/Vol_Report_Eyes_on_the_Aggies.aspx?path=football

https://www.tennessean.com/story/sports/college/ut/2016/10/06/report-vols-jalen-hurd-expected-miss-texas-m-game/91703844/

http://www.utsports.com/news/2016/10/8/Postgame_Quotes_Texas_A_amp_M_45_Vols_38_2OT_.aspx?path=football

http://www.utsports.com/news/2016/10/15/Postgame_Quotes_Vols_10_Alabama_49.aspx?path=football

http://www.utsports.com/news/2016/10/24/Vol_Report_Back_From_The_Bye.aspx?path=football

http://www.utsports.com/news/2016/10/30/Postgame_Quotes_South_Carolina_24_Vols_21.aspx?path=football

https://www.seccountry.com/tennessee/man-purportedly-close-to-jalen-hurd-goes-on-epic-rant-defending-former-tennessee-rb

https://www.seccountry.com/tennessee/now-jalen-hurds-mother-weighs-in-on-his-decision-to-transfer-from-tennessee

https://www.tennessean.com/story/sports/college/ut/2016/11/06/jalen-hurd-breaks-silence-why-he-left-tennessee/93409694/

https://www.seccountry.com/tennessee/former-vols-rb-jalen-hurd-writes-letter-to-tennessee-after-transfer-decision

http://www.rockytopinsider.com/2017/10/03/32-vols-since-2013-class-transferred-butch-jones/

http://www.utsports.com/news/2016/10/31/Vol_Report_Homecoming_Week_Begins.aspx?path=football

Chapter 13

https://www.knoxnews.com/story/sports/college/university-of-tennessee/2017/02/28/source-tennessee-hires-john-currie-new-athletic-director/98525888/

https://www.knoxnews.com/story/sports/college/university-of-tennessee/2017/02/28/charles-davis-thinks-currie-big-get-ut-ad/98539168/

https://www.knoxnews.com/story/sports/college/university-of-tennessee/football/2017/06/20/phillip-fulmer-named-special-advisor-university-tennessee-president/412117001/

https://247sports.com/college/tennessee/Article/Butch-Jones-Tennessee-Vols-football-targeting-five-star-heart-on-51062601

http://www.utsports.com/news/2017/1/10/Gullickson_Named_Director_of_Strength_amp_Conditioning.aspx?path=football

http://www.utsports.com/news/2017/2/22/Azzanni_Accepts_Position_with_Chicago_Bears.aspx?path=football

http://www.utsports.com/news/2017/1/10/Gullickson_Named_Director_of_Strength_amp_Conditioning.aspx?path=football

http://asapsports.com/show_interview.php?id=131752

http://www.utsports.com/news/2017/9/5/football-postgame-quotes-25-24-vols-42-georgia-tech-41.aspx?path=football

http://www.utsports.com/news/2017/9/30/football-postgame-quotes-7-8-georgia-41-vols-0.aspx?path=football

Chapter 14

http://utsports.com/news/2017/10/9/football-vol-report-south-carolina-week-begins.aspx?path=football

http://www.thestate.com/sports/college/university-of-south-carolina/sec/article178288121.html

http://www.utsports.com/news/2017/10/14/football-postgame-quotes-tennessee-9-south-carolina-15.aspx?path=football

http://utsports.com/news/2017/10/17/football-vol-report-focused-on-alabama.aspx?path=football

http://www.espn.com/college-football/recap?gameId=400933910

http://utsports.com/news/2017/11/12/currie-announces-head-football-coach-transition.aspx?path=football

http://utsports.com/news/2017/11/12/football-john-currie-press-conference-transcript-11-12.aspx?path=football

Chapter 15

https://www.dropbox.com/sh/ojyeg96gwsqfml0/AABTaH8am8iLi7BD_G8y91i9a?dl=0

http://www.espn.com/college-football/recap?gameId=400933938

http://utsports.com/news/2017/11/25/football-postgame-quotes-tennessee-24-vanderbilt-42.aspx?path=football

http://www.nj.com/rutgersfootball/index.ssf/2017/09/the_24_hours_that_changed_rutgers_football_history.html

https://www.si.com/2014/11/04/nfl-greg-schiano-year-off

https://deadspin.com/greg-schiano-tried-to-kick-a-buccaneers-hero-out-of-pra-1448815091

http://tampa.cbslocal.com/2013/10/20/tampa-bay-buccaneers-coach-greg-schiano-denies-super-bowl-mvp-dexter-jackson-access-to-practice-kids-told-not-to-come-to-one-buc-place-on-fridays-because-they-are-a-distraction/

http://www.nj.com/rutgersfootball/index.ssf/2014/01/49ers_tackle_anthony_davis_on_greg_schiano_he_was_an_expletive_but_thats_old_now.html

https://www.bucsnation.com/2012/9/21/3369732/greg-schiano-ibully-hated-by-nfl-scouts-mike-silver

http://www.nj.com/rutgersfootball/index.ssf/2014/01/49ers_tackle_anthony_davis_on_greg_schiano_he_was_an_expletive_but_thats_old_now.html

http://www.ohiostatebuckeyes.com/sports/m-footbl/spec-rel/121115aai.html

http://www.cleveland.com/osu/2015/12/greg_schiano_explains_his_new.html

https://www.cbssports.com/nfl/news/jon-gruden-talking-to-tennessee-volunteers-about-coaching-vacancy/

Chapter 16

https://www.knoxnews.com/story/sports/college/university-of-tennessee/football/2017/12/11/ut-vols-greg-schiano-mou-signatures-binding-john-currie-beverly-davenport-tennessee-volunteers-tn/940152001/

Chapter 17

https://www.seccountry.com/tennessee/peyton-manning-agreed-tennessee-hiring-greg-schiano-kirk-herbstreit-reveals

http://www.espn.com/video/clip?id=21586845

https://nypost.com/2017/11/27/disgraceful-tennessee-mob-just-used-a-child-sex-scandal-as-cover/

https://www.cbssports.com/college-football/news/urban-meyer-bill-belichick-stand-by-greg-schiano-after-tennessee-debacle/

Chapter 18

http://www.espn.com/college-football/story/_/id/21591832/david-cutcliffe-duke-told-tennessee-not-interested-vols-head-coaching-vacancy

http://www.wbir.com/article/sports/college/vols/fans-chant-fire-currie-at-tennessee-basketball-game/51-495650612

http://www.al.com/sports/index.ssf/2017/11/lane_kiffin_on_tennessee_job_j.html

https://www.rockytoptalk.com/2017/11/28/16710392/college-football-coaching-search-mike-gundy-to-meet-with-tennessee-in-dallas-john-currie

https://www.pressconnects.com/story/sports/college/purdue/football/2017/07/27/lets-play-football-follows-purdues-jeff-brohm/514924001/

https://www.knoxnews.com/story/sports/college/university-of-tennessee/football/2017/11/29/ut-vols-jeff-brohm-purdue-tennessee-coaching-search-buyout-john-currie-tennessee-volunteers/904180001/

http://www.newsobserver.com/sports/article182852126.html

https://247sports.com/college/tennessee/Article/Tennessee-Vols-football-Former-AD-John-Currie-in-legal-battle-with-Tennessee-per-Kirk-Schulz-112046143

Chapter 19

https://news.utk.edu/2017/12/01/chancellor-davenport-announces-athletic-department-leadership/

https://twitter.com/UTPresidentJoe/status/936732068888940544/photo/1

http://utsports.com/news/2017/12/1/ut-presser-120117.aspx

https://www.usatoday.com/story/sports/ncaaf/2017/12/18/washington-states-leach-agrees-to-20-million-extension/108732390/

http://www.espn.com/college-football/news/story?id=1710617

http://gridironnow.com/phil-fulmer-continuing-interview-candidates-volunteers-opening/

http://www.al.com/sports/index.ssf/2010/07/sec_media_days_begins_top_10_e.html

https://www.cbssports.com/college-football/news/usc-oc-tee-martin-disappointed-not-to-get-interview-with-tennessee/

https://www.dawgnation.com/football/team-news/georgia-defesnsive-coordiator-mel-tucker-interview-tennessee

https://www.ohio.com/akron/sports/playing-for-high-stakes

http://www.sptimes.com/2004/10/20/Sports/In_Alabama__Fulmer_pu.shtml

Chapter 20

http://utsports.com/news/2017/12/7/football-introductory-press-conference-jeremy-pruitt.aspx?path=football

http://utsports.com/news/2017/12/7/football-what-they-re-saying-about-jeremy-pruitt.aspx?path=football

http://utsports.com/news/2017/12/19/-domin18-tennessee-football-early-signing-period.aspx?path=football

http://utsports.com/news/2018/2/8/football-pruitt-officially-announces-coaching-staff-hires.aspx?path=football

https://247sports.com/college/tennessee/Bolt/Phillip-Fulmer-addresses-removal-of-Butch-Jones-image-from-Jumbotron-113923379

Epilogue

http://utsports.com/news/2018/3/3/mens-basketball-postgame-press-conference-tennessee-vs-georgia.aspx?path=mbball

https://www.knoxnews.com/story/news/2018/05/02/statement-soon-ut-chancellor-davenport/573782002/